# I Am a Stranger Here Myself

 River Teeth Literary Nonfiction Prize
Daniel Lehman and Joe Mackall, SERIES EDITORS

The River Teeth Literary Nonfiction Prize is awarded to the best work of literary nonfiction submitted to the annual contest sponsored by *River Teeth: A Journal of Nonfiction Narrative.*

Also available in the River Teeth Literary Nonfiction Prize series:

*MINE: Essays* by Sarah Viren
*Rough Crossing: An Alaskan Fisherwoman's Memoir* by Rosemary McGuire
*The Girls in My Town: Essays* by Angela Morales

# I Am
# a Stranger
# Here
# Myself

Debra Gwartney

University of New Mexico Press ∾ Albuquerque

Library of Congress Cataloging-in-Publication Data
Names: Gwartney, Debra, author.
Title: I am a stranger here myself / Debra Gwartney.
Description: First edition. | Albuquerque: University of New Mexico Press, 2019. |
Series: River teeth literary nonfiction series | "Part history, part memoir, I Am a
Stranger Here Myself taps dimensions of human yearning: the need to belong, the
snarl of family history, and embracing womanhood in the patriarchal American West.
Gwartney becomes fascinated with the missionary Narcissa Prentiss Whitman, the first
Caucasian woman to cross the Rocky Mountains and one of fourteen people killed at
the Whitman Mission in 1847 by Cayuse Indians. Whitman's role as a white woman
drawn in to "settle" the West reflects the tough-as-nails women in Gwartney's own
family. Arranged in four sections as a series of interlocking explorations and rumina-
tions, Gwartney uses Whitman as a touchstone to spin a tightly woven narrative about
identity, the power of womanhood, and coming to peace with one's most cherished
place."—Provided by publisher. | Includes bibliographical references. |
Identifiers: LCCN 2018048380 (print) | LCCN 2018049743 (e-book) |
ISBN 9780826360724 (e-book) | ISBN 9780826360717 (pbk.: alk. paper)
Subjects: LCSH: Gwartney, Debra—Family. | Women—Idaho—Biography. |
Idaho—Social life and customs. | Salmon (Idaho)—Biography. | Women—
West (U.S.)—Social conditions. | Whitman, Narcissa Prentiss, 1808–1847. |
Cayuse Indians—Missions. | Whitman Massacre, 1847.
Classification: LCC CT3262.I2 (e-book) | LCC CT3262.I2 G93 2019 (print) |
DDC 920.72009796—dc23
LC record available at https://lccn.loc.gov/2018048380

Cover photograph and author photograph by John Clark
Designed by Felicia Cedillos
Composed in Palatino LT Std 10.25/14

*For my grandmothers*
*Lillian Lydia Mae Keizer Burke and*
*Lois Alline Rawls Gwartney*

Therefore love the stranger,
for you were strangers in the land.

—DEUTERONOMY 10:19

They are strangers to the language, and the manners,
to the advantages and wants of the people whose lives
they would model and whose evil they would remedy.

—DR. SAMUEL JOHNSON

# Author's Note

I approached this material as neither scholar nor historian. My intent with this book is to offer a personal account rather than an exhaustive examination or analysis of historical events. The interpretation of those events is my own.

Parts of this manuscript, in somewhat different forms, were published in *The American Scholar, Crab Orchard Review, True Story (Creative Nonfiction), The Normal School, Oregon Quarterly,* and *Oregon Humanities,* as well as in two anthologies, *Man In the Moon: Essays on Fathers and Fatherhood,* edited by Stephanie G'Schwind, and *West of 98: Living and Writing the New American West,* edited by Lynn Stegner and Russell Rowland. I am deeply grateful to the editors of these publications for supporting my work.

# 1

# The End of Something

# 1

A man is following me on US-93 in Idaho, his red truck a fire-cracker in my rearview mirror. It's a rumbling diesel truck with a toothy grille and road-gobbling tires, and when the sun's rays tilt just right as we wend through the narrow can-yon, the RAM on his side panel glints like a neon sign. After about an hour of this guy on my bumper, I start to wonder if it's what he's planning to do to me. One good ram.

I'm a little pissed at the bubble of fear rising in my throat. I should be able to hold my own, even on an isolated road in Idaho with brilliant sun splashing across an empty June day, but I don't like how near he is or how alone I am. I'm betting he's spotted my Oregon plates and my "I'm With Her" sticker and wants me (and my kind) off his road. It's not like he's honking or flashing his lights, but his truck is twice the size of my hatchback, and the rifle rack behind his head holds a weapon clicked in tight. Plus, the man keeps closing in on me.

We're on a windy two-lane stretch between the towns of Salmon and Challis with no cars in either direction when he looms again in my mirror and revs his engine. I think about sticking my arm out the window to flip him off, but instead I do what this Idaho man wants and pull over. I need to pee any-way, so what the hell. I tap on the brake and veer into a rest area at the top of a piney rise.

He roars off, and I step out on cracked asphalt, awash in frus-tration and disappointment. But disappointment about what, exactly? That he found me out? That he stared into the tan vinyl interior of this car with its fuel-efficient engine and pegged me as a late-middle-aged white and left-leaning woman? Nail on the head, buddy, and it was the right thing that we parted ways, though I sort of wish I'd waved him over to park next to me so we could, I don't know, talk.

Could we talk?

Mostly I want to let him know that I'm a fifth-generation Idahoan and have the right to drive along the river's edge and weave through the undulating landscape without someone pushing me to hurry along. I'd tell him that when I was a kid, with my father at the wheel easing through these same curves, I felt in my body every bend and straightaway from our house in Boise to Salmon while smells of river and sagebrush and baked earth poured in the open window. I knew the drive by heart, but I stuck my face out anyway to imagine how all this around me was formed by a herd of lumbering dinosaurs that one day plopped down and turned into the tawny, mottled hills of Eastern Idaho. But of course when I was a kid, half dozing in the back seat of the station wagon heading to my one and only best place on earth, I let myself believe a lot of things I can't anymore.

It surprises me that I'm here again, staring out at the hills of my youth, the mahogany cliffs. It's an out-of-the-way place, our wedge of Idaho. I take a minute to soak it in, the wide fields below me dotted with black cattle and an occasional white-tailed deer. If I'm lucky, a few sleek antelope will happen along. If I'm super lucky, some clattering bighorn sheep. In the distance are gleaming mountains we sang about in school. A bright-blue sky.

I know the place about as well as the lines on my face.

Would the truck driver, long gone down the road, care about this affinity of mine? Probably not. But I wonder what he might say if he were standing next to me. I wonder if he'd be willing to listen in a way most men aren't. Most men, all my life, certain they can tell my story better than I can.

First I would lay out my legacy, my great-great-great-grandparents who moved West and bore my great-great-grandmother Iona, who begat Lucy, who begat Lois, who begat my father, Mike, who begat me. Every one of us an Idahoan. More Idahoan than the truck man, I'm betting.

I like thinking, anyway, that I'm rare with my forebears showing up in the early days of the West.

The town I've driven away from, Salmon, is where generations of my family lived, from those early days until now, and it's also my birthplace. I've just spent two days there because my grandfather died. Two days because I couldn't manage any longer, though I still consider the town my Elysium. Only in Salmon has my mouth slacked easy around the word *home* and its cousin, *belong*, and yet I've itched at the same time, from babyhood on, with the rash of not belonging. For years I boomeranged in and out to see if I could get it right. Salmon is snugged into a valley, cupped by the Bitterroots, the Beaverheads, under a sky that fools you into thinking you are slung into the interior of an egg. I was held in just that way for a long time, believing the town had an innate ability to deliver up the truth about who I am.

If the truck driver were standing next to me, listening to me wax on, he might scratch his head at this pronouncement and ask why I gave the place up if I claim to love it so much. *Didn't you forfeit everything that Idaho means by turning against it?*

It's true that I have never shot a gun. I've never stood behind a taut bow with an arrow aimed at an animal's heart. I have little use for horses and no gut for whisky. I've gone forty years without venison or elk or grouse on my table. I've let my skin

5

wrinkle and my belly sag. Decades ago I divorced an Idaho man who once marked the calendar with the days I owed him sex. I raised four daughters without once lamenting a lack of sons.

What I have instead are Idaho stories that, knit together, would stretch as long as the highway to Boise. There's the one about my great-grandfather and my Grandpa Bob at nine years old riding with those who shot the last wolves in the state back in 1925. I despise that story, but it validates the Idaho in me, and I would tell it to a truck man for that reason. I also have a photo of my maternal grandmother Mamie holding up a hooked steelhead, at least a four-footer and for a time the largest caught in the Salmon River. I could tell stories about my great-grandmother's pies and biscuits and pots of stew cooked up for a table of twenty ranch hands and how, six hours later, she would get herself up and do it all again. And I have tales about the men in my family who've set up hunting camp in the same place in the Lemhi Mountains for nearly a hundred years.

*And you've been to that camp?*

I am forced to admit I have not.

*Then you've got nothing. Get back in your putt-putt car and go home.*

My made-up interlocutor is in his early thirties and wears Lee jeans tight enough to show the arc of his kneecaps, a plaid shirt, beat-up Tony Lamas, and a red ball cap. He returns to his truck dressed this way, shoulders square. He swaggers as he walks. A dip of chew bumps from his jaw. The confidence emanating from him, down to the dust clouds he makes with shuffling feet, illustrates the dilemma I'm in with myself. Where's my ease like that, my comfort with who I am and where I'm from?

For reasons I have yet to decipher, I can't seem to make peace with the place I've loved best on this earth.

# 2

My grandmother—my father's mother, Lois—is the one who loaded me with myths and legends when I was a kid. She taught me the names of Lear's daughters and Hamlet's drowned lover; she read to me about gods and monsters. Every car we passed with a headlight burned out caused us to call out *Cyclops!* Every jealous man in the Owl Club bar, she muttered hot in my ear, was another Iago out for blood.

I loved those tales. I loved that she insisted I read *Babar* in French, though I spoke not a word, and that she encouraged me to read every *Oz* volume before I saw the film (advice I did not heed). And yet the folklore that's mostly stuck with me has to do with the town she lived in. Salmon. Both her home and her trap, this berg in the mountains that she and I couldn't talk about honestly because, I think, so much of her wanted out and so much of me wanted in. Or was it vice versa?

Back in childhood, when we were in Salmon for any stretch of time, my sisters and brothers and I might be invited to tag along with our cousins to the Carmen Grange on a Saturday night. Grandma Lois would drive us. They treated her kindly, but I saw how she sometimes confused the Carmen crowd. The way she'd get agitated, for example, over the apostrophes on an A&W sign ("Fry's, $.79") or her insistence on explaining, again, why you don't *lay* down for a nap.

Grandma Lois's oldest son, my father, along with his wife and children, had moved to Boise so he could become the

7

family's first executive for a corporation; he was the first man in our clan to toss off terms like *pension* and *stock options*. But, if I can speak for my siblings, we preferred our original home. In Salmon I could head off in the morning to the newspaper office owned by my mother's folks and find my grandfather at the massive pedals of the printing press. He'd let me climb up and set my hands on top of his chapped ones as he pulled the levers, and later he'd ask one of the operators at the octopus-like lino-type machines to peck out letters in lead so I could stamp my childhood name on end-roll paper, *Debbie, Debbie, Debbie*.

Down Main Street at the implements store owned by my great-grandparents, my sister and I would swing—until we were chased off by our broom-wielding great-grandmother—from scales meant to weigh sacks of nails and screws. Our great-granddad, smelling of whiskey by mid-morning, was usually the one who plunked us on the cement floor and, with a big, happy laugh, fished out a dime from the cash register so we could buy a pack of Juicy Fruit at the City News Stand across the street. We flew out the door, tinkling the bells that signaled *customer*.

After the town siren blew exactly at noon, our Grandpa Bob might drive us in his Scout truck up into the scrub hills where he'd call to his horses—a whistle to bring April, Amber, and Crow in from miles away. I remember him dipping into a pocket for apples gone soft, giving them out to kids who wanted to feed a horse. *Keep it flat*, our grandpa warned about outstretched palms. *Those fingers will get bit clean off.*

And on some weekends we'd all drive out to Carmen, a few miles from downtown Salmon, sliding into the outlying ranch-ing territory as if we were long-lost sheep.

It struck me at age nine or ten that people at the grange had a solid idea of what they meant. I saw it in the plain way they greeted each other, no hugs or pecks on the cheeks but a nod, a grunted hello while Aunt Janice set down world-famous biscuits still warm from her stove and Uncle Jack stepped into a circle of men. Plaid shirts, the monotony of Wrangler jeans, felt hats clutched in their hands, and a stubborn line of sunburn across each man's forehead. My sisters and I followed our five cousins around the musty building, boards complaining under our feet, dipping into potato and Jell-O salads, fried chicken you never wanted to stop eating. A handful of men sauntered to the stage, twanging on guitars and banjos, warming up, while teenagers moved shyly to the edges, gauging interest, working up the nerve for a dance. Soon these young people would be paired off for good, sent out to make a life prescribed by their parents and their parents' parents, whose ranching outfit was not a mile down the road; a life that began at dawn and ended long after dark, their compact homes with utility rooms in the back where milk cooled and separated in stainless steel buckets; where sick lambs were brought in for tending or, if too far gone, dispatched with a twist of the neck.

I realize it's my own long-held perspective, not theirs, that my ranching relations had something I didn't—a single road to travel down. In Boise our parents were more unsettled than settled, and for many years we teetered on that edge with them. As a couple they were driven to go after something better than what they'd had in Salmon—fancier, larger, shinier, whatever tangible evidence they could conjure to prove to everyone back in their small town that they'd made it big.

It's not that I desired my version of what the ranch kids at the grange had; I didn't. There was no missing the stifle of having your future handed to you like a plate of cold leftovers. But being around that measure of stability made me feel, if I recall correctly, lonely.

9

Let's say that is my chief affliction, loneliness. Loneliness boiling up from an empty place inside of me. It has to do with growing up in what many still consider the deep backcountry, in a family steeped in the mythology of the West, square-backed men who were the embodiment of patriarchy and tough women who mostly kept trouble to themselves. As a kid I lived in dread of letting down the men or failing to meet the standard of women carved into me like a talisman. Now it's too late to be one of those women from my past, nor do I want that. But what is it I need to remember about my grandmothers so I can finally be me?

# 3

Making up the truck man was just so much chatter inside my head after I pulled over and stepped out of the ticking car. I had to defend myself to someone, I suppose, in the wake of my brief visit to Salmon.

I'd packed the back of the car with a small suitcase, a couple of my dead grandfather's shirts, and, in the passenger seat, books nabbed from long-dead Grandma Lois's library, a few of those having to do with the founding of the West. One in particular I planned on reading when I got home was a biography of Narcissa Prentiss Whitman, a woman I remembered learning about in grade school and who my four daughters learned about when they played the Oregon Trail video game at school in the '90s. I remember my girls hanging over the screen, strategizing to do whatever they could to keep their digital settlers heading west. ("Your wagon tipped over." "Someone stole six of your oxen." "You have died of dysentery.")

Something about Narcissa Whitman drew me in when I saw the book on my grandmother's shelf this time. She was the first Caucasian woman (so say the history books) to cross the Rocky Mountains, the first white woman to give birth to a white baby on the frontier (same history books). A missionary killed by the people she aimed to convert—her death, some say, changing the course of the settling of the West.

I'd left Salmon agitated, looking for some way to get beyond the notion that I was nothing but a misfit in a town still ensconced in a cowboy ethos that held no room for someone like me. I suppose that's why I promised myself I'd get to my grandmother's book about Narcissa Whitman right off the bat and would find other books about her too. Not so I could fawn, but so I could reject a woman I'd already pegged as odious. She was shaping up to be my ideal nemesis in the way she believed the land was hers to take, in her insistence that she alone held the one and only path to God. Putting an end to an entire culture was justified in Narcissa's mind as long as it was done in the name of Progress and Providence. I would let myself despise her for that squirt of narrow-mindedness and her proclivity to judge, even while managing to ignore my own such propensities. So what if she was trapped in others' expectations—her mother's, and later her husband's, and also her time's and her church's? I wouldn't forgive her for building a good part of her cage.

I stood in the middle of the rest stop lot for longer than I meant to. I was alone in the cool forest breeze, a small creek gurgling not ten feet away. I jumped a few logs in the woods to get to an even wider vista that opened up every pore of my skin, prickled the hair on my neck, lifted my heart. And I decided right then that this was probably enough. I'd found the perfect ending. I could go on home and call it quits with Salmon. Except for an old, niggling need to stay put and meet the woman I'd have become if I'd stuck it out in Idaho, a woman who'd be skinnier and more burnished and could grill a steak to medium rare and, well, I don't know what else because she's a balloon enigma floating just beyond my reach.

I was pretty sure Grandpa Bob, dead for three days, would scoff about my rest-area angst. *Damned useless meanderings of the mind*, he'd say. *Just get yourself out of the bed before dawn, put in an honest day's work fixing whatever broken baler or wagon comes through your door. Challenge your kid to a game of HORSE if there's still daylight in the sky when you're back from feeding the actual horses; read a dozen pages of Louis L'Amour while supper's put on the table. Head for bed at a decent hour so you can do it all the next day. There's a life worth living. What's your bother about?*

I don't know. But I have to say, I was bothered.

I got back in the car and was reaching to turn the key in the ignition when I noticed the book again. I picked it up and opened it to the title page. Narcissa Prentiss Whitman. A version of history set down in black and white, never to be altered. And hadn't I done the same with my own? Told and retold the stories of my childhood so often that the memories finally calcified. Probably time to break it apart, my own past and, for some reason I had yet to decipher, hers.

# 4

Narcissa Whitman died alone, her body crumpled like paper, her head a cracked melon. She was shot a dozen times on a cold day in 1847, men whipping her laid-bare back while she was still breathing. As darkness was coming on, as temperatures fell below zero, she was rolled into an irrigation ditch and left to die.

The Whitmans' compound in the broad Columbia Basin, about eight miles from current day Walla Walla, Washington, is where she was killed. A small band of Cayuse led the raid, having set their knifepoints and rifle barrels on the woman and on her husband, Marcus, though a pair of young girls died too, as did a dozen men and boys—the wrong place at the wrong time for that lot. One was Nathan Kimball, a man who'd left Missouri with a wife and $1,500 in cash and seven children, until two died on the trail. Kimball had asked to overwinter at the mission (one heck of an ill-fated decision) with his remaining family, including other sick children, and on the morning of November 29 he was one among a group of men stomping their feet to stay warm in the center of the compound. Their job was to butcher a steer, and they hoisted the dead animal on a derrick to make the first long cuts. They worked for hours, with few words passing among them. It was when they were finished, when they were cleaning up and distributing the dripping meat, that the first shot rang out. Kimball was as stunned and stock-still as the others when the man next to him was hit in the chest and fell to the ground. Before he could think to *run*, Kimball was shot too, his arm broken and bleeding, but he managed to wrench himself away to fly toward the house with the mission's wounded scholar, Andrew Rodgers, close behind. He crashed through the kitchen door, shouting to those holed up inside, "I don't know why the hell they're trying to kill *me*." His statement made the children giggle—despite a kitchen splattered with blood, despite a boy in the corner with his throat cut, despite their patriarch lying before the fire mortally wounded and the women clustered together in fear—as they were unaccustomed to hearing a man swear.

Glacial temperatures had rumbled in a few days before the attack, encasing the compound in ice, doming it in a winter glow. This place called Waiilatpu, the name Marcus gave his mission in the fall of 1836, to honor, he said, the Native people whose traditional grounds he and Narcissa settled on. The word means "home of the ryegrass people." Tall grasses and bulrushes—tule sedge that the Cayuse used primarily to cover their long houses—were imperative to the tribe's way of life, a fact that Marcus, in what strikes me as one of his first acts of colonial indifference, ignored.

In short order the missionary man/doctor burned great swaths of that grass, churned the rich soil, planted a large, cheery garden, set in an orchard of stone fruit and apples, and began sowing acre after acre of the white man's favorite grain, wheat. In the late 1840s a visitor to the mission wrote in his travel journal that Marcus Whitman had planted a good two thousand acres of crops, largely wheat, to provide for the mission. But back in the early months, when he was just getting started, Marcus wrote the American Board of Commissioners for Foreign Mission with a shopping list: Send more plows. Send more tools for repair when the plows broke down. Send more wheat seed for the plows to plow under. Besides prodigious prayer and the lure of everlasting life, this is how he'd civilize the Natives—he'd create an agrarian culture where none had existed. "All my plans require time and distance," he once wrote. *Be patient*, that statement seems to emphasize, *and I can make the impossible happen.*

Croplands lay fallow on November 29, Marcus and Narcissa's last day on earth. The mission's plows were piled like crooked spines in a shed, with seventy-some souls in the compound moving as little as possible, huddling together against the cold. They scooted up near their fires and exchanged rumors about simmering discontent among the Cayuse. Some were sure an attack was coming, Marcus and Narcissa among that clutch. The couple had stayed up half the night, or so a survivor reported, speaking in hushed voices about threats that Marcus had heard while on the road tending to the sick: Cayuse men were on their way, and they intended to kill.

Beyond her religious ardor (she was indeed a zealot), what Narcissa mostly did at the mission was organize each day so they could *get by*. Storing food against rot and insects. Plugging holes in shelters. Gathering wood for warmth. Providing never-ending care for the sick. Not a single volume I've read about the Whitman venture fails to mention the rampant illness. Narcissa was one of the few who contracted neither measles nor typhoid (neither did Marcus). She did not come down with the dysentery or cholera that spilled from wagon trains that showed up almost daily after 1843, full of desperate overlanders—sick, hungry, lost. Week after week wagons sought succor and food; the Whitmans provided both if they had the means and energy, and they almost always had the energy. But even if she wasn't pockmarked or burning with fever, Narcissa had her troubles. A deep ache in her chest that Marcus diagnosed as a heart ailment, for one, and in a letter home Narcissa lamented that her eyesight, already poor, had failed another notch—the world around her was blurry now. She also fussed about her weight, 162 pounds, a "fleshy" softness that, she said, didn't suit her. "My sisters would laugh."

Plus, she had come to hate her job.

Narcissa was slow to rise the last morning of her life—so unlike her, this stickler for the 4:30 a.m. recitation of scripture, this ardent keeper of schedules, that the children in the house were silent in astonishment, especially after one girl returned from the bedroom to report their steely matriarch was weeping. The dress Narcissa put on once she was on her feet—a dainty flower print that she'd once told her mother "would please the savages"—was crisp and freshly laundered. Of course. That was her standard. It was bath day, so she went to work filling tubs in the living room with hot water. She pulled pale girls, arms bent like snapped twigs, from their sick beds and laid them in the bath, scrubbed them apple red, and lifted them out again.

Around noon a small group of Cayuse men pounded on the kitchen door, a rustle of trouble on the porch that Marcus got up to deal with, and then came the first blast of gunfire. Kimball and Rodgers stumbled in, shouting for help. Naked children fresh from the bath and frightened by the screams of dying men outside darted about the house, screaming too, while Narcissa ordered them to *get dressed immediately.* She checked the doors, gathered the children to her, and eventually made her way to her living-room window—a rare piece of glass that Marcus had bought for her through the Hudson Bay Company—trying to sort the mayhem outside. *Who was dead?* Her husband for one. She'd already dragged Marcus into the living room from the kitchen after a tomahawk was planted in his brain. She'd packed the gash with ashes from their fireplace. He muttered a few words to her, and she knelt next to him believing, for one disoriented split second, that he might survive the blade's strike and the gunshot to his neck, but he died before the ashes cooled. She must have figured then that she'd be next, there was no way out—although perhaps a sliver of hope, thin as an icicle beetling from her house's eaves, rose up in her; perhaps she let herself believe that she and the eleven children under her charge might live on. *If God so willed it.*

But then a pop and a burn at the top of her arm as if it had been ripped from her body. She fell to the floor, pulling along with her a girl who'd been clinging to her skirts. The child had nearly been hit too by the ball lodged in Mother Whitman's shoulder, and they both cried out for being alive. "Hold me tight," Narcissa said, drenching the girl's dress in blood.

The child and Kimball helped Narcissa upstairs to a small bedroom, where two other children were gripped by the worst of the measles. Their wounded matriarch was moved to the bed with them while Rodgers and Kimball and a few teenagers—the ones not hiding in a loft with the younger children—did their best to comfort Narcissa and staunch her bleeding.

One of the instigators of the attack, a man called Tamsucky, who'd been fomenting revenge against the missionaries for a decade, called up the stairs to Narcissa. They were ready to make peace, he said. The killing was over. He and the others asked the woman to come outside to parlay.

The children begged her not to go. The two men in the room cautioned her against meeting with the Cayuse. Not yet. Let things settle down first. Kimball had seen the carpenter Peter Hall run from the compound toward the fort. Maybe he was bringing help even now. But she sat up in the bed, holding a compress to her shoulder. "God has raised us up a friend," Narcissa said.

Rodgers managed to get her down the stairs. At the bottom she fainted—from loss of blood, from the overwhelming experience of the last hours, from the sight of Marcus's now smashed-in skull. She was lifted, barely conscious, onto a settee, and Rodgers took one end and a teenage girl the other until a man named Joe Lewis stepped in and moved the girl aside. The two men carried Narcissa out the kitchen door into the cold afternoon and a line of fire—the lady of the mission was riddled with bullets before she could speak a word. Rodgers fell dead, Lewis having ducked away on cue. Narcissa collapsed to the ground.

A Cayuse man lifted her head and struck her with a quirt—a short, fringed-leather whip, an example of which I once saw under glass at the Tamástslikt Cultural Institute near Pendleton (creepily lethal for such a small weapon, held tight in the palm). Night fell and the motherless children who'd considered Narcissa as near a parent as they'd ever had remained upstairs together, too afraid to leave despite thirst and hunger and icy cold, furiously wondering what might happen to them. They heard Narcissa cry out, and those who could moved to the window, though there was nothing to see in the dark but indecipherable lumps, one of which was the woman who'd fed and sheltered them when they had nowhere else to go.

These children, all girls but one, sucked in the smell of death through the night. The fetid remains of the butchered cow. Human entrails hanging from the fence. The children could not help but smell their dying sisters, the pair of girls clinging to the last threads of light and begging for water. Nathan Kimball was still in the room and had dipped a cloth into the only pitcher to clean his wounds, rendering the water undrinkable for children who would die without it. To his credit the man wrapped himself in a blanket in the wee hours of the morning and slipped off to the river. Before he left, he asked one of the girls to pull out a cotton sheet, tear it into strips, and wrap his wounds. She protested that Mrs. Whitman would be irate if her sheets were ruined. "Don't you know," Kimball told her, "that your mother has no more use for sheets?"

Ten minutes later, on his way back to the house with a full bucket, Kimball was shot by a Cayuse scout, who called out, one of the children later wrote, "See how I make the white man tumble?"

Morning came, and on this last day of November 1847, dawn leaking in the pale sky, a Cayuse man returned to the ditch to smash in Narcissa's skull too. This was an assurance, the tribe believed, that the missionaries who'd lived as increasingly unwelcome neighbors for eleven years would be barred from the afterlife they'd so loudly glorified.

News of violence at Waiilatpu stirred outrage all the way back to Washington, DC, where legislators made haste to give this newly acquired territory an official name, Oregon, and to hire a US Marshall, Joe Meek, and to assign a governor of the provisional government, George Abernathy. One of the latter's first acts as head of the state was to declare war on the Cayuse Nation, Narcissa's death alone justification enough to raise an army, to strike out in retribution.

Thus began revenge on a tribe that did not let up until the Cayuse lost their land for good. They were weak, many of them sick, and hiding in the woods. Five Cayuse chiefs turned themselves over to authorities so, they said, the rest of the tribe might be saved. The chiefs were transported to Oregon City and sat through four days of questionable witness testimony and scant hours of jury deliberation. It was common knowledge that two of the accused had been nowhere near the mission on November 29, 1847. Several witnesses were also not present at Waiilatpu during the attack but were put on the stand to recite what they'd heard from others. The verdict was a swift *guilty*. The chiefs were hung without family or tribe present, without ceremony. They were cut down and buried in unmarked graves so that no one could visit a final resting place to pay tribute or to sit in grief and prayer. The grave has never been located again.

# 5

Even though he was old, in his 90s, and ready to go, I'd dreaded my own grandfather's passing. Still, I couldn't have predicted how unhinged I would feel when this last grandparent was no longer around. Not that I was close to him, my father's father. I wish I'd been but I wasn't. My belief in him as our family patriarch was nearly biblical despite my secular Sundays reading the *New York Times* far from any candlelit pew. As long as Grandpa Bob was planted in Salmon, steady on as always, I was steady too.

One June afternoon when I was fifty-five years old, my grandfather who'd hardly ever left Salmon told my aunt he was going to die that night. The next morning she raised her eyebrows and greeted her father sauntering into the kitchen. He said a message had drifted in while he was asleep: furniture had to be rearranged up there to accommodate him, but the wait wouldn't be long. Two nights later he called for my aunt again, and, when she got to his bed, he asked for his alarm clock. He tucked it into the crook of his arm. He woke her again about an hour later and asked for a flashlight. She said, "Why do you need a flashlight, Daddy?" He answered, "So I can see the goddamn alarm clock." By morning he was dead.

The following afternoon, one sister (of two) and one brother (of two) and I met in Salmon. I was a grandmother myself, making it unlikely for me to still have a living grandfather as mine had been only hours before. I figured that hardly a speck remained of the girl me who once lolled in the shade of Jessie Creek behind his house, though maybe a few cells clung to the cottonwoods or were suspended in the sparkling mist on top of the water. I liked to think, anyway, that not all sign of me was gone.

Soon after I arrived we climbed into my father's truck to travel across town to see our grandfather. Grandpa Bob was in a box at the funeral home, the lumber store's stamp at one end of the nailed-together plywood, grade B in bright-orange letters, which meant he wasn't in his rocking chair in the house tuned to the golf channel and keeping an eye peeled for Tiger's Swedish wife, who'd long before split. He wasn't in his shop or at the Salmon River Inn sipping near-beer. He wasn't telling his story about shooting the last wolves—a male, a female, and two pups  in their den, or entertaining a crowd with his tale about a bear cub he kept for a day in a suitcase. Nor would he regale us with another old yarn about two *fellers* he worked with in a logging camp. He called the pair in this tale "Sven and Sven" and told how they'd set themselves at either end of the crosscut saw for crazy-long stretches in the Idaho forest, jamming chewing tobacco into the hairy pockets of their underarms, their singlets soon drenched with sweat the stink and color of diarrhea. The twin Svens, my grandfather said, were ablaze on that wood. They ground their teeth, bulked the rippling muscles of their backs, elbows swinging in and out, wild-eyed from the wet chaw soaking into their bloodstreams and shirts and skin as, one after another, massive trees around them were reduced to transportable logs.

Those were his stories, but now Grandpa Bob was dead at ninety-two, and my brother Ron and sister Cindy and our father walked to the far end of the dank funeral chapel and stared down on the man who'd held us all together, our father

23

shifting from foot to foot as if he thought he could fool everyone into believing he wasn't jarred by a grief that was immeasurable.

I kept my distance from him, my father, caution already tingling the back of my neck. In a state of mourning he could blow up, and I'd be a handy target. What was I doing here in Salmon? That's what I was afraid he'd ask me. *What makes you think any of this is still yours?*

I actually live farther west than my father does. Our house is not far from the ultimate destination of hundreds of thousands of Oregon Trail emigrants—the largest migration in this nation's history begun, basically, by Marcus and Narcissa Whitman. After the Whitmans opened the trail (they were the first to transport women and a wagon of domestic goods across the Rocky Mountains, or so it was reported back in 1836), hordes of others got worked up about traversing it too, to take up land given over to about any overlander who could manage to ford untamed rivers and hack through the tangled woods to reach the land of plenty. Many of those 300,000 Oregon Trail pioneers were bound for a well-advertised paradise, the Willamette Valley in Western Oregon. Here there was no illness, no extreme weather; here you need only toss in a few seeds, cast grain to the wind, or so promised brochures coaxing folks out to take up their share of river-bottom land, while ignoring the people who'd inhabited said land for generations. (Laura Ingalls Wilder, in *Little House on the Prairie*, expresses the attitude succinctly when one of the settlers in her novel insists, "There were no people. Only Indians lived there.")

It was all sunny tranquility in the untamed West if the brochures told the truth: crops were easy to grow, animals thrived, children prospered. One advertisement even swore that a dead man who'd fallen into nutrient-rich Willamette Valley soil rose again after a couple of days, hale and hearty, better than ever.

The home I live in with my husband is tucked in the Cascade woods. I'm hugged in by acre upon acre of soaring Douglas fir trees and cedar, one hundred feet straight up, one hundred fifty feet up, up. A couple decades ago I wouldn't have believed I could be this settled, for back then I resembled nothing more than a frayed electric cord sizzling at the peeled-away end. I'd signed away a bad marriage and swept my four daughters out of Arizona, where I'd attended graduate school, to a new state, Oregon. I thought I could do it all—take care of my kids, support my family on a lousy salary, keep us from danger in a little house at the edge of town—only to discover that mine were mostly days of failure piled on failure. I was broke and alone, and finally it was my father who bailed me out by giving me money. I remember the spring afternoon we sat on a bench in a park near my house, his body stiff with his usual sternness that insists, *You better the hell not stay down,* while he wrote out a check. Just the same as when we were kids—*Get up, walk it off,* he'd say if one of us got hurt. *Rub it hard. You're all right.* What I wanted was permission to curl up like a hurt dog, do nothing for a while, but he wasn't one to give it.

These days I stand on our deck in the summer with the *whoo-hoos* of church-group rafting excursions bouncing off the river. Osprey chirp and dive in for fat, stocked trout and keep up this daily hunt until chicks fledge and rainy season chases them off to sunnier climes. Rain falls in the autumn and through the winter and on into spring while I stand on the deck once again, walk in the woods again and again, curious why I still can't get quite right with myself. I have a lot. Kids grown and gone, hours of peace yawning before me, but I churn. I'm a churner. I hike through land my husband has protected with a rare diligence for half a century, rain dripping off the trees and dribbling from the old man's beard moss, rain on maple leaves, on alder and cottonwood, like a high piano key struck over and over again, *plink, plink, plink.*

At the base of the Bitterroots, the valley is dry. The corners feel sharper in Idaho's conifer forests, and the ground crunches when you walk over it. Aspen and spruce grow tall in the summit. I remember stepping out of my grandparents' squat red house and, though I'd seen them a thousand times, a thousand-thousand times, gasping at the shining white mountains that pierce a shimmering sky, so near it seemed to me the peaks might drive right up my nose if I leaned in.

The old house my husband and I live in now in the lush woods was built a century after the Oregon Trail rush and during the logging rush and it's far enough west that the Pacific Ocean might lap at my door someday if the prediction of a shattering earthquake comes true, a good chunk of the coast crumbling into the boiling ocean.

My father wouldn't mind if that happened—if the western half of our state floated away. He calls it the phony West, populated by socialists. The title of Westerner is ours only by accident of geography. He holds Eastern Oregonians, across the mountains from where I live, in a different regard. This is where the Utah interlopers, Ammon Bundy and his followers, held up in a visitors' center in the middle of the high desert. The Bundys who plotted to stay *right there*, burning the cheese on their frozen pizzas in the center's microwave while occupying a tract of public land until kingdom come. This Bundy version of Manifest Destiny is based on neither history nor fact, and yet, in our new America, it is acceptable. The Bundys and their followers faced few legal consequences. They went home with their beliefs intact, reinforced, and my father approved maybe not of their tactics but certainly of their vigilante spirit. Snip government, especially the federal government, clean out of your lives. Go at it on your own or die. Let freedom ring.

All to say that politics could not come up between my father and me during my brief time in Salmon, they just couldn't, and especially not at the funeral home, please. Nor could I let the other subject that caused an inevitable clench—beginning in my jaw, ending somewhere around my knees—gain traction. That subject being my mother, the person he most loved to hate (she returned the sentiment). I'd lately realized I'd become a punch line to a tired joke: Did you hear the one about the woman well into her fifties who cowered like a child in front of her long-divorced parents? I stood silent as one argued that the other was the villain, the parent to never speak to again if I had integrity or backbone. Thus I visited when obligation or duty dragged me across the state line, but rarely drove over just to hang out in ease with my family. For thirty years I made myself as scarce as possible.

Now I stayed silent, too, at the mortuary lest I say the wrong thing, which is my special inclination around my family. What I wanted, what all of us wanted, was one last glimpse of our grandfather before he went to the fire. Grandpa Bob's body, which looked downright puny compared to his huge presence for the whole of my life, would soon be burned to ash. The essence of him would drift out the chimney to seed the pancake clouds over the Beaverhead Mountains. He'd spill down upon us. He was dead, and our family, the family I rubbed against and held tight to, with its many generations of making and breaking, drinking and brawling, with our habit of forging on no matter what and pissing each other off royally, had lost its center. Now who would we be?

# 6

A tale of two grandmothers, one known as mad and the other as sad. The sad grandmother was Mamie. Four of her five children, my mother the only survivor, died at birth from what was later identified as an Rh-negative blood factor. Robert, Ronald, Steven, Trudy Lou. In my earliest memories of Mamie she is laden. This made sense to me, that my grandmother had not recovered from four dead newborns in a row, though I didn't ask her about it. My mother said we must never bring up the babies in front of Mamie. It would destroy her. Our mother told a friend once in my presence that our grandmother, after the last infant died, refused to sign her name for many years. She didn't deserve a name.

Except a few years ago I studied my grandmother's sepia-toned wedding picture, a slim and jaunty Grandpa Ron at her side with both sides of the family surrounding them like curved petals around two tall stamen, and I noticed in that picture—before the pregnancies, before the birth of my mother—my grandmother's face was drawn and taut, her eyes hollow. She was a sorrowful woman, even before the Great Sorrow. I'll never know the cause of the rabbit warren of grief excavated through her body, probably starting from when she was a child, the oldest of four thin siblings scraping by with their parents during the Depression. I likely couldn't draw insight from my grandmother about her blue period of half a century if she was sitting next to me this day. She didn't think in those ways.

Grandma Lois was the mad one. Mad as in angry, not crazy. She would not have tolerated having her sanity scrutinized, whapping upside the head anyone who suggested such a thing.

Grandma Lois taught English at Salmon High for nearly four decades—specialty Shakespeare, specialty Tennyson (in particular "Ulysses," which she recited when prompted by a recalcitrant grandchild or stubborn husband, "to seek, to strive, but not to yield!") and Coleridge. She was well known around town for her rages. She raged inside the A&W Drive-In, she raged at the post office, she raged at the butcher in the IGA who'd trimmed too much fat off the chops. My plump grandmother had a booming voice and a wide nose, both inherited from the father she barely knew, a man who left her and her mother and brother in Boise when Lois was a toddler.

This grandmother never much liked me. Or maybe she did. I toggled back and forth, in the course of a single hour sometimes, trying to decide. Was I in or out with Grandma Lois? She liked my aunt's children and my uncle's children and took them on trips to Hawaii and bought them clothes at the beginning of the school year, and once when my youngest sister was brave enough to ask about a trip for us, and what about school shoes?, we were reminded that Lois and Bob had weathered their son and his trouble making wife through the Crisis—a baby too early. They paid the bills while Mike, now a father, finished high school. They helped with his family while their son went to college. And had it really been necessary to produce four children lined up like corncobs before that golden son was even twenty-one? Enough, in Grandma Lois's estimation, was *enough*. She had no more to give to us.

When I first read the story of Red Riding Hood and came to the part about the wolf eating the old woman, I thought, *Well, it depends on the grandmother.* Mamie, all dolefully pleasant, would have apologized to the wolf for being a wisp of a thing, not even a slice of fat to please he who would consume her. My Salmon great-grandmother, taciturn Hazel, with a slight crook in her back that made her look like she was fighting a wind, would have stared him down until he laid down his ears and slunk away. Grandma Lois would have kicked the wolf in the nuts, shouting at him to keep that nasty breath of his out of her face. She'd have gutted and roasted him for dinner.

I saw her not long before she died, Grandma Lois, her lungs thick now from too many years of cigarettes, her feet black and swollen as two butternut squash left out in the rain to rot. She lay on her old sofa, the one she'd rested on even when she was young and plump and lively and seeking its comfort as soon she got home from school. I remember her there, kicking off her shoes and digging into the tub of IGA potato salad. Near the time of her impending death, a sign of which was a cannula squirting oxygen up her nose, my grandmother remained most of the time on the sofa, and one day out of nowhere she decided to order wallpaper with a nature scene, copious Amazon foliage and snaking vines, green upon jungle green, to be hung on the wall next to her. Never mind that the most beautiful view on the planet, or so some of us believe, was a few feet away out the window—a shine on the land as seen only in Salmon. Not so much green as metallic, bronze hills, silver mountains, a molten river that flexed its shining muscles as it moved through its bed. But at the end of her time in this town where she'd raised three kids and lost a fourth, and lived with a man who was funny and strong and a philanderer, my grandmother preferred to stare into her verdant two-dimensional view of paradise.

The other three walls of her den held bookcases, floor to ceiling books. Books upon books. I have yet to meet another person who read as much as my grandmother, and in particular she went for books about the end of civilization, or at least a suggestion of the end. She reveled over stories of our culture's demise. Starting with *Idylls of the King*, her man Tennyson, and the *Oz* series set on the shelf in exact order, the bony lion on each cover next to the timid girl. The Baum books, Grandma Lois informed me, conveyed a truth about the darkness and smallness of the human soul that was nothing like the happy tale peddled by Hollywood. Never let yourself believe, she told me, Hollywood's happy tales.

The books she handed off early on were benign. *Mouse and the Motorcycle* and a Shakespeare coloring book featuring Juliet, Puck, Rosalind. Once she thought I was old enough, eight or nine, Grandma Lois set me down with Shirley Jackson's story, "The Lottery," and then *The Haunting of Hill House*. Later, Flannery O'Connor's *The Violent Bear it Away*. In between I read, at her bidding, her favorites: the crash-and-burn tales, the tester-of-wills stories. I don't remember the order exactly, but to my mind first is *Alas, Babylon*, by Pat Frank, an introduction to the mushroom cloud. Then James Hilton's *Lost Horizon* and his Shangri-La. Others followed. *Canticle for Leibowitz, The Penultimate Truth* (she was, naturally, a fan of Philip K. Dick), *On The Beach*, LeGuin's *Left Hand of Darkness*. And then the book she cherished most and offered to me with an admonition to either like it or keep my damn opinions to myself: *Earth Abides* by George R. Stewart.

George R. Stewart. I was surprised by the author's name on this dystopian novel from my youth when I saw it again some months ago. I tucked a scuffed, used copy under my arm, heading for a chair in the Oregon sunshine to read, filled with memories of childhood afternoons stretched out on a scratchy hide of a small bear that was shot by my grandfather when I was a first grader. I liked to rest my head on the hard nub of the skull when I was a kid, the bear's intact cranium solidly reassuring as I read about the end days in my grandmother's paperback of *Earth Abides*. My husband had picked up a used copy for me and he, too, was surprised by the revelation of the author. Stewart's *Names on the Land* has been important to his way of parsing the American landscape. To discover Stewart also wrote the novel that occupied me when I was a pre-pubescent child: that was wild.

As that girl I roamed my grandparents' property thinking about the survivors in Grandma Lois's end-of-the-world books. I believed down to the bone that catastrophe just might happen, as I was a child of the Cuban Missile Crisis, stopping, dropping, and-rolling under my desk on command. With my knees jammed into my chest, I waited for the burst and swell of radiation. Rumor had it that Idaho, with its subterranean storage of nuclear warheads, was second or third on the list of national targets, so, as a child, I slid down the sweep of crabgrass field that led to the Jessie Creek bridge, plotting how my family would manage if we were the last humans in this part of the world. If poison killed off nearly everyone but left us untouched on our mountain, unscathed, the ones to reinvent society. I'd be assigned duties. I'd find helpful work and please the adults in a way I couldn't seem to in real life. My grandfather would forge us a shelter, my father and brother would shoot an elk and cure the meat, my grandmothers would plant a garden, tend to sheep and chickens and, if we're talking Grandma Lois, recite to us some Victorian-era poems ("Work without hope is like nectar in a sieve!"). We'd take care of what needed taken care of, and I would never again resort to the trance of boredom I often fell into at home. A fugue state I'd perfected on the afternoons my mother left me in the back of the family station wagon while she shopped for clothes, while she dropped in on her friends for a chat, while she picked up day-old Wonder Bread at the Wonder Bread store. The idea of massive change thrilled me: to finally be useful, torpor abolished. Fully awake and *useful*. Not like my normally dull self twitching in the hot car, and not like the victims of disaster in my grandmother's novels. Even as a child I couldn't tolerate ridiculous characters who hid in the wrong buildings and relied on the wrong people and forgot how to feed themselves. They were placid, with little drive and no stir of creativity.

My people were mighty.

I worried, of course, how I'd keep up. I had no training in the use of hand tools and had a lousy sense of direction. I couldn't gut a grouse or find a rodent's innards if you paid me. A snowstorm or days without milk to warm my belly could do me in. I was downright terrified to be tested by hardship, and yet I realize now how much I yearned for that very test.

I wonder, Why this collection of dystopian books for my grandmother, who preferred the company of the wry and smart and dismissed any fools? What was it that captured Lois's imagination? I wish I'd asked her. My guess is that this woman who became my father's mother probably never should have married the charming Grand Robert, as she called him; she should have stayed in Boise with her mother and grandmother and watched the town grow into a thriving city, and she should have traveled to Europe as a young woman instead of an old one. She might have dressed in her generation's version of the hoop skirt, her youthful take on my great-great-grandmother's layers of taffeta and tulle that Lois hung in a closet for an unreasonably long time (though I wish she'd hung onto them longer and given one to me). Instead Lois landed in Salmon at age twenty-five, laid flat by the Great Depression. She'd lost her teaching job in Boise and was forced to take a job selling washing machines, one or two saggy dresses to her name and a blue hat that appears in most of the early photos. She married a Salmon fellow with whom she'd spent five days. Five days. After that her reality was work and worry—how would they get by when everything was so razor thin?

The books gave my grandmother a way out. She didn't ever say so, but that's my take on it. A way out of the mountains, out of a marriage she refused to put an end to—she wasn't about to squeeze her children like she had been by divorced parents. Better to give her lackluster union little weight and instead put her mind on the problem of what to do after the near finish of Earth's population, because no errant germ would knock Lois over. No meteor would smash her into the ground. No radiation cloud, by god, was going to dribble its toxins on my grandmother. She was too determined for such trouble. Maybe my grandmother pictured herself roaming through the IGA and McPhersons Mercantile in Salmon, stepping over bloated bodies and grabbing everything she'd once picked up and put back, items she'd desired but couldn't afford. Or she planned to slog her way through ruin and move in to her grandmother's Boise mansion, an impressive home reduced when her family fell on hard times. She'd retrieve the fine European furniture and French wind-up bird in a cage from the attic, the best wine from vacated shops. No one could tell her ever again that she had to settle for a meager existence, a small pot of goodies when everyone else enjoyed abundance. I can see Lois on a hilltop, alive and alone after so many others perished, fashioning an existence in just the way she, and no one else, desired.

My grandmother had many desires.

If Grandma Lois weren't dead, I'd send her other apocalyptic tales—*The Road*, and also *Station Eleven*, Saramago's *Blindness*. I'd get her to watch *A Handmaid's Tale* and call her to talk about the anguished flinches of Elisabeth Moss's face. We might read together later Le Guin novels. We'd talk for hours on the phone about books and films, safe territory between us. Do I long for that conversation because I'm after my own escape from a dreary trudge and she'd be the one with whom to commiserate? Maybe. Mostly I like the idea of hatching with her what I'd make new, how I'd start over if I were forced to begin again, creating something fresh out of the rubble. No more glancing up at the clock and thinking, *Where did this day go, so little accomplished?* No more wondering if I've done enough to earn my life.

# 7

I tried to recall some details of what I'd been taught of Narcissa Whitman in the fourth grade, the year children are given a unit in Idaho history. What I remembered was the feeling of a general pleasure back then, an embrace of whatever history was handed to me by teachers and adults. I absorbed the stories presented in the classroom and in the books I read because . . . why wouldn't I? Why would someone print a historical record that wasn't wholly accurate and true, and why would my teacher recite anything not dependable? I was given to an ineffable civic warmth blooming in my chest when I read about the courageous founders of the intermountain West, the same glow that rose to my cheeks when I pledged allegiance to the flag as a young girl, Mrs. Anderson at the head of the class leading us in "God Bless America" with her patriotic high notes and moist eyes.

As fourth graders we read accounts—all favorable no doubt—of Narcissa, a missionary, and her husband, Marcus, a doctor and a missionary, along with their missionary companions Henry and Eliza Spalding, who crossed the Rocky Mountains with a wagon in 1836, Narcissa just a few steps ahead of Eliza. They arrived in what would soon be officially designated as Oregon Territory, and both women soon gave birth to the first white babies of the West—Narcissa first, naturally, because Narcissa was first at everything.

The babies might have been spoken of by our teacher, but

Narcissa's end wasn't. Or maybe I'm wrong, maybe we cringed at her death and shivered at the portrayal of Indians who'd struck her down, those Native people portrayed as enemies, as bloodthirsty evildoers, people whose traditions, whose families, whose losses were given no room in our textbooks.

New settlers in the West surely cringed over the Whitman deaths, and they let it be known that after all of their sacrifices to get out to settle this land as the government had practically begged them to do, they would not abide attacks on white people. The new inhabitants of the West wanted protection from Native tribes and laws that delineated ownership of land, as well as punishment for anyone who crossed newly established and often invisible boundaries. The debate over ownership of land was underway long before anyone died at the Whitman Mission, but it was spurred to crackling energy by the bloody limbs of missionaries tossed like doll parts across frozen grasslands. As a fourth grader I heard nothing of the stump of Narcissa's leg in the mouth of a coyote or wolf as it was dragged across the ground, though I appreciate the visceral potency now. Stories like that must have shaken everyone to the core.

It's a mystery why, in 1809 in the village of Prattsburg, New York, Clarissa Prentiss named her temperamental first daughter Narcissa. The other girls, the ones to come, would be called Harriet and Jane and Mary, and there's the matriarch's namesake, Clarissa, at the end. So, why Narcissa? Maybe a clever rhyme with the mother's name, or maybe the flower. It had to be the latter. Clarissa didn't go for trite or clever, though it's possible she had a fondness for the cousin of the iris. Doubtful that Clarissa or her husband—not well-educated people, though Father Prentiss served as the local judge and was known for sentencing wrongdoers to public whippings that he liked to watch—read the myth of Narcissus. If they had, they would have rejected it as pagan storytelling. For the rest of us, Ovid's version of the myth goes something like this: Beautiful Narcissus, dearly loved and admired for his ideal physique, is followed through the woods by the adoring nymph Echo. Narcissus calls out, "Who's there?" only to be answered by, "Who's there?" When Echo steps out to proclaim her love, Narcissus shoos her away, breaking Echo's heart and thus infuriating the goddess of revenge, Nemesis. It's this goddess who puts a spell on the boy. Forevermore he'll be entranced by his own image in a pond. Staring at his rippling reflection, Narcissus loses contact with every other person and even his own body; he can't be bothered to eat or drink while gazing at his beloved. He soon dies of starvation—although other versions of the story have him stabbing himself, his spilled blood providing the nourishment for the spring flower and its faint spot of red.

If Narcissus's vanities were legendary, so were—to the handful who knew her well when she was a girl—Narcissa's. She wrapped her long, strawberry-blonde hair on top of her head and dazzled everyone with her singing voice. People jammed into the Prentiss living room, some riding over from the far corners of Steuben County, if Narcissa was putting on a performance. Yet she intentionally kept herself out of the glow. She sang to glorify her savior. Because of her mother's strict rules, and Narcissa's desire to be just as devout, every melody was a solemn celebration of God.

"Christians were melted to tears, and hardened sinners bowed their heads and wept bitterly," wrote a man from her village who once squeezed into the house for a concert.

Clarissa, whose religious dictates were so severe her own husband balked at times, didn't much like Narcissa's music. Mother Prentiss stressed to her children that it was best not to sing too much, or to grin—"It was a rare thing to see any of them indulge in laughter," wrote one family friend of the couple. Mother Clarissa certainly showed little emotion on her own, restraint being the reflection of piety. She stressed to her eldest daughter that it was necessary to contain one's pleasure. "I wish Narcissa would not always have so much company," she once muttered to the judge.

It was soon after Narcissa's birth that lonely young Clarissa began attending religious meetings and helped start her town's first Presbyterian Church (though Judge Prentiss refused to join in—owner of a distillery, he was disgusted by rules of temperance). She got caught up in what was later named the Second Great Awakening, a movement that promised a relationship with God different from the doddering Calvinistic tradition: A direct connection with the divine. Tenderness and mercy granted to each person who spread the Word (ministering to others was of upmost importance) and who helped prepare the way for the return of Christ. The Second Great Awakening quickly spread its tendrils, catching hold like no movement before, a spiritual enthusiasm that's been called "the most widespread intellectual force ever liberated in the United States."

When I asked a Western historian about the movement, she said that the Second Great Awakening began among Scotch Irish pioneers and caught on with others, particularly in New York State, where a man named Charles Finney and his wife were responsible for month-long revivals in places like Rochester, many of which Clarissa must have attended. The area was soon referred to as the Burnt Over District, focused mostly on upstate New York, home not only to evangelism but Millerism (they believed the end was imminent), socialist phalanxes, Utopian societies, and even women's suffrage.

"It must have been a lively place!" she told me.

In large, empty fields, some relatively close to the Prentiss home, believers set up tents, musicians jangled and strummed, and preachers preached the word while newcomers swooned over theological tenets of personal salvation and the belief that "every person can be saved through revivals." The main task of new believers was converting nonbelievers to the faith. That included—maybe most especially for Narcissa's Presbyterian Church—the Native people of the frontier West. Encountered thus far by precious few whites, the Natives were wide open for the taking (or so it was assumed).

Here's how another scholar says it: "Mixed with Puritanism and Calvinism, with Jeffersonian democracy and the frontier spirit, [the Second Great Awakening] became a highly explosive force."

When Narcissa turned eleven, Clarissa decided it was time to take her daughter to a camp meeting, where women wailed and men threw themselves on the ground, speaking in tongues. Once mother and daughter were sharing the Word of God with others gathered on the dusty lot, diving into the fervor, young Narcissa was done in, forever sold. She'd known since infancy that her life would be given over to God (with Clarissa's aid and at Clarissa's bidding), but after the revival she thought about nothing else. She called subsequent gatherings "the melting seasons," with melty souls flowing toward Christ, and it became her life's ambition to lead others to the altar. By age fifteen she had declared that she would get herself a western missionary post, and she wrote to the ABCFM board in Boston to volunteer, a youthful exuberance she was later critical of: "I frequently desired to go to the heathen, but only half-heartedly." Although she sounds wholehearted when, as that same fifteen-year-old, she continues, "I consecrate myself without reserve to the missionary work awaiting the leadings of Providence concerning me." While waiting for an answer she moved on to attend a well-reputed Female Seminary in Troy, New York, to learn to be a teacher, and then, with her father pulling a few strings, she continued her education at the Franklin Academy in her hometown of Prattsburg. She was instructed on the tenets of a spiritual life rather than one pre-scribed for pretty girls in the Fingerlake District. There'd be no ordinary marriage for Narcissa. No house full of squabbling babies or delicate vases and fine furniture. Her mother had already disavowed the reading of novels (fiction was "light and vain trash") and social evenings around the piano. Claris-sa's daughter was destined for greater things.

The missionary board refused Narcissa's first application. And her second. If she was to travel west, as she desired, Nar-cissa must marry. ("I don't think we have missions among the Indians where unmarried females are valuable right now," was the corresponding secretary's response.) The board believed marriage would keep missionary men from tempting liaisons with Native women, and so it was marriage that Narcissa would have to pursue.

For a long time Narcissa showed little interest in finding a husband. Or maybe she couldn't find a man willing to make the long trek into the darkest corner of the continent with her, a young fellow in her crowd willing to give up every last thing for God.

Discouraged by the board's refusal of her as the church's witness in the West, Narcissa turned to closer matters: she taught physics classes and also kindergarten and began to help other students at Franklin Academy—a school her father helped start and unusual for being co-ed—refine their religious standards. Some afternoons after classes, after prayers, lovely

Narcissa spent hours talking with a certain young man. She tolerated him though he was a sniveler, a whiner, who gave off a stench in the only suit he owned. He needed her counsel and her strict views on practicing their mutual ideals; he required her patient tutelage as he had poor reading skills and could only write "after copy." She sat with him though he tended to be pissy when there was no reason to mope. In general, he thought of himself as ostracized and mistreated by others because of the circumstances of his birth—his mother was unmarried when he was born, and that was an unforgiveable flaw for a child back then. His stepfather loathed the boy, a reminder of his wife's tawdry past. The bastard child was whipped daily and cast out of the house as soon as he could possibly make it on his own.

This was Henry Spalding, who used his unhappy childhood to turn himself into a complaining and manipulative man. Everyone said so. Yet here at their school was the enchanting (and bossy—everyone said so) Narcissa, offering him her attention and—a bit of self-satisfaction he chewed on like a nut—her affection.

A benefactor had provided the money for Henry to attend the Franklin Academy and then to go on to seminary, where he'd be ordained as a minister. The irony was that her eventual husband, Marcus Whitman, who Narcissa knew nothing about during these school years, spent his youth desperately trying to find funds for religious training. Marcus's father—who ran a tavern and was the Rushville, New York, tanner, currier, and shoemaker—died at age thirty-seven, and this third of six children was sent to Massachusetts to live with an uncle, Freedom Whitman. For the next decade Marcus was shaped into a "pious boy," including a life of rigid Presbyterian worship not unlike Narcissa's, which directed him to a soulful missionary life. But there was no benefactor, so there'd be no expensive seminary. Instead the family scraped up dollars for medical school. With no other choice, Marcus spent six weeks riding with a doctor, Ira Bryant, uncle of William Cullen Bryant, who happened to be a schoolmate of Marcus and who also happened to be the first to use the word "Oregon" in his poem "Thanatopsis": ". . . Where rolls the Oregon, and hears no sound / Save his own dashings—yet the dead are there." The two, the old doctor and the new, traveled through small villages, with Marcus learning to tend to wounds (digging out shrapnel became a specialty) and, since germ theory was well in the future, to comfort the ill. Marcus was forced to settle for the designation of Dr. before his Whitman, instead of Rev. The physician title was considered a lesser one, which Henry Spalding never let him forget.

Long before Marcus was on the scene, back in the school days, Spalding was utterly taken with the generous-hearted and unyielding-in-her-faith Narcissa. All that kittenish, flowing hair. All those pretty songs from her pretty throat. She listened to his carping and urged him in his prayerful quests. Maybe she was surprised, but no one else was, when he announced that he could accept no other for his wife. Henry told her that he, too, was fated to be a missionary out at the far ends of the world as they knew it. The two of them would journey to the frontier, where they would bring enlightenment to the heathens, apart from friends and family, relying exclusively on each other.

Narcissa refused him flat out, no need to think it over.

Which made him furious. At first Henry wouldn't let her rejection lie, and he hounded her with letters, missives, with visits to her home that she did not welcome. *Mr. Spalding, leave me alone.* When Henry persisted, the judge got up in the man's face. Stay clear of my daughter, or else.

The beloved, the darling Narcissa, was after that regarded as Henry's worst enemy. The most selfish of women, to be quashed and denigrated. As one biographer writes of Henry Spalding, "He would not forgive her until she was dead."

There was no way for Narcissa to know then that eight years after meeting and spurning Henry Spalding—a period during which he wrote to the mission board to defame her, urging members to turn away the spinster Prentiss—he would be the only choice to accompany her and her new husband on the journey to the frontier. Henry and his frail and mousy wife, Eliza.

Soon after Narcissa and Marcus met, which was the same day they announced their betrothal, Marcus left for the West—a trial journey in 1835 to check out the situation to which he would soon commit himself and his future spouse. He'd been invited to travel with Rev. Samuel Parker, a minister who'd inspired Narcissa to new passion about the missionary life when he'd given a series of talks at her church. She considered Parker a moral compass and guide. (Narcissa, in her journal, excitedly wrote, "I have had an interview with the Rev. Samuel Parker upon the subject of Missions and have determined to offer myself to the Board for a mission beyond the Rocky Mountains.")

On their long journey Marcus found the minister to be lazy and often conniving, a burden and a troublemaker. For one thing, Parker promised the Cayuse that when Protestant missionaries returned the tribe would be paid handsomely for whatever land was required for the mission station, a pledge that later ramped up the heat between the two factions. Marcus came home from the disappointing trip with the reverend hoping never to lay eyes on the man again. The young doctor didn't arrive alone, however, as he carted along two young

Nez Perce boys who, I suppose, he meant to put on display as he made his fundraising rounds. There are several versions of what happened in subsequent years to these children, none of them favorable. One tells that one boy died and the other was sent back, no longer able to integrate well with his tribe.

Once in New England Marcus pushed hard on the Boston-based board, his bosses, to choose new co-missionaries in order to get the next trek, the *real* journey, underway. The board insisted that one member of the party be an ordained minister—the only way to get their financial support. Marcus went after Henry Spalding, a prospect anathema to Narcissa. When the board discovered that Eliza was pregnant, the Spaldings were suddenly off. Relief. But later came the message that Eliza's baby was stillborn, and the couple was back on—as if making the journey with a newborn would be too much, but five months of travel was considered tolerable for the grieving, weak, and often ill young mother.

Narcissa, with this will-they-or-won't they Spalding question hanging over her head, married Marcus in her family's church—the bride wore black bombazine. The man she'd agreed to call husband after their brief encounter was set on getting out to the frontier immediately to save souls, as he had already laid that groundwork for their mission. (Other historians believe they might have spotted each other at least one other time, at a church function. What's known for sure is that after a series of letters, the two met in earnest in early 1835 and decided that very afternoon, for the pleasure of God and the missionary trek, to get hitched.) She liked his tendency of dogged planning. She'd decided from his letters that he was nice enough. Marcus was a fairly docile man until he was pushed, and then his temper flared. He was a little sickly with a pain in his side that he couldn't self-diagnose, and yet he was industrious. He'd build her a decent house and grow food while she began their work of filling Native souls with God's love. She was certain of it.

In March of 1836 the newlywed Whitmans and the Spaldings—Eliza hardly able to stand—met in Cincinnati. The missionary board still had worries about the pairing; maybe it wasn't too late to amend the arrangement. A letter to Marcus warned that it was "better to go alone than with unsuitable associates, therefore use great caution in finding and recommending men." Neither couple was happy about being together, but they nevertheless decided to forge on rather than see the mission trip botched. They would march and ride side by side for over two thousand miles. Little fresh food. One real chance along the way (in what's now Laramie, Wyoming) to give clothing more than a perfunctory wash. Their only bed the hard ground, and their only fuel for most fires the buffalo chips that Narcissa and Eliza would gather in grimy aprons.

Off they went, then, a snarl unfolding among them on this first-ever Oregon Trail overland journey. The cast of characters strikes me as a perfect setup for one of the end-of-the-world novels my grandmother was fond of reading. Or at least a juicy prospect for a reality TV show hosted by a sniveling bully.

On one side is the rebuffed Henry, ladling on insults every time he can think of one, especially if his dig is directed straight at Narcissa. On the other side is Marcus, too put off by the nastiness spewing from an ordained minister in regard to another man's wife (Marcus's own wife, that is) to slug Henry in the paunchy gut. William Gray, the hired-on mechanic, grumbles and protests that he should have been given significant duties and not stuck with tasks clearly beneath him, work he agreed to when he was hired. Eliza is doing everything she can to not keel over and die (the rest think she will—soon). And here is morning-sick Narcissa, left to wonder why God stuck her in a cauldron of misery with her nasty former suitor. "He is one who never ought to have come," Narcissa wrote her mother about Spalding in one of her heavy letters home (loads of letters home, many with judiciously worded complaints about her lonely existence, her friendless days). "My dear husband has suffered more from him in consequence of his wicked jealousy, and his great pique toward me, than can be known in this world."

*He would not forgive her until she was dead.*

8

People I'm related to arrived in the Whitmans' wake to make something of themselves and to make something of land ripe for settlement, for farms and ranches and thrumming towns. The West by then, by the mid-1860s, was calmed to a relative purr for white settlers after a string of violence—not just the sixteen dead at the mission (I'm counting the girls) but whole local tribes beaten down, quashed, forced to move onto reservations in the name of white progress. The Cayuse, Nez Perce, Chinook, Walla Walla, and others, including the nomadic Agaidika (Salmon eater) Shoshone. For centuries this tribe lived near current-day Salmon, Idaho, until, around 1907, most remaining Agaidika were sent against their will to the Fort Hall Reservation. The band was Sacajawea's, she who was supposedly born in a copse of cottonwoods just a handful of miles from where my mother gave birth to me in the Steele Memorial Hospital in Salmon.

I could go on here about my objection to the injustices toward Native people in this country, how sick and sad I am about it, but at the same time I have to admit it's possible, had I been around in the 1830s, that I probably would have agreed with Narcissa Whitman's convictions. I like to think I'd have been more enlightened than she was, but there's no denying my white heritage, and as a white woman back then I'd likely be in a cozy home in, say, St. Louis, or Prattsburg, New York, or Boston, reading the newspapers, as she did, as persuaded by a course of action as she was.

One of the most persuasive newspaper articles had to do with four Native men, who traveled some thousands of miles in 1831 to seek out General William Clark in St. Louis. This is where the sixty-year-old Clark lived now, head of the Bureau of Indian Affairs, his deeply troubled pal Meriwether Lewis dead by his own hand. It was the time of the annual Rendezvous on the Green River, a raucous gathering where furs were traded, goods were purchased, partying ensued, and proselytizers shouted their warnings of hell from upturned crates. But beyond the bare outline of a tale—four men seeking General Clark in this hubbub—the story gets muddled. Some tellers said the men were Flathead and insisted they had sloped foreheads (reputedly having had boards tied to their heads as infants). Others said they were Nez Perce (reputedly having punched metal through their noses). Most versions report that two of the men died from illness as soon as they reached the filthy, overcrowded Rendezvous. Some say one, maybe both, died on the way back home.

Whatever the facts, a man named G. P. Disoway collected that which suited his ecclesiastical bent and wrote a column that was subsequently published in several newspapers. It was read by the likes of the first missionary to the West, Jason Lee, and the likes of Narcissa Prentiss, of Marcus Whitman, of Henry Spalding, and anyone else with an itch to save Native souls. In his article Disoway claims that the meeting with Clark (who had, by then, forgotten his rudimentary knowledge of indigenous languages and had a great deal of trouble understanding what the men were after) had one purpose, and one purpose only: to find out about the "White man's book of heaven."

Whatever the actual reason for a reconnection with their "white father," who several tribes remembered from his journey through their country nearly three decades earlier, Disoway transformed a loose anecdote into a national calling. He insisted that his friend William Walker, a Wyandote man, had been in on the meeting, and that the Native men in Walker's presence *begged* Clark for white missionaries to travel to the frontier for the purpose of offering Christian salvation.

Except Walker was not in St. Louis at the time of the Rendezvous. He did not meet the Native men, and whatever story he passed on to Disoway, which he'd heard second- or thirdhand himself, was further embellished by the writer, including an entirely fabricated final section where Disoway describes a feast during which one of the Native men stood to say, "I came to you, the Great Father of White men, with one eye partly opened. I am to return to my people, beyond the mountains of snow, at the setting sun, with both eyes in darkness and both arms broken. I came for teachers and am going back without them. I came to you for the book of God. You have not led me to it."

Disoway's concocted story was first published in a Protestant newspaper called the *American Advocate*, and it laid out the dilemma in stark black and white, ending with an admonition: "Let the church awake from her slumbers, and go forth in her strength to the salvation of these wandering sons of our native forests."

In 1892 the ethnologist Alice C. Fletcher, well known for her early studies of Native American culture (that Alice Fletcher is also the name of the main character on a recent HBO Western can't be a coincidence), published an account of interviews she'd undertaken with a Niimíipuu (Nez Perce) elder. She'd come to him, she noted in those documents, to better chronicle the tribe's response to the arrival of the rush of settlers to the Pacific Northwest. When she asked about the story of four men who'd traveled to the Rendezvous, the elder gave her the version that had been passed down to him. In Fletcher's words, "Old Speaking Eagle [a chief] was of a philosophic turn of mind, and the question as to whether the sun was father and the earth the mother of the human race was one question that occupied him. When Speaking Eagle heard about the white man's Jesus, son of God, he wondered, 'How can the sun make a boy?'"

Fletcher continues, "It was the discussion of such questions as these that led the four men to determine to find the trail of Lewis and Clark, and to ask them about facts concerning the sun and the earth."

It's hard to know what to do with Fletcher's white-woman account, or with Disoway's column, which was illustrated with a drawing of a crudely flattened forehead. Some tribes, including several Cayuse bands, flattened heads, but that wasn't a Niimíipuu Tribe practice, according to descriptions I've read. Also, one historian notes that it was at this very Rendezvous (when the four men came to meet with General Clark) that members of the Niimíipuu tribe were first referred to as *Nez Perce*. No one seems to know why, as piercing one's nose was not a common practice either, and yet from then until now the name has been attached to these particular people.

What Narcissa saw in the newspaper was a picture of a flat-headed man with a dour expression, blank eyes, and a visage that agitated her greatly, and she swore to herself and her family that she would go to these untamed people and offer them civility. She would instill the proper faith in an Edenic land and await the return of the savior. If the indigenous people of the West wanted the Bible, she would carry it to them. If tribes wished to avoid the harsh ends their eastern counterparts had suffered, she would teach them to avoid that fate. She'd instruct them to cook as white people did, to raise their children as white parents raised theirs (Narcissa was known to rampage through the Cayuse encampment, untying infants from their cradleboards). To stop their nomadic travels and take up the plow. She and Marcus would lead them. She and Marcus would *redeem* the Natives because, most of all, she believed the tribes of the West would happily give up superstitious notions—the Cayuse believed in the spiritual nature of all living things—in favor of her God. Bible in hand, scripture in her mouth, this was Narcissa's purpose.

I'm fairly certain that my great-grandparents shared something of the same mind-set when they moved to Salmon at the turn of the twentieth century to live near the last encampment of Shoshone, renamed (by the Mormons, after one of their prophets) Lemhi. The Gwartneys didn't care so much about the religious conversion of Native people, as far as I know, but they did join other new settlers in supporting the idea that the Shoshone needed to move on, needed to give up most of their land to make way for white culture.

I don't exactly get to be appalled by this, my family's former or current xenophobia. Not as long as I'm the beneficiary of their way of life. The truth is, I have thrived because of what my family made in the West from the 1860s until now. The elk backstrap men brought down from hunting camps fed me as a girl, and so did the rainbow trout my grandfather hooked from the creek, the quail and pheasants my cousins shot in clearings, the pears and beans and choke cherry syrups my grandmothers put up in their kitchens. Wood was burned to keep me warm at night. I've never not had a roof over my head.

Still, memories fester in me. One, when I was traveling with my mother's folks, sitting between my grandparents in the front seat of their Wagoneer. Late at night, a ribbon of highway in southern Idaho, out where my mother's father grew up near Wendell. It's cold in the car. Mamie has wrapped me in her arms; she's pulled me close. No seat belts, so I fold into her for safety, too, and press one ear against her sweater to mute the sound under the tires. The thump, thump, thumping for miles. I've stopped watching out the windshield while my grandfather plows through hordes of jackrabbits crowding the highway as if he's running over clods of dirt.

"Grandpa," I mutter, but Mamie yanks on me, *Quiet now.*

My grandfather says, "It's best to be rid of vermin."

It's too dark to see the road behind us in the side mirrors. I don't wrench my neck to try. I've already imagined the burst rabbits, the umber stains they've left on the asphalt. And what can I do but remind myself that some things have to die so we can live as we do?

Including, maybe, the Native people around Salmon, the local band that had lived on this land for twelve thousand years. Chief Tendoy was their leader. It was Tendoy who in 1875 negotiated a reservation near Salmon with President Ulysses H. Grant, allowing the tribe to retain one hundred square miles of ancestral property. Within days the treaty was challenged by local settlers and governmental officials, and those challenges continued until the treaty was completely rescinded in 1907, the land sold to white people for seven cents per acre, perhaps my great-grandparents among the buyers. The tribe, down to a few people living outside of town, had hardly any presence when I was born at the end of the 1950s.

I often went downtown with a grandmother, to that single street in Salmon lined with shops and cafés, taverns, my maternal grandparents' newspaper, my great-grandparents' implements store, the mercantile where my grandmothers bought us hand-beaded moccasins at the start of summer that we wore until the bottoms were rock solid as the boulders we jumped on in Jessie Creek. Here came a caravan puttering down Main Street, three or four tall black cars that put me in mind of cereal boxes. Out stepped men in tight jeans and western shirts with snaps rather than buttons, cowboy hats on their heads and long, shiny braids down their backs. The women wore shapeless buckskin dresses, their hair in braids too.

I wanted to stare at them and study what was going on, but whatever grandmother I was with jerked me into the Rexall Drug Store or the City News Stand, where I bought my usuals, Juicy Fruit gum and *Archie* comics. "Don't look," the grandmother said. But I wanted to look, and I stepped to the window. "Stay away," she said. "They're dirty."

This I couldn't comprehend. I'd watched, several times in my girlhood, as the men and women from the cereal cars went into Gwartney Equipment for what was sold there: nails, screws, rope, chain, baling wire, barbed wire, copper wire, lanterns and Dutch ovens, and the fine screen needed to sieve gold. My great-grandparents accepted only cash from customers. But Grandpa Bob, co-owner, was willing to trade with the Lemhi. He liked their beautiful things. Their beautiful things were displayed in my grandparents' living room. Beads hung from the set of antlers, gloves and hair ties and a parfleche were laid out in a lawyer's bookcase. My grandfather and father both wore buckskin jackets to hunt in, hand sewn and beaded by Camille George, wife of Chief Willy George. I snugged onto my feet, most summer days, a pair of those moccasins made by people my grandmothers were sure would tarnish me.

# 9

The day after my grandfather died, we spent a few minutes staring at him in his box and then drove back to his house to eat Aunt Janice's hamburger stew, mix a few drinks, wander from room to room and out to the yard. I absorbed as much of the old cat smell and creaky-floor sound, the scruffy texture of the house, as I could manage. Who knew when I'd be back. Maybe never. I went into my aunt's childhood room, where Cindy and I slept when we were kids, and found the framed photo of our father's sister being crowned as an Honored Queen of Job's Daughters. I took it off the hook and remembered how I stood on the bed as a child, reaching out to touch the glittering tiara on my aunt's head, hardly believing such a reign was attainable by a Salmon girl, but there it was: a thick, purple robe swept wide around her feet, a scepter gripped with one hand, passages of scripture tripping off her tongue. And at the far reach of the photograph, I counted the men, Masons all, beaming an approval I longed for myself back then. I suppose in some ways I long for it still.

My aunt's room was located around a sharp corner and down the hall of my grandparents' house, far enough from the main door that I wasn't kept up by the late-night kitchen fights between warring couples or the bellowing of Grandpa Bob (before he cold-turkey quit in his mid-40s) or my looped uncle crashing through the living room toward bed. The open window in my aunt's room floated in the sounds of gurgling Jessie Creek behind the house and, maybe a quarter mile beyond, the roar of the Salmon River that let me sleep. Grandma Lois's family clock, which she set high on a living-room shelf and told us to keep our grimy selves from touching, was the other night sound I counted on. For years I thought I couldn't rest without the dual rhythm of time and water, and for many years I missed it.

I remember a dawn on one of those mornings in the days of my childhood, sometime in the late fall. I hear my grandfather in the basement shoveling coal, the clink of shovel metal against furnace steel. I shake Cindy awake, and we wait for the hum of first heat before we get up and pad on bare feet to the one register in the house. My sister and I tent our nightgowns over the hot air, curling our toes back from the edge so as not to get scorched, smug in the knowledge that our grandfather in the basement will keep us warm and safe. Coal air blows from the raging furnace, heat rising up my legs and through the neck-hole of my nightgown and around my ears to lift my hair, and I give in to the rare comfort that I'm okay here, that I'll be taken care of. That I'll be taken care of no matter what.

Coal heat disappeared before I was in grade school, and the stove was shut down, left frigid in the basement, useless as the broken-down cars that these days rust away in Salmon driveways. My grandmother had electric baseboards installed in the living room; after that, your legs got warm but your neck and nose stayed chilled. Though the old furnace was dormant, a faint trickle of cold air blowing from the vent in the hall its only reminder, I could hardly think of my grandfather without black dust on his shirt, on his hands, and ground under his fingernails.

I pictured him that way, the grit of the man, as I made my way to his room and climbed into his musty bed with the others, burrowing into the very spot where he'd passed (too much, probably, to imagine the sheets were still warm of him). By "others" I mean the women. My sister, my father's sister, my father's wife, our great-aunt Janice, me. We drank cups of whiskey, and then Cindy got up and I did, too, to poke through Grandpa's closet, a dark edge of his room (a room I had entered only one other time in my life, on a dare from my brother), pungently sweet from the worn leather of his boots and felt hats stored away for maybe half a century. Cindy and I each removed from a hanger one of his scratchy wool shirts, pulling them on, and so did our aunt, and so did unsentimental Aunt Janice. Now we all smelled like him. Cindy and I went back to rifling through the always-before-forbidden closet with our uncle, our father's younger brother, fidgeting in the doorway. This was his house now. Meaning everything in it. I was afraid to ask, though I pined for it, for the rocking chair in the living room, the one my mother had rocked me in it when I was a baby. My uncle's new wife liked the chair, and the chipped dishes in the cupboard, and our grandmother's books, so those would remain. My father, when I asked him to advocate for me to get the rocker, snorted and walked away—*Don't get me involved.*

I was late in professing an attachment to the things in this house. Too late. It's not like I'd stuck around to help take care of any of it, to rub kitchen grease off the strings of beads or wash the sheets or scrape snow from the porch so Grandpa wouldn't slip going out to the barn. I didn't run for the school board in Salmon or take over my maternal grandparents' newspaper to keep it in the family. When I returned I stayed for a day or two at most, and only so I could sit with my grandfather while he drank a caramel milkshake I'd brought him from the Artic Circle Drive-In. I roamed the streets in front of other grandparents' and great-grandparents' houses, each inhabited by new owners I'd decided instantly to hate.

I planned to cart home the wool shirt on my back and a few belongings small enough to stash into my bag, including books, including one about Narcissa Whitman from my grandmother's shelf. Otherwise best not to get riled about what I'd have to leave behind. I was discovering in my first house an aspect of myself that struck me as unseemly: my need for physical objects to believe that my childhood happened and that I'd actually been involved in it.

In Grandpa's room, just when I thought we'd about finished snooping through his closet, my sister Cindy pulled out a dress from the far end. White buckskin, hand beaded around the neck and down the sleeves, fringed at the bottom. Aunt Janice, who was settled on the edge of her dead brother's bed in a blue-and-black plaid shirt that was one of his favorites, and who usually kept to herself about matters large and small, drew in a noisy breath. She pointed at the dress. "That belongs in a museum," she said. Janice is a docent at the Lemhi County Museum, and maybe she'd become weary of the moth-chewed and worn examples of Shoshone heritage hanging in the Plexiglas displays, though I don't picture her as a big advocate. She's not been against the tribe either. To each his own has been her steady eighty-some-year attitude. But here was an item of near perfection, unmarred and likely unworn, probably as old as she was. Cindy split open the plastic and released the scent of tanned hide. We stepped in to study the handwork, every knot a work of art.

The Lemhi pieces stored in the dusty living-room case, I assumed, would remain. I didn't bother asking. These things my grandfather had procured in trade from the tribe some fifty, sixty, seventy years back belonged to our uncle's new wife now.

I could form no argument for why I should get anything from the case, but that didn't quell my desire. I'd stared through the glass pretty much my whole life, aching to touch but not touching, as both grandparents strictly prohibited the handling of what was stored inside. Even when I was a kid I felt a strange hankering to steal everything and deliver it back to the cereal-box people, who, I worried, waited for the return. Not because I had noble insight at a young age. I didn't. When my grandmother called on small me to perform for her friends, I bounced out my version of "Ten Little Indians" on wagging fingers. Until I woke up to it, the term *squaw* did not ruffle me. But I suspected for some reason that ill could land on us for keeping things that should never have been bartered away.

So what about the dress. Janice had spoken up about putting it in a museum. I wanted to say we should give it back to the Lemhi, now living at Fort Hall, as if I knew what such a return entailed. I sure didn't. Besides, no one was going to go for that, and I was too cowardly to defend my position, so I said museum too.

The dress had been promised to his new wife, our uncle said, and that ended the discussion because he was the only one with a say according to the notarized and signed documents, though the bad taste in our mouths couldn't be washed down no matter how many beers we consumed. And a couple of years after Grandpa Bob's death our uncle's thin, blonde wife left the house and the marriage and took the dress with her, and, though I can't say for certain, I'm guessing she hauled off the parfleche and the blue hair decorations and the gloves and probably the fine-grained oak and glass case that had held them, and if she accidentally left a few things, maybe they were sold to cover the liquor tab at the Owl Club, who knows.

Your eyes close, they open again, and just like that a stranger has entered to dismantle your past.

# 2 Plucked from the Grave

# 1

Fall shoved in to take on summer, and I was a girl traveling from Boise toward the town of Moscow. The year was 1977. There were four of us in the car, returning to a college our parents were sure would reinforce in us—would beat right up against our hearts—what it meant to be a citizen of the West.

Before I'd left my parents' house, my father had stuck a folded-up page from a legal pad in my hand. I had yet to read it over, but I knew what it was: the classes he had in mind for my sophomore year. A course or two in business, maybe accounting, a political science seminar to keep open the option of law school. Not too different, in other words, than his schedule fifteen years earlier at the same university, and the means, in his mind, for me to find a proper job after graduation and to convene with the right kind of people. I suppose he pictured me as an officer at Idaho First National Bank, where I'd worked as a teller that summer between freshman and sophomore year, or as an aide to a right-wing senator in training to become an industry lobbyist or an assistant to a CEO. Business, business, and for-profit business, otherwise education is wasted. He likely figured I'd pick up a husband, too, in an econ class or at an afternoon marketing club mixer. A boy born and raised in Idaho, who'd become a man spending about every sunny Saturday on the golf course and most snapping-cold fall Saturdays at hunting camp. A man who had a good grasp of engines, whether those of four-wheelers or tractors, and who slammed back (without overdoing it) Maker's Mark at my father's bar.

It's not like my father and I discussed such things, but I assumed he wanted to shape my college days in a way that he wished his had gone. I was unencumbered, in a sky's-the-limit time of youth, while he'd moved to college with a wife and two daughters. A boy arrived a year later. Another girl soon after that. Four mouths wide open, peeping for food before our father's twenty-first birthday. He rose before dawn to deliver milk then went on to classes. In the evenings he fixed cars at a local service station, our mother delivering his dinner in a metal pail. I remember watching out the backseat window of our car while she took it to him, this man I hardly recognized leaning under a yawning hood, his white T-shirt like a search light at the far end of the garage. Some days he put my sister and me on the hydraulic lift in one of the docks. "Hang on," he shouted, and pushed the button to raise us up a few feet then to lower us down, our arms wrapped tight, our hearts pounding in glee and fear.

As for my own college years, I hadn't yet told my father, or my mother, that in the waning days of my freshman year, the professor who taught the overly crowded and auditorium-style Literature of Western Civilization class, having read my clumsy final term paper on Shelley's poem "Mont Blanc" (an essay that somehow rose above most of the other two hundred clumsier essays), had called me into his office. If I changed my major to English before the end of the year, he said, he could promise me a scholarship. The deed was done the same afternoon, a swift check of a box in front of a registrar's assistant, while I convinced myself that my father would be pleased enough about tuition savings that he wouldn't mind. Anyway, we wouldn't speak of it. I wouldn't speak of it. He'd learn nothing from me about classes in the contemporary novel and linguistics, or about my friends, the handful of us who got together to quote T. S. Eliot and drink coffee laced with cheap brandy and for the most part eschew golf courses and right-wing senators and, in our current state of frivolity, the institution of marriage.

We pretended to be unconventional, this group of English majors, but most of us were destined for Idaho lives and we knew it. And why not? Ours was the land of bounty and stability.

After he finished his own run at college, my father took a job on the executive track with the state's largest timber business, and my parents fell in with other young executives and their wives who tended to stick around small-town Boise only until the man of the family climbed the ladder. A year or two maybe. Then off he'd go with wife and kids to Denver, St. Louis, Chicago. But no promise of instant status (he was still promoted, but maybe not as quickly as those willing to relocate) or money would get our father to give up his home. So we stayed.

That home was in Boise, with weekend and long summer visits to Salmon, and my father traveled out from our center, spoking to distant reaches of the country, gone so often that for a while I couldn't sort out who he was. One of my earliest memories: I'm sitting in our small living room snapping together Lincoln Logs, which always struck me as the brown of poo and not of trees, and the door swings open, cold air streaming in. My mother, who's been folding clothes on the sofa, stands up. A skinny man in a gray suit, briefcase in hand, moves into the room, and she greets him. Who is he? He is called Daddy, but I can't wrap my head around what that means exactly. When he's away, our tired, cranky mother shouts at us, she goes red in the face over our misdeeds, our jumping on the beds to Nancy Sinatra's boots song, our knocking the barometer off the wall and rolling loose balls of mercury across the floor, our breaking into the medicine chest to eat Chalks vitamins by the handful. *You're going to get it*, she shouts. *Just wait until he gets here.* When he returns, when the daddy is in the house again, she tells us, he will dole out the punishment we deserve.

What I remember about the night of this homecoming when I am five or six is that he puts the briefcase on the sofa and snaps open the lid. He reaches in and pulls out a scarf that he whips out into the living-room space by one slick corner. It floats there above my head, reds and oranges and blues, while my mother barely mutters acknowledgement, as if nothing, nothing he can bring her will erase her empty days with four small children in a broken-down house. The scarf falls back into his hands. He folds in half, in quarters, presents it to his wife, who takes it in her own hands even as her face says *thanks but no thanks* and he scowls, too, and I promise myself to stay clear of them, to find the crannies of our Boise house where I won't be seen or heard or thought of.

Still, I don't remember dreaming of a place other than Idaho. I had no ability to picture myself in a flat city in the Midwest, standing on a flat roof to see forever, or a noisy skyscraper apartment in New York City (where my father traveled often), or a kudzu-wrapped antebellum home in the South. How does an isolated girl fathom such a thing? Idaho was the ideal, that's what I was taught, and everyone who lived elsewhere secretly yearned for what we had. When a wealthy New York businessman, friend of my parents, came to dinner one night I asked him, "Who's the richest person you've ever met?" Without a pause he said, "Your Grandpa Bob." That cemented it for me at about age ten. Any impulse to step out into other parts of the country, other regions of the world, was beat down to the basement, shut behind a cellar door. Idaho would be my still point, at least for a stretch of years, with every other geographic curiosity in me quelled.

During my childhood my parents met my mother's folks once a year or so at Flathead Lake in Montana, or Grandma Lois might transport Cindy and me to Missoula for lunch—the cream of mushroom soup at the Red Lion restaurant was worth the zigzag trip over Lost Trail Pass, she told us, though my stomach suggested otherwise. When our father had time off in the summer, we went camping in Idaho. At Red Fish Lake near Stanley, or up the other direction to Cascade or Donnelly, though most of the time we simply drove the six hours from Boise to Salmon. Back and forth, back and forth. On the endless return drives to our house, hairpin turns forcing me to keep a bucket in my hands in case I had to throw up, I cracked the window open so fresh air blew in my face. If a Styrofoam cooler in the back squeaked, our father yelled at us to jiggle the lid. Quiet descended except for Jim Nabors's voice crooning from the radio and our brother deviling a sister. Somewhere around the halfway point on our return trip back to Boise, my siblings and I would inevitably start up a chant, begging our father to stop. Just this once. A hotel *just once*. Can't we? A swimming pool, breakfast in a restaurant, in Stanley, in Lowman, even in Bliss, to break up the same old six-hour drive. Please?

*Okay, okay*, he'd say. *Pipe down and we'll stop at Le Bois.*

That would shut us up, even me, even after I'd figured out his ploy. The promise of it pleased me, as it was so unlike our father to say more than flat-out no. We'd fall asleep and hours later find ourselves in our own beds. *Le Bois.*

On one of those weekend camping trips, I was huddled in the back seat of our clunky Volkswagen van with my sisters, sharing a sense of dread: that of our father spotting a California license plate on a passing car. If this occurred while he was ranging up the sharp curves of a gravel road in the mountains, he'd jerk the steering wheel, turn the van around, and we'd be off on an altogether different route before anyone could sputter a complaint. His rule was to drive at least twenty miles in any direction to get the California stench off us. He'd roar ahead with his sulking wife, our mother, next to him, while he ground through third gear to fourth, his kids squeezed in between coolers and sleeping bags, the lot of us hoping to hell he didn't see another CA on a metal plate attached to some sedan or truck or van—no intruder from Sacramento or Los Angeles or Death Valley, places we'd been told were so clogged with smog they were inhabitable—because, unless night was falling hard, the twenty-mile tick could start again.

All to say that when I was small and skinny and mostly too scared to speak up, I understood loyalty. To geography and to family. I understood I was not to give my father guff or bother him with what was on my mind. I was to stay on the sidelines and cheer on the men of the family while they played basketball on the concrete court Grandpa Bob had poured beside the house, erecting a pole and a net and hanging a sign Grandma Lois had made that said "Acres and Paynes" (her idea of a pun; punny enough that only she got the joke). Grandpa piped in a drinking fountain that spouted water so cold it hurt your teeth. The girls were to sit on the crabgrass and keep score and keep the noise down. "This is not Giggleville!" We stood by as the men packed up for weeks of fall hunting camp, my father and brother. Never ask why we couldn't go along, and forget about inquiring why certain women—Aunt Janice among them—were accepted at camp while most were not (actually, there was no one who didn't want to spend time with Aunt Janice, so we were fine with her inclusion). We tagged along to summer picnics at the river, where the adults grilled up steelhead and steaks, where we swatted away mosquitoes and drank orange pop and watched the grown-ups down another whiskey. And another. The stories got louder; the flames shot higher.

No one had to say the words aloud. I knew my job as a girl in my family and my job as an Idahoan: stay loyal to a certain set of values. Keep the government out and the guns close by. Remember that the land is your land to use as you want. Tromp into the woods, camp in the wilderness, douse the fires when you leave, organize your tools, clean up your waste—every last beer flip-top and gum wrapper—and catch enough fish to jam your winter freezer. Let no strangers in. Abide no strangers here.

# 2

My difficulty was that I was one of those strangers. The child born to children still in high school, and not all that welcomed, I suspect, by either set of grandparents. It was as if both nonplussed women, Mamie and Grandma Lois, turned to the doorway on a late June day in 1957 to let me know that my timing was definitely off. *Who said you could be here?*

I once heard from my mother that her future mother-in-law, Lois, tried to push her down a set of high school gym bleachers on a winter day to, with luck, bring on a miscarriage. Who knows if that's true. My mother said she was told to fold up on the floor of the family car, blanket over her head, while she drove through town with her parents so no one could see the family's humiliation. Another apocryphal tale, though both made it obvious to me that no one was much pleased about the baby on the way. My grandmothers never quite got over what I'd done to muck up the works by being born, and now that they're long dead, Mamie and Grandma Lois, I'm left to sort out for myself the mark I left on them and on the family, whether sear or blemish.

My grandmothers in the waiting room of the Steele Memorial Hospital in Salmon. Mamie in a straight shift dress, green stripes and gray, and her cat-eye glasses, Grandma Lois with her ballooning ankles, though neither woman had yet reached the age of forty. The doctor reported what they already knew: my mother was in labor too soon. She'd gained only twelve pounds, making for a small baby at term, and term wasn't for another seven weeks.

My father's mother had been told in this same hospital some years earlier that her daughter was stillborn. My mother's mother had lived through the news on four dim mornings. So these were women who'd proven such tragedy was survivable, and they were, as the doctor suggested they should be, ready for another infant to emerge from the womb cold and silent, its skin a color as if blue had been turned inside out. Eyelids sealed and toes folded like petals. My grandmothers, not particularly close, not terribly friendly with each other—a fissure I would soon enough exploit for my own benefit—scooted closer together on this one day and waited.

A day earlier the boy who was my father had slipped out of work. He locked the shop's door and hurried down the Main Street sidewalk, though he'd get an earful from his boss, Grandpa Bob, for quitting early. The welding shop was located in back of Gwartney Equipment, owned by my great-grandparents, and it was here that my father wore a helmet to cover his face and head, where he pulled on gloves up to his elbows to keep sparks from lighting on the fine hairs of his forearms. Mike helped fabricate parts for balers and tractors and welded springs and latches for horse trailers and gates, soot nesting in his hair.

Grandpa Bob had already left the shop that afternoon, off for a cup of coffee laced with whatever whiskey was handy under a table at Wally's Café, and Mike left no note of explanation, only his scorched equipment on the shelf. He met up with his friend Sandy, and the two made their way to a pasture. They saddled horses and headed toward the mountains, riding over hills picked with gray sagebrush (a man with a stubbled beard was how I thought of the Salmon foothills) and through slate-blue creeks gurgling high in the pine forest. They rode toward the snow-packed Bitterroots, which must have risen in front of them like a shining mirror. Summer had begun. School was out, and everything was about to change. Everything.

They were sixteen years old.

It wasn't deer season or elk season, not legal to go after even a grouse at the end of June, but my father was going to show his mettle by riding into the Lemhi Mountains where he'd hunted since the age of four. He'd given himself and Sandy until nightfall to bring back a buck to butcher into roasts and steaks and packages of ground burger to store in his parents' freezer.

Some snow-heavy day ahead, when it was too dark and slick to walk on Salmon streets after the sun went down, when you didn't dare hold to the iron railing up the hill to my grandparents' house for fear of tearing skin, Mike would fry the liver to a grizzled crust in his mother's cast-iron pan, and he'd fork a chewed-up bite into his child's mouth—a boy child's mouth, at least it had to be that, a boy. He'd buy a .22 to put in the kid's hands as soon as the pointer finger could pull a trigger. More sophisticated rifles would come as the boy grew up, with scopes and straps and dusty boxes of ammunition. Chilled autumn days set aside for hunting, the campfires where four generations of family men sipped whiskey while someone started up on guitar, another on harmonica, to play the familiar tunes, the best to drink by, to brawl by. The boy has a spot there. My father has planned it. A stump in the circle just for his son.

But my father is bushwhacking through the woods on my birthday, not a boy's, and he carries a map. The map is in his head, etched over years in this terrain, a topography as familiar to him as every inch of the half acre behind his parents' house up to the line of shuddering cottonwoods on the banks of Jessie

Creek. Here in the forest my father recognizes downed logs in the shadows, fallen trees nursing feathery hemlock and ponderosa. He knows which slopes have burned and which were only licked by flames. He walks through milkvetch and larkspur blooming across the rise, forest duff crunching under his boots, a sharp-shined hawk circling overhead. He stealths through the trees, watching for a flash of tawny hide, the angle of an antler.

What he doesn't see are one or two humps of tree roots, a jackrabbit hole, an errant cracked stone. Maybe I'm the one who's placed impediments like that in his path so he might catch the toe of his boot and go flying, slamming a hip on hard ground, a shoulder, waking him up to what's happening today—me moving toward him and him moving toward me, like it or not. If he was paying attention he might sniff out the earliest hint of our long pattern, the one already welling through the decades ahead: this is the day he begins his role of the disappointed man while I become the child who disappoints. The daughter who'll be in his arms in a matter of hours, a girl who'll squall and stink and keep him up at night, who'll require a snap of his nail against her foot so she'll stay awake long enough to eat. A girl gumming up his youth, his prospects for college, his ability to make money, to pursue any kind of notoriety. Mike has been told all his life that he's *somebody*. That he's on his way out of Salmon. He's the smartest boy, the best looking, the most capable. The hardest of hard workers. But apparently he can fuck up too, because he got a girl pregnant when he was fifteen and she was sixteen and now they—we— are bound, inextricably.

In the first hour of their hunting trip, one of the two, Mike or Sandy, shot a six-point buck. The boys decided they needed help getting the animal out before the sun set, before bears or lions moved in, before a ranger caught wind of what had transpired. Mike buried the entrails off in the trees while Sandy secured ropes, and then they picked up their packs, their weapons, and left the kill hanging from a high-enough limb. They swung onto their horses and headed for town.

Before there was a baby on the way or a romance leading to a baby on the way, the two boys spent considerable time in these hills. Mike and Sandy, practically inseparable. One afternoon in their fifteenth year, they were roaming as they tended to and stopped to rest their horses. The boys jammed long sticks into a rocky escarpment they'd climbed on—a scrabble of shale under their feet—and when Sandy heard a subterranean rustle, he let out a sharp, quick whistle at Mike across the expanse of rock. "Hey," he said. He pointed at a craggy hole. "Snakes."

They'd happened on a nest of rattlers.

Mike knelt down and so did Sandy. They put their ears to the ground. Then the boys toed back down the scree to their horses and galloped to the valley floor. Sandy's father had a construction job at the railroad and kept a load of explosives at the farm in a shed that every kid was forbidden to enter. But Sandy's father wasn't due home for another hour, and Sandy's mother was reliably distracted.

Back on the outcropping Sandy lit a stick and Mike lit a stick and they shoved in the dynamite and ran for cover. Years later, in a most unusual storytelling mood, my father told what happened after the *boom*—a sky of snakes over his head. Not the ten or twenty they'd predicted, but dozens. Raining rattlesnakes. Some dead but others alive, mottled skin arced and taut. The snakes landed with mouths hissing, ready for strike, falling around Mike's neck and Sandy's, sliding down their shirts and across their boots, the horses rearing up and snorting, pulling free of tethers and tearing toward town so that he boys were forced to run home on their own feet.

If this day was a warning from the gods—watch out, kid, what you go poking into if you are not prepared for the consequences—my father did not heed it.

Ten months after the eruption of the rattlers, Mike was still a ways from voting or buying a pint at the Owl Club. He was two years from tacking a high school diploma on his wall. But he had, as a man did, as a provider did, shot a deer. It was hanging in the woods, and he needed help getting it out, though such help wouldn't be coming from the best hunter in town, his father, who was not in general opposed to poaching but who was generally pissed off these days at his son. So the boys got to town and talked Barbara, Mike's wife of two weeks, into driving the Scout so they could load the kill before trouble came calling.

My mother went because he, her young husband, wanted her to. This boy she hardly knew, really, whose family despised her with a fury she returned. A Salmon High basketball player who'd sat on the seat next to her on the stone-cold night of their first kiss. She'd seen him around school before that kiss, but he was in the class below hers, and she hadn't talked to him until they were on a musky school bus along with the team and three other cheerleaders traveling to an away game in Pocatello. Mike put his arm around her when she said she was chilly next to the icy window in her skirt and thin sweater with her name, Barbie, stitched over her breast. He slid his arm around my beautiful mother, my tiny, vivacious mother, and held her close, in just the way she longed to be held.

Over the course of a marriage that was mostly scotch-taped together, my mother had no problem refusing my father. She set those dark eyes of hers until she got her way. But I suspect she was nothing but solicitous as a new bride. Here was the boy-man who'd get her out of a house of gloom, of overattention. Soon there'd be a baby to be Barbara's new family, slicing her like cold butter from her parents.

Barbara was sick of hearing from teachers and her mother's friends about potential dashed, done with being dragged to the attorney's office to face adoption papers she probably should have signed but didn't. She climbed in the truck. All ninety-eight pounds of her, seven months pregnant, with her bushy brown hair, smooth skin, and happy smile got in the driver's seat, her fingers tight on the gear shift and foot on the clutch. She drove an hour on bumpy, winding roads as if she were unable, unwilling to gauge the danger of such a venture. She drove out again, the back of the Scout filled with bloody game, a slumped head. When she stepped out of the truck, she was in labor.

Dr. Blackadar got my mother to down shots of whiskey to stop the contractions, but even 90 Proof Old Grandad didn't work, no matter the heat in her belly. In the waiting room Mamie wrung her hands in her lap. Grandma Lois stared out the window at the river, while both grandmothers avoided saying the words seared on their minds. *Wouldn't it almost be better if the child didn't make it? Let's get these teenagers back to high school. Let's get them off to different universities. Let's pack a coat of mud over their past so they won't have to look at it ever again.*

But I was born alive. Four pounds and some ounces of wriggling infant, no eyelashes, no eyebrows, but lungs that functioned enough to grab a breath and wimp out a first cry. I was a girl; my father backed away. Venison liver tossed in pasture grass for birds to peck at. My grandfathers decided to meet up at the welding shop to rig Salmon's first incubator with parts they'd procured at the feed store and from Grandpa's back room: warming lights from a chick hatchery, a box welded from scrap metal with tall sides and a solid base, a brooding thermometer hung in one corner. Grandma Lois walked to her house on Jessie Creek, set on a scoop of land that was once the thousand-year place of the Shoshone, which would now be my first home. She moved the rocking chair to the living room; she stacked blankets and diapers on the bureau and shoved pins into a flaky bar of Ivory soap. She took over the domain of her son, who'd finished his sophomore year of high school a month earlier. This was not what he wanted, not what she wanted, not what anyone had yearned for in regard to these bright, promising children. But I was here.

Nothing to do but get on with it.

# 3

On the trip back to college in Moscow, I was two decades past my birth and in tangled relationships still with the people who'd attended it (the following year Dr. Blackadar, one of the world's preeminent kayakers, would be sucked under a strainer on the Payette River and drowned). I was in the back seat with another thin girl dressed in Levi 501s, button fly. She wore a soft polyester blouse like I did, like we all did. Hers gathered at the waist and tied at the top; the loose ties dangled fetchingly across her breasts. We both had long hair, straight as a board, a defiant style for the end of a decade whose main tenet was liberation. Our Idaho version of liberation, that is— thimble sized. We knew not to go too far with such notions.

The girl, too, grew up in Boise. We were oddly estranged from each other because we'd pledged to different sororities a year earlier. What this whole sorority thing was about I can hardly comprehend in retrospect, except that it strikes me as the perfect test for an Idaho girl. As in: any sense of belonging and acceptance you might feel is conditional. As in: those more powerful than you can take acceptance away on a whim. If the sound of your voice, your actions, the look on your face are deemed not up to snuff, you're out. It was this wobbling on the edge of favor that made sorority life thrilling, I suppose. Am I wanted or unwanted? Joining had been impressed upon me as a necessity; I'd be a nobody without it. I went along because that's what I did in my younger years: I went along. Grandma

Lois especially insisted I endure the week of rush—she'd gone through it years earlier at the same college—and move into one of the white mansions on the hill with musty furniture and narrow beds, single-paned windows we leaned out of to smoke our first cigarettes. When it was my turn I'd ding my glass in the middle of dinner so I could lead the other girls in devotional songs, devotion aimed at God, at boys, at finding a party with all the cheap wine we could manage to slurp down before we passed out in a pool of our own spit.

My own reasons for staying with the sorority, an arrangement that stopped appealing to me early on and which brought with it an inviolable boundary that meant I could not easily speak to this girl in the car, escape me now. The lesson, I suppose, was to learn to stick with your own.

The Gamma Phi in the back seat with me pressed her sharp hip against her door, staring out her window, and I, being a Pi Phi, stayed close to my own door, calculating the best moment to ask the driver, a fraternity man himself, for a cigarette break. We four would stand outside the Chevy sedan breathing in the soft air of Northern Idaho, turning our bodies in the direction of the ruddy hills instead of each other, drinking one Coors Light each from the cooler in the trunk, puffing on our Marlboros, kicking the gravel with our new tan Puma shoes. Then we'd get on to Moscow, to the hilly campus, which in autumn glowed umber and which in winter was ice caked and snot slick. We'd return to the weekend parties where we drank a concoction called Rocket Fuel to shoot us to the moon.

I knew who to be at our tucked-away university. I could drink beer until I was blithering and still memorize Anne Sexton poems for class and write an essay on the hand images in *Macbeth*. I could swim in the cold streams at the edge of town to stave off an emptiness best not to look at. Put on a white gown with a silver rope tie and whisper the password to enter secret meetings. Earn good grades and pins and ribbons to send home to my father while ignoring the buzz saw in my head, the one reminding me I had no idea who to be once I was booted from the college town, degree in hand. I ignored a thrum, the one that insisted I'd be settled in Idaho only if I found a man. Get married, have children, focus on domesticity. Become one of those women who typed her husband's manuscripts or kept accounts for his business, women who left their babies with a sitter for an hour each day so they could take a quick run— slipping on coordinated jogging outfits and pumping over hills until their bodies were shaped like arrows pointed nowhere. Did I want that? I think not. But any other future was as hidden from me as a boulder half buried in the silt of Jessie Creek, one of those rocks I squatted on as a girl, wondering if I should topple into the water and float away.

After our break, after we'd returned to the car for a last hour of driving, we soon entered the switchbacks of White Bird Hill, and the beer I'd slammed sloshed around in my stomach, the residue of cigarette acrid in my mouth. I closed my eyes and tipped my head to hold back the urge to heave. I'd lived in the state since the day of my birth, but it turns out a heritage of mountain living isn't enough: my belly has not dealt well, not ever, with the switchbacks you must endure if you want to go anywhere in the West. The best I could do on the late August afternoon was breathe deep, swallow the first spurt of bile at the back of my mouth, and remind myself of the flatter landscape ahead—over the last pass was calmer ground, the variations of yellow, the textures, the subtle relief of the stretch of land called the Palouse. The North Idaho edge of the Palouse, that is, with its far edge in Eastern Oregon: humps and hollows formed in the last ice age, made fertile from a glacial silt known

as loess, soil that's exactly right for growing the long, thick bulrushes that the first people in North America, including the
Cayuse, required. Palouse loess soil, also ideal for growing
wheat.

Though I was around twenty years old on this drive through
the wheat farms of Idaho, I probably acted younger. Line me
up with girls from New York, Boston, Paris, or even, I don't
know, Omaha, and I'm pretty sure I would have come off as
vapid. I knew nothing about the cosmopolitan life that poked
at me from magazines and books. Mostly I was guided by a
desire to be the girl others wanted me to be. I didn't bother
considering what I wanted—or, more accurately, what I wanted
wasn't a consideration I was aware I could entertain. There'd
be no exploration outside the reality my family had built
around me, though adventure is what, I think, some part of me
yearned for. Secretly. The secret kept mostly from myself.

By the time I went to college, I'd been on an airplane three
times. Rare journeys outside Idaho unless I can count the ones
by book, and in that case I departed regularly. In a freshman
English class I'd read Hemingway's short stories. It was "Hills
Like White Elephants" that struck me as truest and saddest,
alive as that story was for a girl who'd hardly parted from
home, a girl aware she might have an imagination but with no
idea how to spark it. The conversation between the man and
the woman in the story was overly cryptic for a callow teenager
like me, but I was enthralled by the bar where they sipped
drinks, the light through the windows, the howl of the train,
and the geologic mounds that rose in the distance. Restless
beasts, those hills, listening in on the quarrel but aiding not in
the least with human foibles.

The hills were stalwart. I had a respect for stalwart.

Once we reached the Palouse and my stomach calmed, I

stuck my head out the open window, singing along to "Hey Nineteen" on the tinny car stereo, and I remembered the girl in the story who drank absinthe (the fanciest liquor I'd seen my parents serve was Lancers from a crockery bottle, so I had to look this one up, absinthe). She said, because she had no idea what else to say, that, "Yes, everything tastes like licorice. Especially all the things you've waited so long for." I thought of that line as we flew past rolling, treeless, wheat-covered hills. Not like white elephants, but golden women. Legs open, mouths agape. The rises and falls of hips, the goddess thighs and breasts, the angled shoulders of wheat crops.

Waving strands of wheat trundled to the horizon, a light and movement that excited and released something in me even as we whizzed by too fast to take it in. Despite the speed and the stuffiness of the car, and deep as I was into the cave of my own reluctance, I still managed to hear something like a whisper of an invitation. Maybe I tasted a bitter sweetness on my tongue. Cloying and black as night. I let it trickle down my throat. A one-time offer issued by the landscape, or so it seemed to me, if only I had the nerve to leap.

How much courage would be required to break most every convention I'd lived by and grab up what was out there for me? More than I could muster.

A beckoning wink of light over the top of a hill. I didn't reach for it. I didn't lean its way. I slid down into my seat, resigned to a small life whose constrictions I could not begin to fathom. I busied myself wondering about the next beer, the next cigarette, about where the party would be that night. The driver, as if he'd read my mind, hit a straightaway, shifted to fourth so he could fly even faster toward Moscow, Idaho, and we were gone.

# 4

Many years past graduation at the University of Idaho, I was in an Oregon auditorium reading an essay about Narcissa Whitman. I strode to the podium with a façade of confidence, though the modicum of authority I exuded came from research. Ask me any password-security question about Narcissa and I'd have at least some kind of an answer: her favorite food, her child's middle name, the name of the family dog (Trapper—eventually eaten by hungry folks at the mission), the man I believe she had a crush on. I knew more about this long-dead woman than just about anyone else alive, or so I told myself. I opened my pages that night swimming in knowledge of her. If you can take history personally, I suppose that's what I'd done. Ever since reading that first book, I'd gobbled up information and let Narcissa's history become personal to me.

After the reading I stood outside in the pleasant evening air and chatted with a few people who'd ventured over to talk, the dreamy afterglow when not a word of praise yet feels faint. A person I'd met briefly, I recognized her, approached me with a smile on her face, and I smiled back, receptive to her show of kindness and the compliment she was about to give. Instead, with that grin stuck to her face like gum, she said, "You know, if you're going to write about Narcissa Whitman, you could at least learn how to pronounce *Waiilatpu*."

I stepped away from the woman and her friend, stammering. I soon went to my room, stung by her comment. How had

I mispronounced Waiilatpu? I'd been there several times. I'd tromped around the grounds and studied artifacts in the visitors' center. I'd watched the twenty-minute film more often than probably any ranger manning the desk. Had I stressed the wrong syllable? Put the wrong inflection on the glottal stop?

The woman's comment, small as it was, flooded me with remorse over my enterprise. Only an hour earlier I was cocky enough to believe that I had a grip on this woman of the West who deeply troubled me, that I was creeping toward insight and perspective about myself as a woman of the West through her—but what had I figured out really? I'd made assumptions about her reasons for coming West, her heart rumbling for God, the ways she rationalized ripping herself away from everyone she loved to convert people to a religion that couldn't, that simply wouldn't, supplant their centuries-long epistemology. I'd thrown punches at this woman who dove headlong into her mother's religious righteousness, who'd fallen for Disoway's fabricated plea to get out to the frontier and preach the Word, who'd given in to Parker's inflated guidance that had nothing to do with what she actually needed. Not to mention Marcus, who took Narcissa away from every comfort she held dear. And yet, that night in my room, I couldn't remember why any of it mattered to me.

And yet it still does. *She* does.

Narcissa rolled onto the Palouse in the fall of 1836. She was a woman whose very being had been shaped for God, delivered by Clarissa for just this purpose, and determined to spread a message of salvation that maybe she didn't even fully comprehend. Her bosses, the missionary board that had hired her and her husband, knew how overzealous she could be about what was *right* and what was *wrong*. The board secretary asked the couple to hold back on the most extreme of their sectarian tendencies. Narcissa and Marcus didn't have to welcome every denomination equally into the fold, their bosses said—in fact, the Catholics were to be excluded and the Methodists only barely tolerated—but maybe they could tone down their rhetoric a notch?

It was a Methodist who'd arrived in the West first. Jason Lee. He, too, had read the Disoway article and in 1835 established a mission near current-day Salem, Oregon. At the time of their arrival in 1836, both the Whitmans and the Spaldings were determined to erode any headway Lee had made in converting local Native people to his faith. The competition was on for saving souls.

Lee might have been the first Protestant missionary to build a religious settlement among the Native people, and his name was certainly recognized among Christian people back in the East, but Narcissa's feats were the talk of the heartland, her adventure tracked by those who cared not a whit about religion. By the late 1830s she was probably admired less for her church affiliation than for the bald fact that she was a woman (though it didn't hurt that she was considered pious). She had completed a journey that that had seemed nearly impossible for an ordinary soft-footed gal, the longed-for journey (Eliza Spalding at her side, of course) across the continent.

On the Fourth of July, 1836, the Whitman/Spalding entourage stepped across an invisible line at South Pass, in what's now Wyoming, progress that set them firmly in the largely unexplored, unsettled frontier. Narcissa didn't realize for a while that she and Eliza had broken the Continental Divide barrier, nor could she have predicted the pop of her own celebrity because of that single feat, another hill climbed on yet another day. But what a hill it was. A woman, newly pregnant, had propelled herself to the other side of the Rockies; she'd walked beside a wagon holding her dishes and household goods and clothes. Because of Narcissa a gate was lifted, or maybe knocked flat into the dirt, and the Oregon Trail was suddenly a real thing, an actual passage for people who had before considered it folly or simply too dangerous for women and children (which, honestly, was often the case).

It's odd that she, who meticulously noted the highlights of her trekking days in her journal, says nothing about passing the Continental Divide. She'd just done that day what she had every other day: she walked. She rode a horse, and did so sidesaddle, and hopped on the back of a wagon for a spell, moving her body from point A to point B. Whatever it would take to put a few more miles behind her. She trudged through the punishing landscape of the intermountain West, heading toward the Palouse, on to the Columbia Basin, without any way to calculate what her trip would mean to those she'd left behind. She—along with Eliza—were paving the way for hundreds of thousands of white women to follow, among them some of my relations.

Back to the start of the Whitmans' journey: in March of 1836, after their wedding and the brief post-wedding travel, and after meeting up with the Spaldings, Narcissa traveled to the last city she'd ever visit, St. Louis, accompanied by the man she was yoked to for the rest of her days, Marcus. Whether they'd met one time or twice, Narcissa and Marcus had spent a total of a couple of hours together before the morning of their wedding ceremony. Once they were in St. Louis, "Husband," as she called him, arranged transport by boat for the first leg of their journey while Narcissa visited friends who shocked her with a stop at a Catholic Mass—a glimpse of the ceremony confirming her distaste for those that Narcissa, as did others, called the

Black Robes, the Papists, men doing the devil's work. She left her friends and the service that disgusted her to go shopping: she bought tin cups and plates for the trip, a few utensils. Later she and the other women who'd be part of the early days of the trip made a tent of oiled bedticking for more comfortable sleep. Marcus went off to purchase twelve head of horses, six mules, seventeen cows.

Now it was real. Narcissa had to know that the trek would only get more trying once they were off the boat at Liberty and on horses or on foot for the remainder of spring and all of summer and a good part of fall. In St. Louis it dawned on her with startling clarity, those clinking tin cups in hand, that she'd left every member of her family forever. "I have been thinking of my beloved parents this evening; of the parting scene & the probability that I shall never see those dear faces while I live."

This was her first chance to turn back, and her first decision not to. At least that's my take on it. She was human, after all—she had to have one or two moments of doubt. But maybe all Narcissa had to picture was her mother's dark frown to squelch her homesickness. Clarissa was not to be disappointed. If every drop of ease and contentment had to be sacrificed for the Lord's work, so be it.

I have a habit of suffusing Narcissa with certain emotions, but the truth is, in no document I've read—nowhere, not in her journal or her letters—does the woman beg to return to her little village in upstate New York, to her piano in the parlor, to the children she taught, to her sisters. So, I could be wrong. Still, I have to guess she spent at least some hours with the desire to go home banging at her insides. But having no choice, she stuck with the course she was given, and she made it through, I'm convinced, by shouting God's plans for her loud enough that her own noise drowned out any festering fear and remorse.

She proclaimed His intentions for her life with every passing day of the trip, every day of the eleven years at the mission. She shouted until her throat was too raw to call out another word.

Narcissa trudged on steadily, eating mostly dried meat, and endlessly repairing her single pair of shoes. At night she slept on the ground in the dress she'd worn for weeks on end. It was near the halfway point of the trip that she realized she was pregnant. The father of her baby, Marcus, probably couldn't much talk to her about her condition given the newness of their relationship, but he did provide perfunctory physician's advice. She managed the pinches and shifts of her body while rising off the ground each morning to walk another ten or twelve miles, and then at night she collapsed to read her Bible next to the fire's warmth—or to take out her portable writing desk to prepare another letter to her family that may or may not reach them, that would never be answered.

At least she had some of her own things, her own valuables from home. Except, when the entourage she was traveling with (a fairly large group of fur traders, who barely tolerated the missionaries) reached Fort Laramie in current-day Wyoming—that noteworthy passage over the Rockies ahead—Marcus and the grouchy fellow of the group, William Gray, the one who'd been hired on as mission mechanic (a regular snake in the grass, this guy), announced they'd all brought too much. Time to winnow. Narcissa was asked to leave behind dishes, books, keepsakes, clothes, and Eliza the same. The men decided that one large freight wagon they'd started with, which they once believed could make the entire trip, was oversized, too cumbersome for the narrow passages to come. The vote was to abandon the behemoth at the fort and for the missionaries to continue on with a smaller wagon that happened to be owned by the Spaldings.

Narcissa insisted that her trunk be preserved. She had packed the simple wood and leather box with care before she'd left her parents' home in upstate New York, and there's no doubt she measured and weighed and reconsidered every item. She and the trunk had departed on her wedding night to begin the journey West with her new husband—the couple made a few brief stops in New England towns whose inhabitants smoldered with faith in the same way she did, as Marcus did. In these nearby locales she and Husband put on some fund-raising events and picked up a pair of man shoes made just for her, stored in the trunk that was a gift from her sister Harriet. Narcissa had also packed dresses she had sewn as well as one pair of girl shoes, a bonnet, a Bible and hymnal, other religious books, her portable writing table, and maybe a prized dish or two. These were the things that would help her maintain, reminding her of home and family. Arranged in her dear trunk from Harriet. Which was, after the first purge, set firmly in the Spalding's wagon.

Eliza's parents had given the couple this Dearborn as a wedding gift, compact and made of hardwood and featuring an innovative kingpin that made turning a simpler chore. The older couple couldn't have realized that it would be, for a time, the most famous wagon in America: it was this Dearborn (well, the highly amended Dearborn) that successfully traversed the Rocky Mountains and inspired thousands of families to take their own wagons over the same pass.

Except few in the East had heard the actual facts—that the Spalding "land canoe," as some Native people called such wagons, barely made it over the Rockies, and did so only because it was reduced in size and scope. After South Pass, Marcus transformed it into a wobbly cart. Now it had two wheels instead of four and was broken and battered, including a busted axle with no possible replacement. By the time the entourage reached the Snake River in current-day Idaho, the cart was about done in. The men talked about ditching it altogether but then decided to reduce the load one last time. Every item was examined and discussed as to its merits. One thing that had to go on this round, the men announced, was the trunk. But, oh no. Narcissa would not have it. She'd put up with everything, every hardship, every horrible meal and every long day of walking and sleeping in puddles and every fire made of buffalo dung, and now she would lose her trunk? *No*, she said. *That's not going to happen.* And perhaps as a sign of the first splinter of what I have to believe became a scratch post of a marriage, Marcus picked up the trunk and threw it over a cliff.

Narcissa's report of the trunk's demise, in a letter home from the next fort, hints of no such husbandly rage or even tensions between the two. Here's her usual forced equanimity on the page, her written acceptance of everything that befalls her, every sorrow and hardship that God sent her way. "Dear Harriet, the little trunk you gave me has come with me so far & now I must leave it here alone. Poor little trunk, I am sorry to leave thee. Thou must abide here alone & no more by this presance remind me of my Dear Harriet. Twenty miles below the falls on Snake River. This shall be thy place of rest. Farewell little Trunk. I thank thee for thy faithful services & that I have been cheered by thy presance so long. Thus we scatter as we go along."

The party did go along, the party did scatter, with Narcissa fuming and Marcus sulking, until one of the men who'd been traveling as protector and scout for the small group of missionaries, one Thomas McKay of the Hudson Bay Company, whose daughter would later be hired to care for the Whitmans' child, backtracked several miles. He scrambled down the cliff wall to retrieve the trunk and return it ceremoniously to Narcissa, who surprised the man with her huffy ingratitude: "Mr. McKay has asked the privaledge of taking the little trunk along, so that my soliloquy about it last night was for nought. [The trunk] will do me no good. It may him."

The rejected-by-all Narcissa trunk was hardly the point. By winter of 1836 thousands of other women were packing their own trunks, buying and outfitting their own wagons, inspired by the Whitman and Spalding wives, who had arrived at their homesteads with goods they'd hauled in. Except that wasn't the case. The Whitmans got to their new mission site without a wagon, and Henry Spalding went on to his Lapwai mission site in what's now North Idaho without a wagon. While the husbands arranged for some kind of semipermanent domicile to get through the first winter, the women stayed at Fort Vancouver, safe and warm. They carried scant items they'd saved from the trip. Nearly everything else had to be ordered new, and the Hudson Bay Company was glad to do the ordering. But never mind about what actually happened. People in the rest of the country believed what they wanted to believe, propelled to action by hearsay and rumor that served their own ambitions and fairy tales of a sparkling new existence.

Maybe Narcissa had her trunk again once she reached the Palouse, maybe she didn't—there's no evidence about whether she took it back from McKay or turned away from his offer. Trunk or no, she missed her sister Harriet. She missed them all. She'd made it to the end, but her future in this place was murky. Here was yet another chance to return to New York, but she didn't, as much as she might have wanted to go back to her sisters and to her Ma. After Marcus had left and she was surrounded by strangers (except for Eliza) at the fort, she expressed nary a word about discomfort with her new land and position. She showed no fear or sorrow, even if that's how she felt, and even if I'm out here postulating that going home before she got her mission started would have been the wisest thing for this woman to do.

# 5

In the last days of 1836, the twenty-eight-year-old Narcissa and her husband decided they'd live on the banks of the Walla Walla River, with acreage flat enough for a garden, a large one, fecund with tomatoes and onions, the bushy tops of carrots and potatoes. Husband would, at some point down the road, get her out of the hut he'd hastily constructed, building her a sweet house with actual window glass if they could find it. First, though, he would fortify this original house and nail together a cradle for their baby. And soon enough they'd meet the nearby Cayuse, the Walla Walla band of several hundred people, feared as warriors and admired for their expert skills with horses, described by early settlers as a "governing tribe, their superiority acknowledged by others."

This was one of the central tribes of the Columbia Plateau, along with the Niimíipuu, the Walla Walla, the Umatilla—and, like other tribes, stuck with a name they didn't chose for themselves. French trappers called the tribe "Callioux," rock people, while the "Cayuse" most likely called themselves Liksiyu, *the* people. The Nez Perce referred to these neighbors as Waiilatpus, people of the ryegrass.

The Cayuse reputation as the finest horsemen on the plateau began in the 1700s after several scouts spotted men from an enemy tribe riding "large deer," though the animals' hooves were not split as with an ungulate. The scouts returned to camp to retrieve others, including a chief who, upon seeing horses for the first time, quickly negotiated a truce and gave up everything the scouting party had with them in exchange for a mare and a stallion. It's said that the Cayuse returned home naked, but with the chief sitting high and proud on horseback.

After a century of refining their skills and building up substantial herds, the Cayuse agreed to sell a few older, weaker horses to the Whitmans for their first winter's meat. As these tribespeople came around the mission to deliver the food and trade for other goods, Narcissa was sure they would be persuaded to become the Whitmans' loyal flock. The Cayuse had been exposed to Christianity back in the days of Lewis and Clark, but now it was time, the Whitmans insisted, to get serious. To recite scripture to herald every sunrise, to sing out hymns in praise of God, to renounce all beliefs except the Presbyterian version of the one true God.

As soon as the snow cleared in the spring of 1837, our most industrious man Marcus made his first major gaff at Waiilatpu if he truly meant to get along with nearby residents. This is when he cut the grass down to bristle, torching the remnant. He tilled the loess soil, scattered the seeds for his first crop of wheat, dug irrigation ditches, and, on the banks of the creek, erected the region's first gristmill. Marcus was one to get things done. The doctor was bent on launching civilization, and fast.

Though at first many Cayuse were curious—particularly about the white man's weapons, far more lethal than the bow and arrow—it didn't take long until members of the tribe were confounded by the insistent woman and the overambitious medicine man, these *Americans* (a term the tribe used as a pejorative) who'd shouldered their way in. The Cayuse had expected the doctor would awe them with his miracles of white-man healing, but his powers of medicine were largely ineffective with the tribe. He was no tewat like the ones they revered (the ones they didn't revere, the ones who failed to heal, were put to death under tribal law). And also, because of Marcus Whitman's rush to cut and burn, the women could no longer walk out onto certain familiar fields to gather familiar, and much-needed, tule.

The Cayuse also heard more than they could stand about the white man's hell. Eternal punishment quickly became the missionaries' loudest threat—do as we say or you'll spend every moment until the end of time writhing in anguish. Cayuse chiefs met with Marcus to request an end to the hell intimidation tactics. Narcissa wrote to her father that several tried to persuade Marcus "not to talk such bad talk to them, as they say, but talk good talk, or tell some story, or history." In another letter Narcissa noted, "Some now threaten to whip [Marcus] and to destroy our crops, and for a long time their cattle were turned into our potato field every night to see if they could not compel him to change his course of instruction with them."

But, as one historian writes, "Marcus would not desist. Hell was too dear to him."

In her journals and letters home, Narcissa, without a waver, asserts that she and Marcus were doing exactly what was necessary to teach the Cayuse a different way of being. The Cayuse had little interest in such instruction, but Narcissa went on instructing, and she went on insisting, for one thing, on a new notion of boundaries. Narcissa, like my great-grandmother Hazel would sixty-some years later, stashed a rifle on the porch to warn Native people away from her door and vegetable patch, and, in the permanent house that Marcus finally did build to replace their first sod dwelling, she made sure an "Indian room" was tacked on toward the back, the one space the Cayuse (though only those dressed in western clothing and recently bathed) were allowed to enter, to keep their muddy feet and sticky hands, their stinking bodies, from her parlor.

The Cayuse had to learn the lines around a new word, "garden," as well. No more could the people of the tribe pick whatever fruit had ripened on whatever vine for their meals, as they always had. Marcus and William Gray—who'd stayed on at Waiilatpu for years snarling at the Cayuse at every turn—got busy pointing out whose fruit was whose, a strange concept to the Cayuse. Several tribal dogs were killed by consuming a pile of meat Gray and Whitman had poisoned and left near the garden to scare away wolves. Gray also mixed up a nasty solution from the doctor's bag and spread the emetic on the outermost melons in the garden, so whoever dipped in on the cantaloupe or honeydew would vomit until he felt like his stomach was scorching its way out his throat.

From the first days of the mission, lines were drawn in the dirt. Don't cross, or else.

Narcissa's journals describe the days she ventured out to the camp to teach a lesson or two in manners, but mostly she's busy praising her Lord on her pages, and expressing, again, her aim of turning souls in His direction. Sometimes under the mighty surface of God's plan she slips in more of her own desires than she probably meant to. She yearns for home, a seat at her mother's table eating pork and potatoes. She pleads for one of her sisters, any of the four she left behind and her favorite, Jane, in particular, to travel to Oregon and relieve her abject loneliness. "Who will come over and help us?" is one line from a letter. "Weak and frail nature cannot endure excessive care and anxiety any great length of time without falling under it."

Soon she is hurt, even furious, that she's had no response to the many letters she's sent home. "It seems like talking to the wind," she wrote to her sister, "or that I am entirely out of the reach of your hearing."

Out on the cold frontier Narcissa started to grow hard. The longer she lived on the harsh Columbia Plateau under the shadow of the Blue Mountains, there in the nascent territory of Oregon, the more bitter she became. After her two-year-old daughter Alice drowned in the river, Narcissa became as impenetrable as stone.

# 6

A few summers ago I asked for a look at a rare book about Marcus Whitman, a single volume within the vast holdings of the American Antiquarian Society in Worcester, Massachusetts. I'd applied for a month-long research fellowship at the library for one reason: to get under the surface of Narcissa Whitman. To learn not about the myth or the icon of the frontier, not the "angel of mercy," but the woman. I was curious about this person who'd lost her only biological child. A woman stuck, I'm guessing, in a terse-at-best marriage. The woman who had no close women friends (she and Eliza Spalding barely tolerated each other, their one-hundred-mile distance giving them necessary cool remove). The real Narcissa, who was eventually beaten and shot and who died in front of the children she had taken in and cared for, kids who probably tried to love her even as they cowered from her stern comportment.

On my way to Massachusetts I'd stopped at the eponymous Whitman College in Walla Walla, where a single lock of Narcissa's hair, tied with a ribbon, sits inside a glassed-in cabinet in the basement archives. The college, and the library at the center of the college, is located a few miles from Waiilatpu (which is now a historical site managed by the US National Park Service). There in the basement I waited at a table while the young archivist, who said he'd known nothing of the Whitmans before he was hired for the job, slid a set of her letters from a metal box. Narcissa had written some on the journey out to

Oregon Territory and others from the houses that Marcus had built at the mission. After she and Marcus died, piles of letters were retrieved from her parents and sisters and stored here, way, way out here where many of the notes had begun, in Walla Walla, Washington.

Narcissa's straight handwriting is barely decipherable on the original paper, now turned crisp and yellow. The archivist wouldn't let me handle the letters—not that I asked—but he said I could lean over and read whichever one he'd flattened on the table. From what I could make out, her message is fairly consistent in tone and flavor (only a bit of a wobble when she allows that yearning for family to seep out onto the page). She describes, in some detail, the marvelous new and unusual landscapes and cultures she'd witnessed. It also makes sense, since she and Marcus were belly-rumbling hungry for most of the trip and expecting a warm and familiar meal once they hit a fort, that she yelps over the unpleasantness of the food on one of their stops: "I thot I would tell what kind of a dish we had set before us this morning. It is called black pudding. It is not a favourite dish with us Americans. It is made of blood & the fat of hogs, spiced and filled into a gut." Still, most of her letters are full of reminders to her readers, and herself, of her Christian duty to save the heathens of the frontier.

"All of us here before God," she states in one. "It is not enough for us alone to be thankful. Will not my beloved friends the deciples of Jesus unite with us in gratitude & praise to God for his great Mercy. It is in answer to your prayers that we are here and are permitted to see this day. To dedicate myself renewedly & unreservedly to his service, among the heathen, and may the Lords hand be as evidently manifest in blessing our labours among them."

Once I arrived in Massachusetts I started in on books about the people who had, it seems to me, swept in to make hay of Narcissa's bloody death, as well as Marcus's, though it was the image of the woman's dead body in a ditch, the whipped and shot-up body of the "angel," that provoked the most outrage.

One book about Marcus Whitman I'd asked for at the American Antiquarian Library was delivered to a small carrel, as was protocol, and I set the book on a dust-free plastic cradle, more protocol, and squeaked open a cover that had, if its stiff and unblemished paper was any indication, remained slammed shut for decades. I peeled away stuck-together pages, one at a time, bored already with the hair-splitting argument that I was skimming through—the point being that Marcus Whitman, though he had led the first major wagon train, which had become lost, over the mountains to safety in 1843, had overly aggrandized his role in settling the West. The author insisted Marcus was no frontiersman but instead an awkward settler and a somewhat lousy missionary. Just when I was considering moving on to a different book, to what I hoped would be a less sour discussion, a piece of paper fell out of the pages I was coaxing apart. It fluttered onto the desk in front of me. A blue square of onionskin, about six inches by four, so delicate I wasn't sure I should handle it. The note was folded in half. I picked it up, spread it flat. I held the paper in my palm and studied what was there: on one side, a pressed feathery green leaf in the shape, nearly, of a Christmas tree. On the other side, written in the leaf's rusty shadow, a notation in miniature, formal handwriting: "Plucked from the grave of Eliza Whitman, October 12, 1848."

I stood up, balancing the note in my palm. I looked around for someone, anyone, to share this with. What a thing to discover so far from my home, from Narcissa's home. Who wrote it? The line he or she penned made me half crazy. Eliza Whitman? What was that mix-up about? For no two women were more different in tenor and approach than Narcissa Whitman and Eliza Spalding.

Eliza, meek and compromising and ever gentle, had gone off with her brute of a husband, Henry, to start a mission in what's now Idaho, living for eleven years among the Nez Perce. Eliza, first thing, taught herself the local language so she could converse with her new acquaintances. She invited them into her home. She shared meals and stories with Nez Perce women. The opposite of Narcissa, who once wrote to her family, "You have no idea how difficult it is to realize any benefit from those who do not understand you."

Eliza asked the tribal women to show her their way of cooking, their ways of tending to children, and she asked them to tell her about their beliefs, their notion of a creator—forbidden subjects when Narcissa was in charge.

Henry may have been despised by much of the tribe he lived among—for one reason because he regularly tied a Nez Perce man or boy to a tree to give him a hearty whipping in front of the others—but Eliza was beloved.

If the leaf dried into the very fabric of the paper in my hand was plucked from any grave, it was Narcissa's (Eliza lived years past 1848 and died of lifelong health problems; she was not shot in the chest or whipped with a quirt). What the note signaled—I held it gingerly in my hand as if it might sprout wings and fly away from me any moment—was that mere months after her death Narcissa had already been confused with another, rather than remembered for the force that she was, confounding as the force may have been.

I abandoned the reading of the book, any book actually, and concentrated instead on the ephemera that had fallen quite literally into my lap. Since the library had a way to do this, I started tracking down the donor of the book: Edwin Marble and Harriet Chase Marble, born in 1828 and 1830 respectively, which would have made them twenty and eighteen years old when the note was written.

Had one of the Marbles gone to Oregon Territory in the late 1840s?

That was my first question. Why had a longtime Massachusetts resident—Edwin seems the more likely of the two—taken it upon himself to ride out all that way and somehow (it doesn't seem possible) manage to stand on the heap of soil over the mass grave of people who'd been killed nearly a year earlier? If Edwin was the one who'd picked the leaf on a cool fall day, he didn't do so near a resting place for Narcissa. There was no interment for her. In the immediate days after her death, her bones had been dug up by animals, coyotes or wolves, not just once but several times, as had the bones and viscera and raggedy chewed clothing and boots of the others. The older children were sent out to gather up the pieces and wrap them in sheets stripped from beds (so much for Narcissa's sheets), hastily buried in a hole and covered with a wagon bed. The wagon belonged to a man, Joseph Stanfield, who'd been friendly to those who'd planned the attack—Stanfield had been promised, the story goes, the hand of one of the widows once the killing was done. Problem was, the widow Hays, his choice, kicked him off her porch with a spit-in-his-face refusal. Anyway, it was Stanfield who scraped up enough frozen dirt to cover the bodies, topping the makeshift grave with the overturned wagon, and scurried back to his corner, enemy that he'd become to the terrified survivors.

In October of 1848, the date on the note, it was dangerous to be anywhere around Waiilatpu. Most everyone had moved away, including the Jesuits who'd begun a mission shortly before the attack but abandoned their efforts soon after. Every Protestant missionary for miles around had closed its doors. Skirmishes between the two sides had broken out around the former Whitman mission—one side made up of reluctant volunteer troops (settlers practically had to be dragged out of their homes to join the militia—they hadn't made the endless journey to the West to fight, after all, but to *live*); the other side made up of perhaps equally reluctant Cayuse.

Proclamation!
The Legislature now in session having authorized me to call on the citizens of this Territory to enlist, for the purpose of carrying on operations against the Cayuse Indians, and to punish them for the murders committed by them on the residents of Waiilatpu: I therefore call on the Counties hereinafter named to furnish the number of men required . . .
—Geo Abernathy, Governor

Despite their familiarity with the region and the battle tactics for which they'd long been celebrated, the Cayuse were losing the war. Less than half were still alive, most hidden in the mountains, sick and starved. They no longer occupied any of the land around Waiilatpu. No one did. The women and children of the Whitman Station had been traded for a few dollars, tobacco and blankets, and, once hostages slipped away in the dead of night, the Cayuse burned most of the buildings. Except for an occasional visit by local mountain men who hoped to find a piece of Narcissa's hair strewn across the vacant compound, the place was empty.

Maybe one of the famous mountain men of the time—Joe Meek, Robert Newell, Wesley Howard, Jim Bridger—was cousin or friend to the Marbles. Is that the connection? If so, why would that man pick a leaf from a plant growing in the dirt? Why would he cart it home, press it flat, ship it (or travel with it) to Massachusetts, and hand it over to the young couple? I wonder, too, about the leaf's recipient—Edwin Marble, say. He, or someone, took the trouble to glue the leaf to paper, to write out an inscription, to place the folded note in a book, and not just any book, but one about Marcus Whitman. The book was put away, eventually donated to the Antiquarian library, undisturbed for 160 years. Now open on the desk in front of me, emptied of a message that was tucked into its pages long ago.

# 7

Maybe whoever wrote the note wasn't thinking of the mother Eliza Spalding but instead of her daughter, also named Eliza. The nine-year-old child was the only member of that family to land in the stark middle of the attack. She'd arrived at Waiilatpu on November 22, 1847, accompanied by her father, to start school at the Whitman Mission, which makes me wonder if Eliza the younger spent the rest of her life wishing her parents had kept her at home until after the holidays. Even if they'd waited a week, past Thanksgiving, or even if they'd let the long-brewing feud between families prevent the Spaldings from trusting the Whitmans with their child that winter, young Eliza would have been spared the mayhem.

A few months before the Spalding girl showed up, Narcissa and Marcus had hired a new schoolteacher, L. W. Saunders, and a helper for that teacher, musician and religious scholar Andrew Rodgers, both of whom had dedicated themselves to offering lessons steeped in Presbyterian values. Henry Spalding approved of these teachers even if he had little praise (if any) for the Whitmans, and he wanted his daughter to benefit from an education. Rodgers soon became Narcissa's dearest friend at the mission. He played violin and, like her, had a penchant for song. I suspect her heart was aflutter around him—there's a hint of *smitten* in her letters home about her new companion.

When tall, young Eliza showed up for school, she joined at

least a dozen other compound children (the school was originally built for Cayuse children who were no longer deemed educable) who'd be under the tutelage of Saunders and Rodgers—children from families that had decided to overwinter at Waiilatpu, as well as the many abandoned or orphaned children the Whitmans now cared for.

Eliza was already friends with girls in the mission's kid pack, including a gaggle of orphaned girls who'd shown up three years earlier, and including Helen Mar Meek, daughter of Joe Meek the mountain man (the soon to be marshal), who'd left his child at Waiilatpu—as in dumped her with the Whitmans and saw her rarely again because he did not want her to be raised by her dead mother's tribe, the Nez Perce. Eliza was friends, too, with Mary Ann Bridger, a child also dispatched to Waiilatpu by her father, another famous mountain man, Jim Bridger. Mary Ann's mother was daughter of the Chief of the Flathead Nation. Like Meek, Bridger wouldn't allow a tribe to raise his girl after the mother died, and he chose Narcissa as the replacement parent. Jim Bridger also neglected to stop in; he hadn't seen his child for years.

When Eliza arrived for school at least half the children were sick with the measles, the same strain of measles that had killed, or was actively killing, almost every Cayuse youth. The cold, the illnesses and deaths, the diminishing stores of food: Waiilatpu was barely holding together. What a place to leave your nine-year-old girl, who was plopped down in the cold and told to fend for herself.

November 29, 1847. *That* day again. One of the orphan girls was the first to rise in the frigid house. She went into the kitchen seeking warmth. She found Marcus at the stove, frying meat, and climbed on a stool to stand next to him. The child told this man, who'd promised that he would soon formally adopt her and her six siblings, that she'd dreamed during the night of death—the Cayuse barging into the house to kill them all.

"Let's hope that doesn't happen," Marcus said without slowing his spoon.

The rest of the children—the ones well enough to get out of bed—soon made their way into the kitchen for breakfast. Late morning Narcissa swept in to take charge, over her bout of worry. In the meantime the Osborn family, one of those over-wintering families, was occupying the "Indian Room" because there was no space for them in the Emigrant's House down the lane. (The Emigrant's House, in the early days of the mission, was built by William Gray for his own use. In year five Gray resigned his post at Waiilatpu and returned to his home in the east. Cheers all around. Except later he came back, this time with the title of Reverend and in service to God and no under-ling of Marcus Whitman's, and, for a time, he moved to Lapwai to live near the Spaldings.) Most of the Osborns were up now, too, looking for warmth and food in the kitchen, though the mother of the family refused to move from bed. A week earlier her infant had been born infected with the measles and died within minutes. Her two-year-old daughter died of the same illness the following day. Now Mother Osborn sent her remain-ing children in for breakfast, but stayed herself in the room, weeping for her lost ones.

Her husband, the compound's most skilled carpenter, was one of five men who met in the frozen compound to butcher that cow, as the store of meat was nearly empty.

Marcus ate his meal and then put on his buckskin coat and left the house, trudging several miles in the fog toward the Cayuse camp. He would attend the burial services that morn-ing for the chief's three young sons, the latest to succumb to the measles. Marcus would offer prayers and he'd offer solace, though many in the tribe would flat out refuse his ministrations. While children at the mission—white children, anyway—were often able to recover, the Cayuse children were not. One after the other, Cayuse youth fell ill and died. Marcus, the doctor, the healer, the white medicine man, could do nothing to help. Nor could he dispel the anger aimed at him and at Narcissa for the misery they'd brought—though of the two, it was usually Marcus who leaned toward the conciliatory. The day the Osborn toddler died, her dead infant sister already arranged in a coffin for burial and both bodies pecked raw with measles, Marcus had reminded Narcissa again about the danger they were in from Cayuse who believed he used his magic doctor powers only on whites. He had no way to understand or explain how antibodies are passed on from grandparent to parent to child, giving white people a speck of genetic immunity. He persuaded Narcissa to ask Mrs. Osborn if certain Cayuse people might be invited in to examine the dead babies, laying the deceased children out on the bed as evidence to the tribe that no race was safe from the scourge. But even after the little Osborns were put on display and a solemn group of viewers took a long look at the dead children, tension did not dissipate between mission and Cayuse camp. Strained relations, not just over illness but also about the white settlers moving in to take over tribal land. One wagon after another, a near daily reminder that the Whitmans had themselves appeared out of the mountains and plunked down without a discussion of payment. Why hadn't the Cayuse been compensated, well compensated, for the vast acreage that Whitman had taken up as his own, building homes, shops, a gristmill, and planting swaths of wheat, a garden, an orchard? After all, Reverend Parker had promised there would be payment, and that it would be generous.

The land dispute had been a problem since the Whitmans' arrival, with threats of death arising even in the early years. A Cayuse chief called Umtippe is one of the first to issue a demand, as the Whitmans were living on land that was well known to be his. Umtippe also insisted that Marcus heal his sick wife. "Doctor, you have come here to give us bad medicines; you come to kill us, and you steal our lands. You had promised to pay me every year, and you have given me nothing. You had better go away; if wife dies, you shall die also."

Nothing infuriated Marcus more than this issue. To Marcus's last day, his answer was stern and swift: *I owe you nothing. The land was mine to take.* A week before his death Marcus penned an angry letter to his friend Alonson Hinman at the Dalles Mission to insist again: no matter how often they demand it, pay the Indians not a single cent for their holdings.

The deaths at Waiilatpu prompted more than one official investigation in the years that followed, many of which are recorded in the annals of Oregon history. White men acquainted with Marcus Whitman were interviewed about the causes of the attack—it seems almost too obvious to point out that no Native people were asked for their side of the story. The new government in Oregon planned to send convincing documents to Washington, DC, to Congress—the body that would act on the results of the investigation if action was deemed necessary, which Abernathy and others hoped to dissuade. They preferred to handle the aftermath of the attack their own way.

Question:
Has the American Congress the least shadow in truth to represent that the taking of the Indians' land by the missionaries (Whitman and Spalding) was one of the alleged causes of the murder of Dr. Whitman and family?

Answer:

I believe and know this to be false.—Geo Abernathy

The most wicked falsehood ever uttered.—A Hinman

Whitman and Spalding took no lands, only the stations they occupied and improved, as the Indians requested them, and upon which they located them on arriving in the country in answer to a call from the Indians, and as authorized by a written permit by the War Department at Washington dated March 1, 1836.—JS Griffin

Marcus, despite his feuds with the Cayuse over money and doctoring and especially land ownership, still hoped to keep at least some peace between the two factions, and so, anticipating the scorn that would certainly meet him, he continued on to the Cayuse encampment to stand near the back of the death ceremony for the chief's three boys on November 29. As he marched over frozen ground that he considered his and that the tribe considered theirs, Marcus might have been thinking about the report he'd heard the day before while he was visiting the outlying camp of a man named Stickus. On the morning of November 28, Marcus had convinced Henry Spalding (still at Waiilatpu), despite their rub with each other, to ride with him to smaller encampments about twenty miles from the mission where the doctor would check on sick families. The men reached Stickus's lodge and entered comfortably, assured that the Cayuse man was friendly toward the missionaries. It was daybreak on the Sabbath, and so Spalding, because he was Spalding, insisted on an impromptu church service for the few people who'd gathered. Whitman, after prayers and breakfast, went about his visits to various other lodges, to the children suffering from measles, and late in the afternoon began to prepare for the long ride home to Waiilatpu. That's when Spalding told Marcus he'd decided to stay on at the camp of another Cayuse man, Five Crows. Spalding had wrenched his knee and thus required rest, so he wouldn't, as originally planned, go back to the mission to see his daughter Eliza. Instead, he'd give himself a chance recover and then head straight to his own mission at Lapwai the following day.

A sore joint and an extra night with friendly Five Crows. That's what saved Spalding's life.

Marcus agreed to give young Eliza her father's best and prepared to leave. Noticing that Whitman's horse was spent, Stickus offered the temporary use of his mule, which Marcus accepted. As they were packing the animal, Stickus whispered to the doctor that a stranger named Joe Lewis was brewing trouble among the people of the tribe. Whitman knew about Lewis and the man's propensity for bad-mouthing the missionaries. Lately, though, Lewis was pouring on gas, claiming Marcus was secretly poisoning the Cayuse while he pretended to treat them and that both Marcus and Narcissa were concocting ways to make the people of the tribe sick, or even dead, so new pioneers could snatch up their land.

Whitman shrugged—he'd heard this kind of rumor before. Lewis was a loudmouth, a problem for sure, but so far all talk and no action. Marcus got on the mule, thanked Stickus again, and headed home for the final time.

It was Mary Saunders, the new schoolteacher's wife, who later wrote in her account about Joe Lewis. She said the Delaware man had showed up at Waiilatpu early in 1847, "sick and in need of clothing," and added that "the doctor clothed and cared for him until he recovered and sent him away with a family going to the Willamette Valley. He returned in three days and refused to leave. It was a case of warming a viper in one's bosom."

Marcus might have at first dismissed Stickus's warning, but Joe Lewis's fearmongering went to work on the doctor's troubled mind as he traveled back to Waiilatpu on the night of the twenty-eighth, as survivors said he arrived late, agitated, and sat up with Narcissa for hours until she went into the kitchen to cry alone. The Cayuse had laid down their terms: The Whitmans needed to go. Pack up their equipment, their Bibles, their friends, their songbooks, and vanish for good.

Joseph Osborn happened to be in the house checking on his grieving wife when Cayuse men fired the first shots, a few hours after Marcus's return from the Cayuse camp. He alone, of the cow-butchering team, survived because Osborn was a quick thinker and a quicker doer. He pried open the bedroom's floorboards as men shouted in anguish outside and as Narcissa called for help to drag Marcus out of the kitchen so she could get him next to the bed of ashes. Osborn shoved his stunned wife and two remaining children into the crawl space and climbed in after, rearranging the boards as best he could. He set a hand across the children's mouths; he pleaded with his wife to huddle in silence on the frozen ground. Not a peep. Once it was completely dark, he led his family into the forest, somehow evading Cayuse guards, somehow enduring the unforgiving temperatures, and then somehow, after hiding his wife and daughter in the forest, making a twenty-mile journey by foot to the nearest bastion, Fort Walla Walla, with his feverish son on his back. At the fort he was refused entry, just as the compound's other carpenter, Peter Hall, had been a few hours earlier. Hall was told it was too dangerous to let in Waiilatpu survivors. The inhabitants of the fort were determined not to further incite the Cayuse. *Keep us out of it.* Hall went on, never to be seen again, though Osborn had better luck. Several men at the gates offered to help, and the lot returned to search the dark woods for his wife and child, who they miraculously—truly, a miracle—found alive.

Not that this family got away without being marked by the experience—the Osborns did slog their way to relative safety (emphasis on the word *relative*), but once they all reached the fort again, the sick child died. Four-year-old John. No wonder, when she was ninety years old, the only surviving offspring, Nancy Osborn, leapt to her death from the third-story window of her Oregon nursing home, shouting, "The Indians are coming to get us!"

While the Osborns held each other under the floor of the Indian Room in silence—if the baby and toddler had lived, the family surely would have been found, which is one of the terrible ironies of that day—Eliza was in the schoolroom with a dozen other children, any child well enough to sit at a desk and concentrate. She heard the first shouts from Mary Ann Bridger, a girl already showing signs of the measles that would end her life in another couple of weeks. Mary Ann ran out of the kitchen door yelling, "They've killed father!" She didn't mean her own father, Jim Bridger, but Marcus. She'd been in the kitchen with the doctor when he stepped to the door to speak to a small group of Cayuse men gathered on the porch. She saw Tomahas jump into the kitchen and strike Marcus in the head with a tomahawk. Some reports stated that another man, perhaps the young chief Tiloukaikt, was the one who shot Marcus in the neck.

Eliza ran to the window to see what was happening in the yard while the schoolteacher Saunders hurried out the schoolroom door to find out for himself about the noisy disruption. In short order Saunders was sliced open and flung over a fence, and Eliza was climbing into the schoolroom loft to hide with the other children. The loft turned out to be not much of a secret space—the children were located quickly and brought down, led outside by Joe Lewis himself. Lewis apparently didn't realize that Eliza was the only one among those left alive who spoke the region's common trade language (some of the other children had learned phrases, but she alone was fluent). Maybe he didn't care what she heard. Eliza stood outside the kitchen door, arms wrapped around her whimpering friends, while she listened to the leaders of the raid debate whether or not to shoot the children. Several Cayuse men lobbied for no survivors—kill every white person and be done with it. Others said no, keep the hostages alive for their rescuers, who'd be showing up as soon as word of the attack reached the fort. Eliza wrote later that she was certain the side pushing for execution would win. She remembered lifting her apron to cover her eyes so she didn't have to watch herself or her friends be killed.

But at that very moment Narcissa was brought to the door of the house on the settee. She cleared the doorway, and the Cayuse opened fire.

Eliza and the other children held tight to each other as the Cayuse turned away, fully occupied with Narcissa now. Mothers pulled their own kids to safety while orphans and stragglers ran up to the room of the main house. They joined the two girls in bed begging for water, for whatever help they might get. A din settled over the compound, except for their plaintive moans and those of Narcissa Whitman.

In the days that followed, it was young Eliza who taught the others how to approach their captors, or so wrote Mary Saunders in her book. Eliza suggested greeting a Cayuse person with the word "Sixtiwah," meaning "Yes, friend," and then stating clearly, "I have a good heart." Repeat it: "I have a good heart." Finish the salutation with an apology—*I'm sorry for the doctor's actions and his wife's.*

Mary Saunders also reports that three teenage girls who'd been given to Cayuse men as wives suddenly reappeared on the day of rescue, to the surprise of everyone else who figured the young women were gone for good. In a letter dated September 1880, Eliza Spalding, well into adulthood, wrote that a silent agreement was formed among the hostages that rescue day. They would say nothing, ever, about what had happened to the teenagers, "and I have purposely refrained from giving personal details. This is to protect the women involved, as they certainly would not want these things to be broadcast."

A month after the attack survivors at Waiilatpu, including the teenage girls, were not saved by a troop of American soldiers nor by American volunteers. No Joe Meek or Jim Bridger. The legends did not charge in to rescue their respective daughters. Instead it was a rather peace-loving fur trader from Canada who showed up at the mission to retrieve whatever survivors he could fit on his boat. Peter Ogden had sent a message to the Cayuse some days earlier: "If you deliver me up the prisoners I shall pay you. On my return, if you wish it, I shall do all I can for you—but I do not promise to prevent war. We remain neutral. Let it not be said among you afterwards that I deceived you."

What Ogden couldn't have conveyed to the Cayuse— because it only became clear to him with the passage of years— was that the timing of this violence could not have been better for the whites or worse for the Cayuse. Less than a year earlier the long battle over Oregon Territory, with both the British and the Americans claiming the land as their own, was finally settled for good. James K. Polk, elected president in 1844, at the apex of the Oregon Trail migration, promised that the Pacific

Northwest would soon be entirely in American hands. His campaign cry of "Fifty-Four Forty or Fight!" helped sail him into office, US voters as a throng supporting the westward expansion of the country. Still, it took Polk until 1846 to settle a matter that became more urgent and embittered the longer it went on. That is, exactly who owned the Pacific Northwest? Every year, tens of thousands of US citizens were wooed to the land of the Whitmans—to seemingly endless swaths of land in what's now Washington State, Oregon, Montana, and Idaho. The settlers claimed land that, actually, the US government had only shaky legal rights to. The newcomers were busy setting up farms and ranches, building log houses, establishing commerce, and they wanted (demanded) guarantees from the federal government about those rights of ownership and safety. That required a big solution: the US federal government had to find a way to procure the region as its own once and for all. Native claims to land were summarily dismissed, ignored, considered no impediment to progress. But the British were another matter. They had been around far longer than the Americans, they inhabited forts and offered supplies through the Hudson Bay Company Trading Posts, and they were determined to stay (except they had no means to move British citizens in to settle the land).

But then, surprisingly, the US-versus-Britain problem rather solved itself: the population of beaver fell off just as the fur was no longer in demand. The place of fading trappers and hunters became so crowded with American settlers that the British, recognizing the tide had turned against them, agreed to close up their posts, including the supply stores that had pretty much defined trade in the frontier, and move beyond the forty-*ninth* degree, not the fifty-fourth (Polk's final concession). The territory known colloquially as Oregon was split, with more than half of the land now officially part of the United States.

By June of 1846 the Whitmans and Spaldings could legitimately claim that they lived in America.

By December of 1847 the Whitmans were dead, and the Spaldings, as well as every other missionary, had closed their missions and moved away in haste.

Joe Meek, new US marshal, went about enforcing with a vengeance laws passed in a rush after the attack on Waiilatpu, included white settlers' rights to take land from Native people and laws that allowed the killing of any Native person deemed a threat to life and/or property. All of this in the name of she who was proclaimed an innocent martyr, Narcissa Prentiss Whitman, and her husband, Marcus.

An editorial from the July 13, 1848, issue of the *Oregon Spectator*: "That country would have been much settled before now but for the efforts made by the lamented Doctor Whitman on behalf of the Cayuse to prevent it. His lips are now sealed in death; massacred by the bloody hands of those for whom he long and so earnestly labored. We see no reason why the Cayuse country should not be open to the settlement of the white man."

# 8

The tribe had many reasons to despise the missionaries. The illnesses—dead child, dead child, dead child lined up on burial grounds—the disputes over land, and also the prickly club of the underworld swung at the Cayuse again and again, a concept so disturbing that after eleven years of pushing for it, the Whitmans had converted not a single person of the tribe to their faith.

Still, only minor acts of subversion and violence had broken out between tribe and mission in the first decade. Windows smashed, a few weapons brandished but not used for harm. Marcus wrote about one such touchy incident the year before the final attack:

> A Cayuse took hold of my ear and pulled it and struck me on the breast ordering me to hear. . . . When he let go I turned the other to him and he pulled that, and in this way I let him pull first one and then the other until he gave over and took my hat and threw it into the mud. I called on the Indians who were at work . . . to give it to me and I put it on my head—when he took it off again . . . and threw it in the mud and water, of which it dripped plentifully. Once more the Indians gave it back to me and I put it on all muddy as it was, and said to him, "Perhaps you are playing."

But then Joe Lewis showed up. Joe Lewis, who had a case to

make about these White Mans. His meetings were held in secret, though the young people of the tribe had no trouble finding out where and when to gather and plot. Tribal elders were opposed to plans involving the deaths of the missionaries: for certain things were bad; for certain the situation would only get worse if white people died. But Lewis's campaign of discontent worked on the younger men. Weren't more wagon trains moving through than ever before? Weren't babies dying every day at the Cayuse camp? Didn't several Cayuse vomit through the night after eating melons from the mission's gardens? Isn't it so that Marcus was heard ordering strychnine from the Hudson Bay's purveyor at Fort Walla Walla? Joe Lewis said aloud what others had thought for some time: there was no remedy for all that had gone wrong for the Cayuse except to end the lives of those who'd brought calamity. And so the attack was planned and executed, and after the dead bodies—torn apart by animals—were regathered, buried again under Joseph Stanfield's wagon, after the teenaged Lorinda Bewley was raped in the open before being taken away by the Cayuse, after two sick boys (one of which was Lorinda's brother) were forced to the center of the compound to be beaten to death, and after one member of the Young family—eleven people living miles above the mission in the sawmill camp—was shot while making a poorly timed delivery of lumber, Joe Lewis slipped away. The new governor of Oregon Territory didn't care about this single rogue individual. He sent no one to search for Lewis. Instead Abarnathy focused on his war with the Cayuse and with any other tribe that might dare offer aid, sending his smattering of volunteer troops out to hunt and kill any suspicious Native person they could locate.

I knew nothing of this history when I drove over the Blue

Mountains and into Walla Walla on a weekend near the end of my senior year of college. I was traveling west from Moscow, through Washington State Palouse country, directly into the valley where Marcus and Narcissa once settled and where they died. But even though Narcissa and Marcus were the ideal of Western fortitude, his statue standing in the National Statuary Hall in the US Capitol, I'd moved on to fifth grade and probably never thought about the missionaries again.

Once I was in Walla Walla, along with my mother and sister, I had no reason to notice the mission a few miles from town, nor did it occur to me to connect Narcissa and Marcus to the college or the fancy hotel downtown. History was simply not on my mind.

I had one task that spring of 1979, and that was to buy a wedding dress.

The three of us had driven over a hundred miles, two and a half hours over the switchbacks of Snoqualmie Pass. We crossed the border of Washington State and entered the Columbia Basin, blanketed with thousands of acres of spring wheat and purple rapeseed. I'm surprised to this day that my mother went along with my lark. There were plenty of dress shops in Boise where I could have found a gown, but I'd seen the one in a magazine, the only one I wanted to wear to my May wedding, acres of lace and, if I had my way, a train that spread down the aisle—I pictured a thin, elegant woman moving in a cloud of white and wondered if, for a day, I could dare to be her. The dress was for sale only in a single tiny shop in Walla Walla, and I, caught up in an overblown romantic illusion about how to make the leap into an adult life, thought I had to wear it. That gown, the color of fresh milk, and no other.

The afternoon drive out of Idaho and into Washington might have given me time to reconsider marriage, if reconsidering was even a twitch in my eye. It wasn't. I'd become adept at ignoring any prick of doubt, shoving it down. I was twenty-one, terrified to leave the predictable rhythm of college, the lofty conversations (or so I imagined) with English-major friends in the daytime about those Hemingway short stories, Bryant's "Thanatopsis" recited by heart, and Ezra Pound, whose papers were archived in our university's library. For Halloween we all dressed as characters from Hawthorne stories, and in general we threw rollicking parties where I drank myself into a blur. I felt incapable of finding a job or applying for graduate school or traveling to some distant place, and I opted instead for what seemed like my only way to adulthood. The option I'd resisted for a time, but now gave into. I'd marry a boy, a boy equally steeped in the legacy of the West, who both awed and worried me.

If I let any hint of my buried panic spurt into the car my mother drove through the Palouse, or into the room of the bridal shop once we'd arrived, nobody paid any attention. My mother would have brushed it aside if she had. She was planning a wedding. She'd already ordered cases of champagne and pink roses for the tables, and nothing was going to keep her from the charge she'd thrown herself into at age thirty-eight, a fancy reception after a solemn ceremony, nothing like her ten minutes in front of Salmon's justice of the peace. So, sure, I'd get married in late May, on my own parents' twenty-first anniversary (not realizing yet they'd be divorced by their twenty-fifth), and we'd all dance into the night. I'd leave with the man called husband, and that would be that. And to start things off my mother would buy me a wedding dress.

I put on the gown from the magazine ad, the one from the picture I'd cut out and pinned above my dresser so I could gaze at it, and stood in front of the tri-mirror at the shop, almost too afraid to study my reflection in case I had even a stab of disappointment or disillusionment. Out of the corner of my eye I could tell: it was beautiful, this dress. It was perfect. But it was also expensive. Even the shopkeeper had raised her eyebrows when I'd asked for it: *Really?* Now my mother hunched on a stool in the corner, my sister behind her, and shook her head. "There must be others," she said, picking up the price tag and staring at it again. "You'll only wear it once."

I could have begged and wailed for the one I thought I had to have, and I might, maybe, have gotten it. But we didn't do that. We didn't complain or stomp feet. I remember little crying in front of our parents. My mother said no, and I silently cursed her and moved on. My sister (who'd marry her own boyfriend a year later than I'd marry mine) and I chose another. A more conventional dress. Lacy, but practical. Cheaper.

I tried on the second choice. Cindy did the same. My sister went back into the fitting room to remove the dress we'd cart home, and I leaned down to tie my shoes, to pick up my purse. My mother stepped to the counter to write the check under a sign that stated "No Returns" in dense red letters, as if the owner had learned a thing or two about the fickle nature of brides-to-be. The gown was purchased, and lunch was ordered at a café down the street before we headed back to Moscow. Another stone set, one more wedding detail to dissuade me from changing my mind.

No returns.

I've let myself sometimes rage at my mother. Why didn't she say something? Why didn't she convince me to buy no wedding dress while pointing out the obvious disaster ahead with this boy-man who was even less prepared for marriage than I was? Of course, I wouldn't have listened. Maybe she put out a few warnings that I knocked like dirt off my shoes while I congratulated myself for doing what young women in Idaho were made to do and that left one small part of me triumphant: I'd found a husband.

Just like my mother was pregnant with me on her wedding day, I, too, was pregnant on this dress-shopping day, though my mother didn't know it. I'd hardly let myself know it. Yet here was the real rock set hard in the wall, a baby on its way. I could not escape the only future I'd let myself consider.

Which makes me think: What if it was Narcissa combing through my life, instead of me rattling my way through hers? What if she lined up my mistakes, one after another, and condemned my delusions? She might have reminded me that while she didn't, I *did* have a choice—that in fact choices had risen up regularly along the way in my last year at the university and of many varieties. I could have taught English in China. I could have hitchhiked to Guatemala. I could have applied to every graduate school program until one took me in with my 3.8 grade point average and Phi Beta Kappa key. Instead I strode right by those on my way to the most predictable path. Narcissa might have reminded me about that day in the car, returning to school as a sophomore, when I could have heeded a call for liberation, for actual freedom, instead of the fake independence I practiced so well. I was perfectly capable back then of asking the fraternity boy, whose name and face are lost to me now, to drop me off in Lewiston. I could have scrambled over the sorority nemesis and made my way to the Greyhound bus station or stuck out my thumb, destination unknown. Anywhere, everywhere, to begin to figure out who I was.

But like Narcissa, I stayed. I did what was expected of me. I stepped into the only adult life I would let myself want.

Some springs ago, divorced many years from that first young husband, our children raised to adulthood, I went to Waiilatpu. I'd been there already, several times. This day was hot, and I sweated to the top of Memorial Hill, a steep promontory at one end of the mission grounds. At the top I stood next to the marble column erected on the fiftieth anniversary of the attack in tribute to the white people who'd lost their lives. There's no memorial here for the Cayuse: not for the Cayuse children who died from disease, not for the tribal members who died in the war, not for the five Cayuse chiefs hung in Oregon City, men who were made a spectacle.

Narcissa. I think about her in those minutes after the first wave of attack on Waiilatpu, when she pulled the tomahawk from Marcus's head and packed his wound with ashes, an act that extended his life by a few minutes. Survivors said he spoke to her before he died and that she spoke to him, whatever bitterness between them forgotten and only the bloom of their years together in the room while he was dying. Then he was gone, and she was left alone to manage the children and the women in the house with her and to endure, somehow, the chaos. Her husband was dead in the living room, her only biological child buried at the bottom of the hill, her mother and sisters long absent from her life. Narcissa was alone, staring into the chasm of her end.

On this visit to Waiilatpu I walked back down the hill and over to the shady section of the grounds, to the communal grave (the bodies had been disinterred, reburied together under a marble slab at the fifty-year mark) of those killed at the mission. Narcissa Prentiss Whitman is listed second among the dead, after her husband's name, on the weather-beaten stone. I stood there for a minute and considered my own failures, with significantly smaller stakes and consequences, except that I have hurt, many times over, the people I profess to love, often out of an ambition to serve myself.

I pulled out a photocopy of the note I'd found in the library in Massachusetts. "Plucked from the grave." I squatted to the ground, searching for a piece of vegetation that matched the picture in my hand. Before long I found it, a feathery green plant growing in shade. Tansy. That was the one. Maybe a descendant of the very plant Marcus had put in the ground here for his medicine bag, related to the one a mystery person had picked and dried, glued to a card, and stuck in a book in 1848. I decided to believe that it was related, without a doubt, to that long-ago foliage. Why not? Connection upon connection, electrically charged synapses that snapped and sizzled from her to me.

I reached over to pluck a leaf of tansy near the grave of Narcissa Whitman. And now that piece of plant rests between two sheets of parchment paper, dried and flat. A sprig of tansy pressed in a book situated on my table. It's from my grandmother's library, a biography of an obdurate woman, Narcissa Prentiss Whitman, who came West and began a movement that I'm still trying to grasp, still attempting to comprehend— because somewhere in the spinning energy of it are glimmers of truth that might just light on me.

# 3 River of No Return

# 1

A Sunday in June of 1839. The bright season, cheerful summer, offering up no hint of tragedy. The Walla Walla River was running with snowmelt and sunshine, dazzling anyone glancing that way—including two-year-old Alice Clarissa Whitman (named for her grandmothers), who stood in the doorway of her family's home a stone's throw from the riverbank.

Behind her was the small house, the simple structure constructed by Marcus shortly before her birth, built of rough-hewn logs and patted-down mud and grass, now crumbling in places. The river had chewed like a rat at weak spots in the foundation through the winter, meaning the family needed a new dwelling, one that didn't miserably flood every time it rained. But construction would have to wait. Marcus and Narcissa felt they needed to stay intent on their duty, their effort to establish themselves as spiritual authorities in the region. The couple had traveled a long way and given up just about everything to bring their message of Providence to the Cayuse, people they referred to in letters home as "heathens," as "savages." Their efforts to bring those *heathens* to God took precedence over all things.

What seems to have surprised the Whitmans after their arrival is how few Cayuse were open to change; the Whitman neighbors did not present themselves, at least not uniformly, as the open, willing, eager searchers for the white man's God that both Narcissa and Marcus had been assured would be waiting for them. A few were curious about the Whitman religion, and others saw the benefits of learning more about white culture, but the Whitmans' new rules for them—well, *no*. The tribe knew nothing of the *American Advocate* story about a meeting with General Clark, nor of Disoway's subsequent appeal (actually, a demand) for God-fearing people to go West and get the Bible into Native hands. Except for the rich land and plentiful water and sunshine in the Columbia Basin, the Cayuse did not know why the Whitmans had chosen their land to settle on, or their tribe to settle among.

Strains that first season between mission and Cayuse (with worse to come) were largely lifted by the birth of Narcissa's baby. She was the first Caucasian infant in the territory, or so the story goes. When pale, blue-eyed, blonde Alice Clarissa was new, the Cayuse gathered around as one chief gave her a name: Te-mi, Cayuse girl.

The tribe's people by that time had a name for Narcissa, too: their word for *haughty*.

Marcus was also given a name when he first set down at Waiilatpu. Early on the Cayuse were willing to call him *Tewat*, mostly because he told them he was one. A healer, a medicine man. But the title didn't hold up for long.

I wonder if the Whitmans, back in those first years of the mission, were forced to admit to each other that they weren't going to sweep in and have things go their way after all. One bit of solace that first year was the affection that the Cayuse people felt for Alice, a girl who quickly learned the language and played among their children and sang their songs and ate from their steaming pots.

And there she was, Alice, on a Sunday afternoon, stepping off the porch and heading toward the river with tin cups in her hands. She'd pulled the bent containers, maybe the very ones

Narcissa had purchased in St. Louis, off a table set for the Sabbath meal. The hired girl, daughter of the commander of a nearby fort (the rescuer of Narcissa's trunk) named Margaret, had laid out cutlery and plates and returned to the cook stove to stir soup and look out at nothing, not noticing Alice nor hearing the child when she raised the cups over her head and announced that she'd slide down the new ryegrass on her bottom to the banks of the Walla Walla and dip water for the meal. Narcissa and Marcus, consumed by the Bibles on their laps, might have even intentionally ignored their daughter's attempt at getting an adult's attention—a reminder that she wasn't to disturb her parents on God's sacred afternoon.

Alice was born on her mother's twenty-ninth birthday, March 14, 1837, delivered by her father in the mud house. After she noticed the delight the baby gave her neighbors, Narcissa agreed to let select Cayuse—ones she'd deemed friendly—into her home. Curious tribal members lined up at the door for a chance at a peek. "The Little Stranger is visited daily by the Chiefs & principal men in camp & the women throng the house continually waiting an opportunity to look at her," Narcissa wrote her mother. "Her whole appearance is so new to them. Her complexion, her size & dress & all excite a good deal of wonder."

Alice, as she grew into a busy, smiling toddler, also brought Narcissa a sense of peace that had eluded her since leaving her home in New York State and since leaving her beloved and tight-knit family. In one letter to her parents, on the occasion of her thirtieth birthday and Alice's first, abject loneliness roars east: "More than two years have passed since I left my father's home and not a single word has been wafted hence, or, perhaps I should say, has greeted my ears to afford consolation in a desponding hour. This long, long silence makes me feel the truth of our situation, that we are far, very far removed from the land of our birth and Christian privileges."

But six months later, in a more cheerful frame of mind, Narcissa wrote to her sister:

> Yes, Jane, you cannot know how much of a comfort our little daughter is to her father and mother. O, how many melancholy hours she has saved me, while living here alone so long, especially when her father is gone for many days together. I wish most sincerely that her aunts could see her, for surely they would love her as well as her parents. She is now eighteen months old, very large and remarkably healthy. She is a great talker. Causes her mother many steps and much anxiety. She is just beginning to sing with us in our family worship.

The girl was a singer, like her mother, and she memorized hymns, trilling as she moved through the house. She knew by heart, Narcissa reported, at least four Nez Perce Christian songs, and on the last day of her life, Alice awoke to request that "Rock of Ages" serve as the music during that day's worship with the Cayuse. As the first notes lifted in the makeshift chapel, Narcissa later wrote to Jane, the child grabbed her mother's hand and looked up to ask, "Mama, should my tears forever flow?"

And now, about a half hour after the child announced she was leaving the house, the air was silent. Narcissa glanced up from her book. "Where's Alice?" she asked her husband. He shrugged.

Narcissa hurried to the kitchen, dress twisted in her hands, as she scrambled to put together the sequence of events. Even as Margaret was saying she hadn't noticed Alice leave the house, in came Mungo, a Hawaiian Island man who'd traveled all that sea-and-land distance to work for the missionaries, as Marcus had reported to the board that he could find no Cayuse man willing to put in the long hours required to make the venture a go. Mungo, for the most part, was miserable in the Pacific Northwest—the cool climate, the food and culture, none of it suited him. His stint at Waiilatpu would be brief. But on this day he reported to Narcissa that he'd just seen two cups bobbing in the river.

"What are they doing there?" Narcissa asked, composure gone now. Marcus stayed in his chair, insisting that she leave the cups be until the next day to keep sacred the Sabbath. But Narcissa ignored her husband. She ran outside and, at her shouts of panic, Marcus was quickly on his feet too, the couple rushing across the yard, calling their daughter's name. The kitchen girl joined them, as did Mungo, and others from around the compound who'd heard the Whitmans' frantic voices.

"By the time I got to the river's brink," Narcissa later wrote her parents, "it flashed across my mind like a dream that I had had a glimpse of her while sitting and reading. On seeing the table set for supper, she exclaimed with her usual animation, 'Mamma, supper is almost ready; let Alice get some water.'

"We thought if we could find her immediately she would not be dead entirely, so that we could bring her to again. We ran down on the brink of the river. We saw an old Indian preparing to enter where she had fallen in. He took her from the water and exclaimed, 'She is found.'"

# 2

It happens that I once fell into the river of my childhood, though I wasn't a girl at the time—not a child still new to the world like Alice. I was twenty-four years old, a mother of two daughters, one about the Whitman child's age and the other a baby of six months. I went rafting on one of the mightiest rivers in the West, the Salmon—the River of No Return, as it was called by the Shoshone—because I ignored a nut of self-protection inside of me that insisted, *Don't.* I fell into the Salmon and, against all odds, I got out. For thirty-some years I've been trying to sort out why.

From the time of my birth, I suppose, I'd bought into the idea that our part of Idaho demanded my loyalty and, in return, it would be fiercely loyal to me. A kind of Western *quid pro quo* that we saw play out weekly on *Gunsmoke* and *Bonanza* and (my favorite because of the wide-shouldered and growling mother) *The Big Valley*, not to mention each and every late-night John Wayne rerun. My family, both sides, had sunk its all into the West. We'd fastened ourselves in, tight as bolts, to a mountainous corner of Idaho, counting on an alliance between family and place.

But on a Fourth of July morning in the early 1980s, I was agitated. My feet were jittery under the table, my butt cheeks and thighs were tense, my hair pulled back in the tightest ponytail I could manage. I sat with a smattering of family at the breakfast table in Grandma Lois and Grandpa Bob's dusty house, listening to the men talk about the Salmon River in flood stage. The more they talked, the more I didn't care for the direction of the discussion. I remember wishing I could pick up my baby's diaper bag and extract my toddler's blocks from the cluttered den and whisk myself back to my home in Spokane. That way I'd be no part of whatever was getting cooked up. I held my nursing daughter to my breast, entirely covered by a blanket so the men would see not an inch of skin, with an arm resting on my grandmother's vinyl tablecloth that was sticky with syrup and grease from the elk sausage crackling away on the stove. I straightened my back and did my best to appear as steady-on as the others in the room.

The high water was nothing to worry about, my uncle was saying. Not for people who'd lived near the river for decades, for nearly a century as a matter of fact, and especially those who'd been on the river so often they knew its meanders and habits and traps. My grandfather, my uncle, my brother among those experts. I wanted to believe it—that we'd be safe because of their many years of practice and experience, their grace on the water, the reliability of equipment the men cared for scrupulously, and also because of our near century-long bond with Salmon—but I was already poking holes in the idea that it was possible to predict a wildly unpredictable river. My uncle went on about the Forest Service's decision to close the Salmon to rafting on the most popular holiday of the year—no reason for such a drastic action, he said. Just tell folks to be careful, and if they're not careful enough then to hell with them for their lack of care. Grandpa Bob tapped his coffee cup against the edge of the table, annoyed too, while Grandma Lois huffed back and forth from the stove with platters of meat and hot cakes.

I sat between Cindy and Ron without saying a word. The night before, when I had a cold beer in my hand and another sloshing in my belly, I'd agreed to go on the trip. Now I squeezed my baby tighter to my chest as if her warm nugget of a body would keep doubt from spurting out about that decision. I knew how it was in my family. Misgiving signaled weakness, and we were going on the river, no matter what. Those who were strong enough, anyway, would hop in a raft within the hour.

We launched at 10:00 a.m. The first raft off on the smooth water was yellow, manned by both Grandpa Bob and my father. My aunt and her husband were on board, too, as was my father's new wife, whom I'd met only a few times. Into the second raft, which was blue, climbed my entire generation except for my youngest brother, who was at home with our mother. My brother Ron, a pair of sisters, our aunt's two children: they all jumped in. As did my young husband and Cindy's young husband. With my uncle and me, nine passengers in a happy mood set off on a cold river that we thought of as ours.

My uncle was at the oars. He'd been a guide and an expert boatman for more than a decade, working on the Middle Fork and the Main. This day was a big nothing for him compared to the lengthy trips he led into the wilderness. We'd encounter no class four rapids, not even class three. Simply a sail through familiar canyons, rock walls lumpy with swallow nests, fireweed and glacier lily blooming from cracks in the soil. Blue sky overhead. A few easy hours on a placid stream, that was it.

He sat back and relaxed into the day. By noon he'd finished a six-pack; by one he'd polished off even more. I counted the cans at his feet, and I told myself that maybe full concentration wasn't required for a quick ride. In at ten and out at three. No later than three, I'd reminded him when we got on. I'd left bottles of pumped breast milk and a few jars of baby food with

Mamie, who was watching my daughters, but by late afternoon the baby would be howling. Not from hunger—she'd have enough food—but because our habit was time for cuddling and nursing in those hours before dinner, her hand entwined in my hair with her sister nearby, bumping against my thigh and rubbing her face in my unbuttoned shirt as if she, too, were hungry for the smell of me.

Before we'd started this trip Cindy and I hunted down a couple of ratty orange life preservers in our grandpa's barn. Lumpy Mae West jackets. My uncle watched us put them on and waved a hand at us. My brother laughed. *Jesus, you guys, you won't even get your feet wet.* But we both kept the jackets on even when, an hour or so into the trip, our younger sister and our girl cousin stripped to bikini tops—*hey, toss me a beer*—and splashed cold water on their bare arms and long necks. The boys pulled off clothes too, T-shirts shoved into bags, cocoa oil passed around until they were slick and shiny and smelled like tourists in the Bahamas or Palm Springs, overwhelming the river redolence of rainbow trout and sun-baked granite.

I clicked the latch on the worn-out vest and wondered why I'd come.

Mamie had told me that morning, point-blank, that I shouldn't. The only wise course was to stay in town. *Those people know what they're doing,* she'd said of the Forest Service. I shrugged at her. My mother's mother was someone, I'm ashamed to admit now, whose opinions we tended to dismiss. She was overly solicitous when it came to authorities, for one thing. She'd probably already wrung her hands and bit at her lips hard enough to bring the taste of blood to her teeth and then called to report us. She'd also likely phoned my mother in Boise to complain about our lawbreaking and my father's bullheaded family and the hours I was going to be away from my kids.

Five hours, I'd told her. No more. We'd be home in time for me to change diapers and snuggle with my daughters, and then I'd help her frost the chocolate cake for a picnic that night, the end of Salmon River Days. Fireworks and a bluegrass band. We'd eat potato salad and burgers off the grill. But before all that, just give me a half day of fun away from the kids, *please*.

But even as I pleaded to go, I knew deep down my grandmother was right.

# 3

While she was alive, living in the mud house, Alice joined her parents in their pursuits around the mission, a plump and bright addition to the flurry of activity. A whiff of hope was still ripe in Narcissa in the early days, and the Boston board members were over the moon with news of the mission's progress. The corresponding secretary wrote that first year to bolster spirits and to celebrate prospects in the West as carved out by the Whitmans and the Spaldings. He also announced that the board had decided to appoint more missionaries to the West. Two couples, in fact, who'd been instructed to settle a new station about a day's ride from the Whitmans. Fresh air for Narcissa, as her loneliness was no secret. Finally, friends for the mistress of Waiilatpu.

Cushing and Myra Eells, of Connecticut, would begin a mission at Tshimakain. Elkanah and Mary Walker were to move to the same place, to live and work with the Eells at a compound not far from the current-day city of Spokane. The four had been on their way to establish a mission in Africa but were recalled suddenly because of the outbreak of war, so there'd been little time to plan for their arrival in the frontier. That meant the new couples would have to spend the winter with the Whitmans, hunkering down at Waiilatpu and waiting for a thaw that would permit them to move on.

A whole winter together: not exactly an ideal proposal, the lot of them living in basically a makeshift cabin, the most habitable building at Waiilatpu, but it was the way it had to happen. In fact, despite the crowded conditions and the cold, it was going to be a wonderful arrangement, the president of the board wrote in a letter. Think of it as a way for the women and men to get to know each other, to pray together and plan until the air was lightened with their supplications and praise of God. And wasn't it fine that Narcissa would finally have the company she had hoped for since she'd stepped foot into Oregon Territory?

Except in short order the three women dug up dirt and slung insults, working up a mutual derision and scorn for one another. No doubt this had to do with the tight space and scant food through the frigid winter, not to mention the fact that both Mary and Myra were pregnant and sickly and Narcissa was still figuring out how to be a mother to Alice. But also: Narcissa was hard to get along with. Add in Mary Walker's sharp tongue, especially in regard to the missions's doyen—"She went out and blustered around and succeeded in melting over her tallow"—with an oft mention in her journal of "all the hardness among us," and Waiilatpu becomes one sodden and unhappy place.

Narcissa had her ways of striking out at the boarders. One such jab is described in Mary Walker's journal: After the birth of her son, Mary had trouble nursing, her breasts hard and swollen. Narcissa stepped in, at first, to offer the baby her own breast, a great relief to the new mother. But when Mary Walker suggested the arrangement might continue for a few weeks while her nipples healed, Narcissa said nothing. She only turned and walked away. Mary writes, "Narcissa that same day weaned her own child."

# 4

Decades after our rafting day on the Salmon River, and having by then read several accounts of Narcissa's prickly nature, and also of Alice Whitman's death by drowning, I formed yet another grudge against the woman. The breastfeeding story got to me, but I especially didn't like how she'd put Sunday religious etiquette before the well-being of her child. I thought about her sitting in a chair and staring at her book while her toddler sailed down the wet grass and into the water, frantically flailing when she hit the current, and I fumed. I fumed more every time I thought of it. Then one day it occurred to me that my judgment was awfully heated, wasn't it? More vitriol from the likes of me than a dead woman deserved. I'd managed to dredge up so little compassion for a young mother who'd lost the most beloved person in her life. What was with that? I remember how strange it was to be suddenly aware of my stinginess, to squirm over my judgment. Especially since I'd been, in my own way, equally as negligent a mother. A hammer of obligation had convinced me to go on the Salmon River back when I was a young woman, just like, I suppose, a hammer of obligation convinced Narcissa to stay intent on her Bible instead of watching over her child.

I could have skipped the raft trip. I could have taken my daughters to Wally's Café for huckleberry pie and foamy milk, to McPherson's Mercantile to buy moccasins (no longer made by Shoshone women, but perhaps by a factory in China). I might have strolled to my great-grandfather's house, where he'd greet us with a cry of "Tucempuck!," a term of endearment he liked to toss out and that he probably made up. He'd offer cold biscuits that Aunt Janice had baked and colder bacon—"You don't mind a little hog teat, do you?" he'd call from the kitchen and then insist I give a hunk to the baby to teeth on (I wouldn't). After that, he'd point at my purse and tell me to fish out a dollar to wage at cribbage.

But if I stayed in Salmon, even to indulge in comfortable nostalgia, I'd be admitting to the rest of the family that I was scared. Too nervous to go along on a mild day on the river. I plain didn't like that version of myself. A lifelong capacity for fear had caused me to be too-often dismissed by my father and grandfather and every other man who happened to be around—*That one, spooked by her own shadow.* I was tired of being the Gwartney kid who couldn't live up to the family creed, our eighty-year history that let us believe we held dominion in the nearby mountains, throughout the canyon, and down to the valley floor. So this time I swallowed an intuition that told me it was crazy to head off on a river closed to all manner of watercraft, crazy to leave my daughters in a little trailer with Mamie, my young girls who'd be waiting for my return and their father's. I shut away the story we'd heard about a local teenager who'd driven off the road in her Volkswagen Beetle, flying through the air over cottonwood trees, over scrappy ash and pine, to plunge into the Salmon River. At least that's what her skid marks suggested. After days of searching, neither she nor her car could be found, so deep was the water in mid-summer and so treacherous the current.

That Fourth of July morning, grandmothers and ancient aunts stood on the front porch, waving us off to a day worthy of native Idahoans. A day worthy of anyone prepared to show mettle and defiance. I climbed into the shuttle truck. I got in the raft. I put on that life jacket that shed mouse shit on my bare legs. I cinched it tight enough that breast milk, a sticky reminder of my real obligation waiting in Mamie's trailer, dripped out of me, hot on my skin.

Our grandfather had welded both frames. He was known as the finest welder of river rafts in the state. Ron told me about working in the shop with Grandpa Bob back in the 1970s when rafting first caught on, a tourist trend no one had seen coming, really, with Salmon thriving in this new recreational maelstrom. Our grandfather was set on being an innovator, inventing a steel frame that could support an inflatable raft and yet remain light enough to easily maneuver in the water. He used old tires, Ron told me, wrapping tubes of steel, his welding torch molding and re-molding, his drill press punching in holes and spaces, until he found the shape and heft he was after. Buoyant frames and, I've heard from guides over the years, ingenious oarlocks invented by our Grandpa Bob. A tribute hanging in the Salmon Historical Museum after his death described my grandfather like this:

> For thirty years, there was nary a river company running the Middle Fork and the Main Salmon who didn't know [Bob Gwartney's] name or had utilized his sturdy welding and creative fabrication skills. Though he first joined the whitewater world through his building of oarlocks, boat frames, and trailers, he hungered to be closer to the action. Bob had easy access to river tripping and spent enough time on the water to become a fine oarsman. Bob was great to have along on a river trip, as he was the first person up and stirring around camp. He had the fire built and cowboy

coffee ready before the first gray streaks of dawn hit the beach. He was truly a river-running man.

The metal bar I hung onto on the side of our blue raft was fused by my grandfather's hands. I searched for him in the steel—nothing he made, ever, was shoddy—and I told myself we'd be fine as long as we were protected by his skill and ingenuity. We'd be home in a few hours, dry and warm and recounting memories of the day over the beer I'd finally let myself drink in a couple of gulps. I gave into the loveliness of the day, the shadow the Beaverhead Mountains cast over the river, with swallows pecking at the surface of the water and wheeling away again. We'd lost sight of the other raft some time earlier. We saw no one on the river in either direction. In fact, except for a dead girl trapped in the current below us, sturgeon nibbling at her bloated face, we were alone.

When I mentioned to people in Spokane, where we lived then, that I was originally from Salmon, Idaho, they assumed I'd gone down the river enough times that my initials were carved in some dinosaur-sized boulder next to names of other frequent river runners. I didn't correct them. I let friends picture me gathering wood for a fire while our tied-up rafts bobbed in the water. Or slicing open the belly of a steelhead I'd caught that afternoon to sluice out its guts, threading it through a stick to hold over the coals. Our tent would be set up with bags, one for me, that I'd slip into every night, exhausted and exhilarated, a shot of whisky warm in my chest. I couldn't explain to my friends, or to myself, why I'd done none of that. I wanted to have done it, and yet most of my life I scurried away every time a chance to *do* was proposed. Maybe my grandmothers cautioned me against the river, though I don't remember such an admonition. Sometimes I rode with Grandma Lois when she was shuttle driver, which got me to the edge of the river to help pull out rafts and gather oars and equipment, overhearing fragments of stories—one rousing time after the other that I'd missed out on again. Did my mother and father forbid me from the river? I doubt it. They weren't the types to care one way or another. If I'd wanted to step into a raft heading into the Salmon, if I'd packed a suit and towel and stuck a bottle of cocoa butter in my pack, grabbed a sleeping bag and a jug of water, I would have been welcome to tag along.

But my habit through childhood and into the years of young adulthood was to retreat to safe places, hoping not to be called out as the family wimp. Mostly I got my wish—I was hardly noticed on those days I made for the bear hide, a stack of books in my hands.

In fact, it was the bear hide that crossed my mind as I folded myself up in the raft. I half wished I was on it again, stretched out on scratchy fur in my grandmother's den doing nothing but turning pages and imagining other worlds. I pulled my knees to my chest, squinting against the brilliant blue on the water, enjoying the breeze on my face. This was fun, right? It was going well. In fact, I promised myself that if this day went as planned then a week-long trip on the Middlefork might be next, and someday a six-day ride down the Main, earning me a standing with my family that I'd sought since I'd tuned in to the necessity for each of us to earn our place, the necessity to prove our fortitude.

Three hours in, our uncle's shoulders had turned a brilliant pink on top of his berry-brown tan. He'd been at the oars from the start, insisting he was the best at handling the fast current, refusing my brother's offer to give him a break. He kept rowing, while others drew beers and wine coolers from bags floating alongside the raft. When the sun came out and warmed us up, we stretched our long legs over the sides to put our toes in the water.

My nine-year-old cousin made a game of climbing over the rest of us to balance on the stern, legs straddled, where he'd pee out the Cokes he'd been drinking. I tipped my head back, letting rays baste my face. I was lulled into the rhythm of our ride as we floated, cans tied to the frame clinking a tinny song.

A halcyon day. But after a while our uncle got fidgety. He set down the oars with a clunk to lean over for another drink. The raft veered toward the left bank, chugging through a mass of uprooted foliage. Ahead of us I saw a cottonwood snag that had been yanked out of the banks by the high stream, slammed across the point of an island.

"How many strokes do you think I need to get around that?" our uncle said to Ron, who'd been half dozing in the warmth. I followed our uncle's outstretched hand and my brother's gaze toward the small patch of exposed land, maybe a hundred yards in the distance. The felled cottonwood's leaves shimmered like coins in the sunshine.

Ron got up on a knee, flat hand over his eyes to better study what our uncle was talking about. "Hey, don't," he said, turning toward him and scooting in the direction of the extra set of oars. "The girls are nervous."

Cindy and I, the nervous ones, sat up. "What's going on?" she said.

Our uncle waved his hand, picked up the oars that groaned and snapped in the locks, and stuck them into the water again, his thighs bending into the effort. After the first couple of strokes he sat up straighter. He'd let the raft drift too far. That's what I'd put together later when we sat at our grandmother's table combing over details. Now he said to Ron, "Get over here." My brother tipped forward, bear-walking toward our uncle, the group of us alert to any flinches and nuanced messages between the two. My husband reached over to squeeze my shoulder while I stared at the island screaming toward us.

"What the fuck?" my husband yelled. Then we were silent. All of this happening in about one minute. Our uncle dug into the water, dug again, his back arched and face in a knot. He dug with the muscles of his arms and legs and his tight red neck.

My sister wrapped her hand around my wrist, tethering the two of us together.

"Hold on," Ron shouted, and he began to pick up loose items—a flip-flop, a half-empty can of Coors, a plastic-wrapped chunk of cheese—to throw overboard. He pulled a cooler from under a bench and tossed it in. It tipped sideways, a happy canoe, and bumped its way downstream.

The cottonwood and the island in the center of the river were in front of us now, maybe two bodies' length from where I gripped the frame of a sturdy boat made by Grandpa Bob. I held onto my sister, who kept a bent knee on a second cooler as if to steady herself, her free hand wrapped around its handle. Before I could get a better purchase, before I could plant my bare feet or tighten the cotton straps of the life jacket, we slammed into the snag. The raft trampolined into the air for a split second then splashed back into the river.

We hit the tree again.

Ron and our youngest sister toppled off the rear. Cindy's husband was already gone. My husband reached over to grab the nine-year-old boy cousin. He flung the child onto the island ahead of us, and I watched as the kid hit the brush with a thud and my husband, without a life jacket just like the others, fell sideways into the water.

The raft backed up, collided a third time with the tree. Now a whirlpool force sucked on the metal and rubber—we were caught in a strainer, which made a noise as if I'd put my palm against a vacuum cleaner's hose. "Get out!" our uncle shouted at the last two passengers, Cindy and me. She leapt for the island but went sideways, tugged in the wrong direction by the cooler attached to her. I jumped right after her, but I missed too. Instead of finding earth under my legs, my feet skidded on the surface of the river.

I had water in my eyes and in my ears. It gurgled around my face. My glasses swirled away, but I didn't notice. I kicked hard, moving against the shocking iciness of the water and the more surprising heat of my bones. I opened my eyes, and what I saw above me was blue. Not the blue of the sky, but the bottom of the raft. Every time I pushed myself in a direction that felt like up, aided by the buoyancy of the life jacket, my head rammed against the thick rubber, held firmly in place by the frame my grandfather had made with his own hands and tools.

I don't remember being afraid. The one almost always afraid, me, was somehow unloosed from fear. It was a pissed-off curiosity that unfurled in my chest. I'd die this way? I couldn't sort out how the river kept me nearly motionless. I was unable to jerk myself left or right, only up a few inches to be pushed down again. I remember thinking that my father and grandfather had to be searching for the main faucet, a huge faucet that would take both of those strong men to turn. They had to shut this water off, make it stop rushing around my body, stop ripping at my skin. Only closing the spout, which was to my mind as real as the splintered logs battering my legs, was going to save me from drowning.

I wish I could say I thought of my small daughters growing up without me, but I didn't. It didn't occur to me yet that my girls might spend the rest of their lives wondering why I had chosen a river trip over them. That thought came later, part of the wave upon wave of regret. Neither did I think while underwater about my grandmother staring at her clock and wondering, *Why aren't they back?*, patting the sobbing infant in her lap, a knot of dread in her gut. I remembered no one, and I soon set aside thoughts of rescue. My legs went limp, my arms went limp. I felt the river against my mouth, wanting in. Knocking at the door of me, demanding entry. This river I knew so little about, though I'd long considered it part of my heritage, as much mine as the cells in my blood. Now the river wanted to take me, to show it owed me nothing. It wanted to show me there was no strength here but its own. Its singular and unrelenting power.

# 5

After Alice's death Narcissa had every reason to quit and go home. No one would have criticized her if she'd resigned her post, packed up her things, and moved back to upstate New York to be with her parents, who now lived in Angelica. I can't figure out why she didn't. She yearned for the care of her family, her sister, her mother—all those loved ones who wouldn't hear news of the child's drowning for a year. Alice was buried, weeks went by, and only then did Narcissa receive a bundle of letters and packages from home—not letters of sympathy, but instead the first notes of congratulations for her new baby, packed alongside clothes and knitted hats and tiny mittens, as well as assurances that Alice Clarissa's name had been entered on the Births page of the family Bible. By the time condolences arrived from the Fingerlake District, Narcissa and Marcus had decided, consciously or unconsciously, that for whatever reason there would be no more Whitman babies.

Narcissa also had nothing left to give the missionary effort. She stopped offering the Cayuse women lessons in cooking. She didn't ring the bell on Sunday mornings to draw the people of the tribe to services. The Cayuse, Narcissa regularly complained now, were beyond redemption. They broke her windows, stole food from her garden, spoke to her harshly. She was finished with them.

Still, she didn't leave. Instead it was Marcus who got on his horse one day in 1842 and headed to Boston without her.

In the years before and after Alice's death, the ABCFM board was bombarded by letters at their office in Boston. The Whitmans, as well as the new recruits, the Eells and the Walkers, wrote to complain about each other, griping about their infighting, their inability to even speak decently to each other, about fractious meetings that led to few lasting agreements. Mostly they carped about William Gray, the man they all most loved to loathe, who'd returned from the East with his wife and the minister credentials he was happy to wave in their faces. In second place was Henry Spalding, his general laziness and self-righteousness, his endless capacity for disturbing the peace. As skinny and contentious Elkanah Walker wrote of the enterprise, "It is enough to make one sick to see what is the state of things at the mission."

The board responded with a letter that Marcus received in the fall of 1842. Fine, the group of Boston men said, we're done listening to your grievances. The Whitman Mission, by unanimous vote, was over. It was to be shuttered. The Grays were out (too late, the Grays had already huffed off on their own). The Spaldings were to return east immediately, dismissed from their post. Marcus and Narcissa would move to Lapwai Station to work among the somewhat friendlier Nez Perce and away from the constant threats of the Cayuse. The Eells and Walkers would also, sooner rather than later, be sent home, burdened with failure.

Even though he'd pushed for Spalding's dismissal, Marcus Whitman was irate. He would have none of this plan. He was not going to tolerate a single word from the distant board about the end of his compound and his fruitful fields, the mission into which he and Narcissa had poured everything they had. The place where their Alice was buried. Within a few days, and against the advice of Cushing Eells and Elkanah Walker, who protested yet another Whitman knee-jerk reaction, Marcus had located a man willing to travel east with him (it happened to be Asa Lovejoy, later known as the founder of Portland, Oregon). Marcus wrapped himself in a bear-sized fur coat, climbed aboard a horse, and departed from his emotionally shaky wife.

He did not return for a year.

And what of Narcissa? How did she stand to see him go without her? Maybe she howled, protested, wept her eyes out, I don't know. It could be that she sent him off with Christian charity overflowing from her heart—that's what most of the histories about the couple claim, that she was exactly that affable. But I can't help but believe she had at least some furious desire to call out to Marcus, to beg him to gather her up, too, and all of their belongings, the last of Alice's clothes and playthings, so that they might both give up an effort that was turning out to be nothing but a chimera.

While Marcus was away Narcissa fell apart. About a week after her husband's departure, she was awakened by the sound of her bedroom door latch being jarred, shaken, and then the door was suddenly shoved open. She screamed, and when help arrived she said a Cayuse man had rampaged to her bed meaning to rape her. Narcissa was unhinged by the event, which the Cayuse adamantly denied. She insisted that the man was intent on not just hurting but killing her. Not long before Marcus's departure, a large group of Cayuse men had barged into the new Whitman house to break windows, beat down doors. Several had waved around weapons, including a gun that was, for a few heart-pounding minutes, pointed at Marcus's chest. The altercation ended before anyone was hurt, but those in the compound and officials at the nearby fort were on high alert. So when news of Narcissa's latest trouble reached the new head of Fort Walla Walla, Archibald McKinlay, he rushed to the mission to get Narcissa out of danger. McKinlay made a bed in the back of his wagon and laid the unnerved, weeping woman in it, arranging her foster children around her. After a few days at the fort, resting and gathering herself, Narcissa received a letter from a group of Methodists running a mission near the Dalles. They offered her shelter. It was the Methodists—a religion she maligned regularly—and not her fellow Presbyterian missionaries who offered to take her in. I could find no invitations from the Walkers, from the Eells. She retreated to a small home on the Columbia River where she spent most of her days alone, often sobbing, writing long letters, admitting finally to those around her that she was finished. She wrote to her father that Waiilatpu had become "a place of moral darkness."

Marcus returned in the fall of 1843. He rode back into his compound—after heroically leading the lost wagon train of settlers to safety—to find it in sad shape. A caretaker had been hired to watch over the mission, but all was not well. Marcus's prized gristmill was burned. More windows broken, shards scattered on dry grass. He soon discovered that emigrants passing through during his absence and Narcissa's had used the station in about any way they wished. Stormed right in like they owned the place. The bedraggled settlers took what they could find before heading off again for the Willamette Valley, including tools, bedding, food. The Cayuse, too, had ransacked the Whitmans' home. Marcus stood amid his torn-apart dream and thought about the news he had to deliver to the others: the board had decided to give them a reprieve. They'd stay on in their respective missions after all, and Waiilatpu would become primarily a way station for Oregon Trail overlanders. Even the Spaldings were kept on at Lapwai. Hardly joyful, this development, in the face of the wreckage. It's a wonder that Marcus didn't turn around and head right back to Boston, where he'd been celebrated by large crowds of admirers for his rough-and-tumble appearance (a true frontiersman in their midst!) as well as his heroism in preparing the West for white settlers. He might also have been tempted to run away from Waiilatpu because, in a matter of hours, he was going to have to fess up to Narcissa that he'd failed her. He had not detoured up to her parents' home after all, even though a visit with her family was her most fervent wish. He had not personally delivered his wife's letters to her loved ones, nor picked up letters and packages for her in return. She lived for those letters. He had not sat with her sisters to spend a few hours describing their darling Alice. He'd brought back no consoling kisses or embraces from Jane or Harriet or the others to broken Narcissa. Perhaps most egregiously, Marcus had forgotten to buy his wife the one item she couldn't do without—a pair of eyeglasses. She would have to stumble around in a world growing fuzzier by the day. He had nothing but sorry news. And yet he hitched his tired horse to a wagon and went first to deliver Myra Eells's latest baby, and then to retrieve his wife from the Methodists.

The reunited Whitmans returned home a week later, in early October. This time they found a couple occupying their bedroom, sleeping in their bed because the woman, a new missionary who'd come along with her husband, had just given birth there. The exhausted Whitmans made a pallet on the floor. Other settlers had moved into the compound buildings after plundering the garden for the last fruits and vegetables, the dwindling stores of wheat. The Whitmans chased most of the strangers away and entered the mayhem of their lives, determined to follow the board's orders to keep on going. Somehow.

If Alice had lived, would this all have gone a different way? The child might have softened her mother, provided her companionship, improving relations with the Cayuse. It could be that other Whitman children would have followed, adding to a bridge of rapport and conversation between tribe and mission. It's possible that Narcissa and Marcus, happy with their family, would have held their wagging tongues about the other missionaries, sending at least neutral reports to the board instead of one diatribe after another, so that Marcus wouldn't have been provoked into fleeing east to plead his case. If only, back on a sunny Sunday in 1839, Narcissa had lifted her head for a moment and told her two-year-old to stay away from the river's edge, or stood up to go out with her. *Yes, Alice, let's dip some water.* And yet such conjecture is useless. We do what we do. We are at times hardwired by our own histories to act in ways we spend the rest of our lives desperately untangling.

# 6

I got out from under my grandfather's raft and out of the froth-
ing Salmon River. My brother got out. My sister's husband
and my husband got out. Both of my sisters were trapped
underwater before they reached safety: Cindy's hand was
stuck in the lid of the cooler, so that when she and it landed in
the water, she had to wrench free, breaking two fingers in the
process, though she then used the cooler's buoyancy to reach
the brushy stretch of island. Our sister Rebecca was caught
in a snarl of tree branches, slapped and whipped by the current. She, the family's best swimmer, says the only reason she
survived was due to her tiny bikini and no life jacket, letting
her dive deep and deeper still to get under the clump of dead-
fall. It's Rebecca who tells me that once we were back at our
grandparents' house I wouldn't stop complaining about the
noise, the sound of the river in my ears.

I don't remember saying that. I don't remember the roar of
the water in my head, though I've been haunted by my plunge
into the Salmon since the day I went in. I'm not sure why, since
everyone in the raft survived. Our story has a good ending, a
happy ending. We returned to our grandparents' house shaken
but *alive*. Was it Providence that saved us? Did we live on as
evidence of our communion with the West? Maybe. Though
even then I suspected something different—it was simply pure
luck that the river didn't swallow every last one of us. And I
am not one to rely on luck.

My sister Cindy, spotting me in the river, had reached under the tumbling logs to grab the edge of my life jacket and pull me out. Another moment and I'd be as drowned as Narcissa's Alice. I crawled on the small island where she and I and our young cousin waited for rescue and waited, too, in dread of news of the others. We spent hours hardly speaking, instead rubbing mosquitos from each other's backs and arms and legs, our underarms and the crooks of our knees, the folds of our necks, thousands of sucking insects covering us like shaggy fur, their invisible needles intent on bleeding us dry. I was panicked and raw, but already a determination was galvanizing in me. I would not go back on this river. I knew I'd be told, by the men in my family in particular, that I had to return, that I must jump off the bridge in town directly into the water or sign up for another raft trip the next day—the only way to face your fears. That's their code of toughness, and I have no quarrel with it. But during those still hours on the island, wondering if I'd make it home to my children, I knew my family's code was no longer my code. If it ever had been.

Two Search and Rescue boats showed up late in the afternoon, one after the other—but neither could negotiate the rapid current to get to the patch of land where Cindy and I called to them, begging them to get to us. *I have children!* I yelled. Actually, I howled at them like a maniac, I screamed and swung my arms at the boat as though I were winding up for a bat. If I shrieked loud enough it would bolster the rescuers' will to get to me. I was sure of it. But they went on, out of sight, and I gave up. I slumped to the ground, resigned to being there overnight, long dark hours before news came of siblings and cousins, our own husbands. But then, rather out of nowhere, we spotted our grandfather sailing toward the island in his yellow raft. He was standing up, oars tight in his hands, back bent in the effort; he fought the current until he was up against the craggy edge of land. Our boy cousin jumped on with him, and then Cindy. I was last, raking the dusky air, half blind without my glasses. I stepped in and sunk to the bottom of the boat, letting out a single, long wail.

"What's all this fuss about?" my grandfather said, looking out at the water to chart his course and not at me.

"Grandpa," I said. "I almost drowned!"

"You did?" he said, shoving us into the center of the current, his eyebrows popping high on his forehead. "When?"

Such was his ability to make small what felt enormous to me. For him, the incident had not heft enough to be anyone's defining moment but instead was one of those things that happen. He'd already told us that everyone was safe, so what was the big deal? And what was there to do but forge on?

But for a long time I couldn't forge on. And Narcissa, whose loss far surpassed anything I've experienced ever in my life, could not forge on. Her savage acrimony, her pain over her lost child, led only to worse trouble with the Cayuse. Ugly tensions and mounting threats until the day the whole thing blew.

I remember the evening of our raft accident, the golden light, the cooling air, when we four siblings and the two young husbands gathered around our grandparents' table. We spoke in hushed voices. My daughters slept on my lap, our three hearts beating, I swear, in a synchronized rhythm. Ron had stretched out a map, and we used the sharp ends of Grandma Lois's pencils to trace the events of the day. *When we were here, where were you?*

We were just kids, twenty-four, twenty-two, twenty, and eighteen, trying to comprehend what it meant to sweep that close to death, close enough that we smelled its rotting breath in our faces.

As we were talking, bent over the map, I detected a presence, a shadow, and I looked up to see our father standing in the opening between the living room and kitchen, his shoulders hunched and his expression a block of stern resolution. "Put that away," he said, pointing at the map. "Put that shit away and stop talking about it." He turned on his heel and left, and though we could have ignored his outburst, we did as he instructed, tossing the pencils back in our grandmother's drawer, rolling up the map, and dusting off the surface of the table before we scattered like birds into the night.

I went home to Spokane the next day, throbbing head to toe with mosquito poison, the world around me made hazy until I could buy new glasses, and after that it was as if my skin could no longer tolerate water. As if I were desert dry, irritable as a cactus. As if I had sand in my sheets and rocks in my shoes. I did not submerge my body in a bathtub for six months. Years went by before I put my head under in a swimming pool. I didn't return to Salmon for nearly a decade. It's been thirty-five years since our raft was sucked away in the whirlpool, never to be located again, and I still have not gone near the water of the Salmon River.

But recently I stood on the deck of my home, overlooking a different river. This one in Oregon, a few yards from our house. It was a warm afternoon, the sun was shining, the water in front of me smooth as glass, laminar. I held a thin book in my hand. I'd just finished it, an account of the killings at the Whitman Mission written by Ernest Thompson who had, for his own reasons, spent years researching the plight of Marcus and Narcissa Whitman.

The book includes a letter that Narcissa wrote to her father soon after Alice's death. She opens herself up in front of her father in ways she maybe couldn't with her mother and sisters.

The letter strikes me as the most vulnerable I've read from her hand, and in the time it took me to take it in, a dose of the anger that had hummed in me toward Narcissa was released, quick as ions snapping on the surface of a stream. Not that I considered her now some kind of angel. I didn't. I don't. But I'd been in a rush to impugn her character, and I now found myself wanting to take back some of my insults. Who was I to condemn this woman from the past who only did what she was destined to do?

I would describe to you, if I could, her bright, lively appearance on Sabbath morning, the day of her death. She had always slept with me until just a week before her death, and that night she proposed, of her own accord, to sleep on a mat on the floor. This gave me a very strange and singular feeling, for I never could persuade her to live away from me, not even in her father's arms, before, and I could not divest myself of the feeling that she was laid away for the grave. It being very warm, and because she preferred it, I let her sleep on the floor all night—but did not sleep much myself. Ever after this, I made a bed for her by the side of mine, where I could lay my hand upon her. When I used to take her into the bed with me, she would lie a while and then wish to go back again. Thus she gradually went out of my arms to the grave, so that I should not feel it so severely as if torn from them at once.

# 7

On a chilly November day in 1844, it was Narcissa Whitman standing outside the door, not her toddler daughter with cups in hand. Narcissa hovered in the doorway to the kitchen of the new house. The family's first home, where Alice was born, where her body had been laid out for burial, the house that had been a shelter for those passing through, including the Eells and Walkers over a tough winter, a house that had held the Whitmans for years, was demolished. It had flooded enough times that it was uninhabitable. Plus, the bad memories. The couple moved on, only a few paces from where they'd once been a family.

From her new porch Narcissa peered out on the repaired mission, the patched-together gardens, the restored gristmill grinding away, and she watched a wagon train of exhausted pioneers pull into the compound. Nothing unusual—trains now regularly used the Whitmans' once-again-tidy and well-stocked station (Waiilatpu reaffirmed as a civilized outpost in a most uncivilized land) at the foot of the Blue Mountains. They came for rest and resupply before the final push to the promised lands in the Willamette Valley and other parts of the territory. But this particular group of wagons had her attention. A scout had ridden in several hours earlier to tell Narcissa and Marcus that among the hundreds of settlers were seven orphaned siblings, ranging in age from fifteen years to four months, the baby no more animated than a sack of cornmeal.

The Sager children, two boys and their five younger sisters, were nearly starved, so filthy and lice infested that, once she saw them, Narcissa believed the children might never be clean again. Or healthy again. Their parents had died on the journey, months earlier, and now the scout's job was to inform the Whitmans that the wagon train master, Captain Shaw, wanted the childless missionaries to adopt the orphans on the spot (with no government established in the region, Oregon still years from becoming, officially, even a territory, the matter would be settled on the porch with a handshake). Captain Shaw had promised the children's dying mother that he would find one home for all seven, and he meant to keep his vow. He would persuade the Whitmans, who he'd not met but certainly had heard of, to raise the Sagers as their own.

The Cayuse were watching this scene unfold, no doubt, as they studied wagon after wagon pulling into Waiilatpu, increasing in numbers every year. Dozens of wagons full of white people sweeping onto Native land asking for food, for medical help, for a warm bed, with some also seeking local property on which to build their own new homes. On this day the Cayuse watched as seven orphans stumbled off a battered wagon to stand in front of the missionaries.

"Here was a scene for the pen of an artist," wrote Catharine Sager, years later, as she remembered meeting the woman who would become her last parent. "Foremost stood our little cart with the tired oxen lying near. Sitting in the front end of the cart was John, weeping bitterly. On the opposite side stood Francis with his arms resting on the wheels and his head resting on them, sobbing aloud. On the near side the little girls stood huddled together, bareheaded and bare footed, looking first at the boys and then at the house, dreading we knew not what. Thus Mrs. Whitman found us."

Earlier, when Narcissa was asked by the scout if she had any of her own offspring, she'd pointed to a small cemetery and said words that were, to my ear, oddly colloquial for her: "My only child lies yonder." What was she thinking about the seven desperate children standing before her, four of them feverish and nearly passed out from a measles strain, pleading for their lives?

The wagon train the Sager family had joined in 1844, to which Henry and Naomi Sager pinned all of their funds, earthly goods, and ambitions, was, similar to other groups headed toward the Pacific, fully loaded with equipment for an overland journey, though it lacked some necessary items they later desperately wish for. Better axes for cutting firewood, for instance, and tools for repairing wagon wheels that were constantly breaking down. The group left St. Joe too late in the season to reach Oregon Territory before cold weather set in, making progress sludge-slow and game hard to locate and hunt. The Sager parents, like many others before and after them, ignored obvious signs of trouble from the start, or at least Henry ("Father was a perfect Nimrod in his love of the chase," Catharine Sager once wrote) convinced his family that he could handle any old problem that might befall them on their way to paradise.

Henry was a true believer: he re-trumpeted every promise spouted by promoters about what waited for families like the Sagers if they'd only move West. The rewards were whispered like hot gossip from family to family: land, freedom, wide-open prospects, all yours if you had the stuff to go get it. Only adventurous spirits ought to partake, no question. Leave the fearful and the lazy behind. Henry Sager liked that command. He considered himself a sprite of adventure.

It was only when they were well on their way that the Sager father discovered there'd be no abundance of animals to shoot or trap, and pregnant Naomi found out how rugged this trail to the distant Willamette Valley would be, day after day, miserable hour after miserable hour. "Not being accustomed to riding in a covered wagon, the motion made us all sick," wrote Catharine, "and the uncomfortable situation was increased by the fact that it had set in to rain, which made it impossible to roll back the cover and let in fresh air."

Well into the second month of travel, the Sagers' wagon overturned on an embankment soon after crossing the South Fork of the Platte River, nearly killing Naomi, who'd just weeks before given birth. ("A tent was set up and Mother carried into it, where for a long time she lay insensible.") Three days later, Catharine herself, the oldest daughter, got her dress caught in a handle on the wagon. Her twisted skirt swung her under moving wheels, crushing her leg (which was clumsily set by her father with sticks and twine) so that she walked with a limp for the rest of her life. Not long after Catharine's accident, and after a two-day stop at Fort Laramie, Henry Sager fell suddenly ill along with several others on the train. He survived only five days after the morning he first complained of headache and fever—"Poor child," he said to Catharine moments before his death at age thirty-eight, "what will become of you?"

A year later, a wagon train would come upon Henry's disturbed grave, parts of him spread across the banks of the stream, "a reminder," one settler wrote in his journal, "that we knew not when we would have to leave some of our loved ones to this same fate."

Naomi, who'd made not a drop of milk for her baby, was to be one of those who'd share Henry's fate. She couldn't fight off the fever sweeping through the community of travelers, and soon she was on the cusp of death.

"[My mother's] suffering was intense, unable to make her wants known, and traveling over a road so dusty that a cloud of dust covered the train all day," Catharine later wrote.

To screen her as much as possible from this, a sheet was hung in front of the wagon, making the air within close and suffocating. She talked continuously of her husband, at times addressing him as though present, and beseeching him in piteous tones to relieve her of her sufferings. As the disease advanced, she became unconscious, making only a low moan. Her babe was cared for by the women of the train. The kind-hearted women were also in the habit of coming in when the train stopped at night to wash the dust from [my mother's] face and otherwise make her comfortable. The day she died, we traveled over a very rough road and she moaned pitifully all day. When we camped at night, one of the women came in as usual to wash her. To her inquiry if she wished her face washed, she made no reply as she had done in former times, and the woman, supposing her to be asleep, washed her face and then taking her hand to cleanse it, she discovered that the pulse was nearly gone and called some others. She lived but a few moments more.

Naomi passed on twenty-six days after her husband and was buried close (likely too close to a waterway others would drink from) to the Snake River, at a place known as Pilgrim Springs. Her last request was made to Captain Shaw. *Keep my children together.*

Before they left the wagon train launching point, way back

in St. Joe, the Sagers had heard about the cholera, dysentery, smallpox, mumps, and measles running rampant through overland caravans—diseases that eventually killed most of the twelve thousand people who perished on the Oregon Trail (not to mention infecting and killing tens of thousands of Native people). But somehow Henry left Missouri with his wife and six children, another soon to be born, believing his family would withstand such germs. Henry and the other men in the outfit had brought along stores of guns and ammunitions, prepared for what they considered the real danger: Indian attacks. Except no Native people circled the wagon train with weapons slicing the air along with their war whoops, nor did they threaten the women and children during their brief run-ins on the road. One of the Sager girls in her journal noted distant drumming and fire light, assumed to be emanating from a Native camp, but that's it.

Also, the men on this train were champing at the bit to shoot a buffalo, not realizing buffalo were largely depleted by then, though this train did come across a large herd on the Platte and had a heyday killing all they wanted to kill, far more than they needed, dead bison bodies left on the plains to rot, and then, astonishingly, because the first day's meat had been improperly dressed (and thus left to rot, too), the hunting party spent a second day slaughtering even more.

The Sagers had joined the '44 train from Missouri and went along with exuberance—well, Henry and the boys went along with exuberance—but soon they were defeated by the trouble most common on the Oregon Trail journey: the parents got sick and died, leaving their children without care, without food, without any hope of getting by without significant help from strangers who had little for themselves.

Henry Sager, as he is remembered in various books about

his family, including his daughters' journals, was just the kind of man to fall for the folklore of the West and to think of himself as "worthy of government largess." That's the way one historian describes the attitude of those heading out to claim their piece of the American pie—the government owed it to them. Henry Sager was one among hundreds of thousands willing to step up to populate the frontier, you bet. But he expected to be compensated for his efforts, paid with plentiful land, with support, and with layers of assurances of safety for himself and his family.

Henry had moved his wife and many kids frequently in the ten-year period before signing up; he was a man after the next big chance, the get-rich-quick scheme that *this time* was going to fill the coffers to the brim. Back in Missouri he'd pleaded with Naomi for months before he finally convinced her to make one last journey with their kids. They'd take up land the government offered for free and settle down for the rest of their lives. Never, ever move again. Nothing could go wrong. They were young, healthy, and vibrant enough to subdue any foe. Or so he swore to his wife. Reluctantly she agreed, though she stepped on the wagon the first day muttering to Catharine, "I will not live to see Oregon."

# 8

A few years ago I was pushing a cart through a co-op store close to where my husband and I live whose inventory might date back to my year of birth. Going down one aisle, I bumped the edge of my cart into a dusty sale rack of DVDs. I stopped to straighten the mess I'd made when a title on the top shelf caught my attention. "Seven Alone," with a cover photo of a blonde teenager holding a swaddled infant. I knew instantly that it had to be about the Sagers. I could hardly wait to get home, stick the disc in my player, and watch this film, for which I'd paid $3.99.

That fourth grade Idaho history class in my Boise elementary school, way back when, reaffirmed much of what I'd learned from being around my parents, two people devoted to politics. My father was a state legislator for years, and my mother worked for a state senator and then for a US senator in Washington, DC, and she sometimes sent my sisters and brother and me off to read the placards hanging in the statehouse to keep us occupied after school. One claimed that the name of our state, Idaho, is a translation of "gem of the mountains" in Nez Perce. Except not long ago I met a Nez Perce elder, a man in his eighties, one of the last fluent speakers of the language, and I asked him about "gem of the mountains." He said no, not even close, that the word *Idaho* means absolutely nothing in his tongue. This confounding revelation sent me on a hunt. Soon I read an account by Berkeley cultural sociologist

George R. Stewart—the very author of my grandmother's favorite novel, *Earth Abides*—who suggested a version of how Idaho got its name.

A group of landowners, some of them perhaps new legislators, were preparing to appeal to the US government for statehood on behalf of their territory. The three or four men sat around one night considering an appropriate title, doodling suggestions on a pad, when one proposed the faintly indigenous-sounding *Idaho*. "Its charm must have been largely melodic, as no one at the table knew what [the word] meant," wrote another historian, who tells a story similar to Stewart's. They decided to try it out on one of the towns that had sprung up, from then on to be called Idaho Springs. Yet in the end the men settled on another title for the state, one that referred to their soaring mountains, including the famous fourteeners: Colorado.

Back to Stewart—he says that some time later, another gathering of well-heeled landowners / local lawmakers began casting about for a place name. One possibility was a word many assumed was Nez Perce, as they'd come across it in newspaper stories in reference to Native people. Since it hadn't been assigned to another state, why not? In the summer of 1890 my home place was brought into the US fold as an official state, shaped like a pan replete with a panhandle, a title imposed upon it that means, basically, nothing: Idaho.

If that's not a confounding enough tale about historical folklore, here's another one from Grandpa Bob. He said once, and not too many years before he died, that he'd been informed by the head of the Lemhi Tribe, his friend Chief Willy George, that there was no such person as Sacajawea. At least not the Sacajawea we think of, the woman with a major role in the Corps of Discovery. The day he said it I was getting ready to go to Sacajawea Days with my mother and her husband. When I mentioned to my grandfather where we were off to, he grumbled. He waved his gnarled hands in the air. "A bunch of nonsense," he said. Meriwether Lewis and William Clark and the rest, during their long trek West to the Pacific Ocean, were accompanied by Native people, yes, and one of those was a Shoshone woman who'd been kidnapped as a child, reunited with her brother and other family when Lewis and Clark brought her through Lemhi Valley. The woman, *all right*, probably helped procure fresh horses and food and good direction for the geographically confused corps (who believed they'd hit the Pacific Ocean far sooner than they did), but she was only one woman among several who traveled with them. There was no single guide, no individual marching along with them from near the beginning to the end. That story of the iconic female Indian guide was simply a good tale to tell and a reason for the town of Salmon to build a Sacajawea Interpretative Center, a big waste of money. Or so opined Grandpa Bob, and allegedly so said Chief Willy George, who was, if I understand the lineage, Sacajawea's great-great-great (maybe one more great) nephew.

What am I to do with that? I find it near impossible to believe, and I can't figure out why my grandfather even said it. But what about the sweep of other stories about the past that have holes poked in them? What's true about the early years of the West, the creation of a regional identity, and what's not: it's a jumble of perplexing misinformation. That includes the *Seven Alone* film, which I watched by myself one cold afternoon in our small TV room and have refused to watch again. When the credits finished rolling by, I turned off the television and the DVD player and went to my computer to order the novel that the ridiculous video was based on, sure that the book would do a better job of presenting the actual Sager story. But if anything, the novel—written by Honore Willsie Morrow—is worse.

Morrow starts with a claim that her fiction is based on "a remarkably true story" and that the book was written in close collaboration with one of the surviving Sagers, which isn't possible if you do simple math around birth dates and death dates. The author, like plenty of others writing about the frontier, uses her pages to go on a romp, exploiting readers' glee in being dished up a giant helping of Western Tall Tale. But a whole lot of what she committed to the page just plain didn't happen.

*On to Oregon!* was published in 1926, while the glib video was produced in 1974, years after Morrow's death. They both infuriated me for the same reason: Didn't the Sagers go through enough? Morrow called her work fiction, which allowed her to take license. But, really, did the Sagers' true story have to be stolen from them in this way? They lost two sets of parents, including the last pair with whom they were just getting settled, and, even more anguishing, Catharine, Elizabeth, and Matilda (also Henrietta, who was three—and not mentioned in accounts of the attack) watched their brothers and a sister die one bloody day at Waiilatpu.

The actual Sager story is, to me, the truest story of the West anyone could ask for. It starts with their father's wild hankering to go to the frontier, a desire that led to several sloppy decisions by Henry and myriad others who rushed to join a wagon train. The men and women who'd obviously never taken such a journey made plenty of mistakes which led to plenty of accidents, and then there were the steady deaths by illness, the drownings, families left suffering in grief and pain. But still, the vast majority of those who started off in wagons survived the trail, harrowing though it was, to become the West's backbone of settlers. Including the final three Sagers: Catharine, Elizabeth, and Matilda.

There's nothing unusual about a writer sensationalizing a

nifty bit of history, so I probably ought to give Morrow—best known for her novel imagining the innermost thoughts of Abraham Lincoln—a break. Except that a small volume written by the three Sager sisters, which was published when they were older women, has mostly been forgotten. Of course, who's to gauge the truth of the Sagers' memories decades after their time at Waiilatpu? By then memory had surely been warped—some of that due to Henry Spalding's pressure on the women to put the blame for the massacre squarely on the backs of the Catholics—and then warped some more to suit their own biased views, political and cultural and otherwise. The point is, Morrow's book has not been forgotten. Because she was married to New York publisher William Morrow, publishing and distribution of her books was a breeze, while the Sagers' *The Whitman Massacre of 1847* was printed in small batches by a defunct tiny press in Washington State and has long (long) been out of print. A few minutes on Google dishes up proof that Morrow's book, even to this day, continues to land in the hands of readers, mostly school kids curious about the history of the West. Grade school teachers rely on the novel and film to, as one teacher writes, "show students the actual challenges of the Oregon Trail." Never mind that few of the challenges in Morrow's pages are actual.

And then there's this: Nicholas Kristof, famed *New York Times* reporter who happened to grow up in Oregon, once listed Morrow's novel as one of the best children's books of all time.

Morrow required a hero for her book, a protagonist for her coming-of-age story, a boy who'd be transformed into a man before our eyes. She wanted us to watch him endure obstacles on his hero's journey until he became a true frontiersman, meaning fiercely independent, meaning that he'd need no one for any reason and could save himself (and those under his protection) from even the most death-defying collisions.

The boy for the job was John Sager.

After the death of Henry (who doesn't die of cholera in the book but is shot by a marauding Indian) and then Naomi, the oldest boy, John, who is fifteen, overhears the other adults hatching a plan to send the Sager children back to relatives in Missouri. Book John is furious. His father's dream of a homestead in the Willamette Valley of Oregon will not be thwarted. And so he concocts—with the unlikely and mysterious aid of Kit Carson (who appears out of nowhere in the novel with bloody scalps tied to his belt)—to take off on his own. In the middle of the night John slips away and carts with him his siblings: Frank, Catharine, Elizabeth, Matilda, Louisa, and Baby Henrietta, age three months.

The children go at it alone for weeks and weeks. In the wilderness. They endure hostile Native people bent on killing them some young-uns, they trudge long stretches without food, they get robbed, they somehow cross treacherous rivers (Morrow's John is a quick weaver of willow branches, making for magical watertight rafts that float as if under a spell; his round-cheeked little sisters don't even lose their bonnets in the brisk wind). Mostly the younger six put up with a brother who constantly chides and berates and threatens to beat the hell out of them if they don't go along with his plan. (In the meantime, who's feeding the baby? Who's changing her diaper—and, wait, where are they getting diapers?) Not one adult steps in to help while John is glorified and reglorifed as the hero of the tale. He is a champion of the West, the symbol of wit and courage.

The fictionalized Sagers trudge ahead, no matter the tribulation or torment; they go and go until they can go no more. Until one wintry day when the girls, one after the other, fall into snowdrifts, tattered blankets flapping in the frozen air. The baby turns blue. John decides to leave his siblings, his "nestlings" as he calls them, in the snow so he can push on. He finds his way through a blinding storm to the Whitman Mission, where he lands in the arms of Narcissa and Marcus. With the aid of these noble adults, the only ones worth trusting for two hundred and some pages, the other six children are retrieved and brought to safety.

As soon as he's dry and fed, book John tells the Whitmans that his stay—and his siblings'—will be brief. Only a few weeks tops while he earns cash by doing chores and allows the baby to get stronger. Then it's *on to Oregon!*, as the title promises. No mention in the novel of the Whitmans' own reason for coming West, their religious fervor, the saving of "savage souls." No hint of the brewing hostility with the neighboring Cayuse, or the attack, three years (almost exactly) after the Sagers' arrival, when John and Frank were murdered and Louisa died of thirst and lack of care.

Instead, Morrow's novel has a happy ending. A guarantee to those brave enough to traverse the far reaches of the 1840s frontier. "If the book has made you live for awhile in those hard, dangerous days," states the afterword, "make an impossible journey without any of those things we think are necessary today, and understand what 'going West' really meant, then the author has succeeded."

The end of the film shows all seven Sagers brimming with good health and smiling, running through a field of wheat, planted at their own homestead in the Willamette Valley. Their father's dream made manifest.

# 9

By the time of the arrival of the Sager orphans in 1844, Alice was long dead. The mission had been saved by Marcus's rushed journey East and home again—meaning meager financial support was still deposited in the mission accounts—but so what? The Whitmans were worn out with any notion of converting the Cayuse. Marcus's new alliance with the board in Boston was nothing but a spindly vine drying up in the sun. And yet here—seven needy white children standing before her—was a chance for Narcissa to revive, a reason to go on with a day-to-day life at Waiilatpu. As one scholar writes, "It is hard to see how she could have turned the Sagers away. They represented a way to retreat honorably from the dilemmas of missionary work." Seven ill and whimpering children gave Narcissa every excuse to distance herself for good from the Cayuse, a people she now considered wretched.

After some wrangling between themselves—Marcus wanted only the boys, Narcissa wanted only the girls, and most of all she wanted the baby—the Whitmans agreed to take in the seven children. The Sagers were scrubbed clean, they were fed, their sores and fevers were tended to by Marcus Whitman, though he still had no treatment for the measles except to keep the patient in bed and hydrated. Marcus was skilled at delivering infants, and he was celebrated for digging shrapnel from under the skin of a mountain man (he did so for Jim Bridger) and setting a broken bone, but he knew zero about viral pathogens. But then, no country doctor did. Marcus was not even aware he was to keep his instruments sterile. That would have been a challenge, anyway, since teetotaler Narcissa would not permit him to carry alcohol in his satchel.

Soon the Sager children had food in their bellies, and their bodies were healing—the physical suffering, which they'd barely survived, was over (for now; a different illness would knock most of them flat in a couple of years), but they'd also stepped into a reality that had to be a rude bump on the head—especially for the boys. A rigid program of activities at Waiilatpu under the watchful eyes of two highly ambitious people, with rules and boundaries the Sagers couldn't have imagined in their earlier lives.

The Sager children hadn't attended church services with their parents back in Missouri, nor had they sat through all that many days at a local school, but now they were slammed by both. The kids were expected to spend the first hours of every day memorizing scripture, and then, after chores, the five eldest were sent off to the schoolhouse. A man named Alonson Hinman had been recently hired to give the children a strict religious education, and for Hinman that stricture included a gnarly green switch, cut each morning from a willow tree, applied to the backside on a regular basis—especially Frank's rear end, as the boy seemed to royally agitate the schoolteacher.

Life continued in this manner for three years (though Hinman, thank goodness, was replaced with Saunders and, for music and devotion, Andrew Rodgers) as hundreds of pioneer families stopped in at Waiilatpu for rest and supplies. Three years, during which the Whitmans' trouble with the Cayuse grew ever more choked. Again, the Cayuse could not understand Marcus's reasons for doing little to save the tribe's children from death and yet adopting seven white children and nursing each one back to high-spirited health.

Early in the fall of 1847, writes Catharine in her account, a particularly headstrong Cayuse man—called "the murderer," Tamahas—showed up at the mission with a bag of corn and demanded that Marcus grind it at the gristmill. Grind it right now, ahead of any other task or chore. Marcus took umbrage at being ordered about on what he considered to be his own property and told Tamahas, one of the five hung in Oregon City some years later, that "he was not in the habit of doing things for people unless asked in a proper manner." Tamahas, the story goes, stormed toward the mill saying he'd grind the corn himself, with no help from the doctor (Marcus had strictly forbade the Cayuse from using or even touching the gristmill, and while he often handed out free wheat to settlers, the Cayuse were forced to pay). But Whitman ran ahead, wrote Catharine, and

> took an iron bar in his hand and retired a short distance and awaited the coming of Tamahas. He soon arrived, and after trying in vain to start the mill, made at the Doctor with his club, but perceiving that he was armed, stopped and ordered him to put down his weapon. To this, the Doctor replied that he would put it down when the Indian put his down. Tamahas dropped his club; but as soon as the Doctor put his down, the Indian came at him again with his club, but he was ready for him and warded off the blow with the bar of iron. The Indian now told [Whitman] to leave the country; that he did not want him here. To this the Doctor replied that if all the Indians said for him to leave, he would gladly do so, but he could not leave just because one Indian told him to. . . . The Doctor, exhausted in body and vexed

in spirit, came into the house, and throwing himself on the settee related the above transaction, said that if the Indians would only say so, he would leave, for he was tried with them beyond endurance.

But he did not pack up and leave the mission, nor did Narcissa.

One reason Marcus refused to abandon his charge had to do with the Catholics. He'd heard talk as early as '42 that the Cayuse were communing with Jesuit missionaries, newly arrived on the Columbia Basin. The Black Robes' first business was learning the Cayuse language. They ate the tribe's food and hunted with the tribal men and sometimes folded Cayuse entreaties to the creator into the Catholic mass. The Cayuse were pleased with this inclusion of their own practices, and many decided the Jesuits would be the outside spiritual guides to the tribe now, not the Whitmans—a shift that Marcus, and even more so Henry over in Lapwai (in regard to the Nez Perce), would not abide.

Their conversion efforts hadn't worked before the Jesuits, so why did they think they'd win over the Native people now? And yet Marcus doggedly persevered at the compound, in part to do just that—to compete with newcomers for Cayuse souls. A gamble that was lost to him long before he could admit it.

While Eliza Spalding saw the attack unfold from her vantage point in the schoolroom, John Sager saw it—the first burst of violence, anyway—from the kitchen table. On that end-of-November day, the eighteen-year-old eldest Sager, a quiet and serious boy who'd caused no trouble for the Whitmans and was about the opposite of the spitfire John of Morrow's novel, sat cutting twine at the table. He was barely recovered from a strain of measles that his sister Louisa, asleep upstairs, would die of in a few days (as would Helen Mar Meek in bed next to Louisa and, a few weeks later, Mary Ann Bridger) and that Elizabeth Sager, staying close to Narcissa that afternoon, was recovering from too. The banging knock came at the door. Narcissa answered and, when she saw the jumpy group of young Cayuse men on the porch, she called to her husband to deal with it. Marcus told her to retreat to the main part of the house and to secure the lock between the kitchen and living room. Moments after she'd shut the door and set the barricade, Marcus was struck by the tomahawk, shot in the neck, and he crumpled to the ground. Cayuse men stormed the kitchen, one shoving John off his chair and slicing the boy's throat then shoving the edge of John's shirt into the neck wound, leaving him on the floor to suffocate.

Elizabeth later wrote that she did not yet realize what had happened to her brother when she ran to the window, along with Narcissa, to look out on the scene of murder. This is when Narcissa was shot in the shoulder. "I was standing right beside her," Elizabeth wrote to her uncle years later. "It seems almost a miracle that [the ball] did not go through my head. Mother dropped right where she was standing. She seemed not to think of herself for her prayers were, 'Oh my dear children, what will become of you?'" Nearly the same words she and her sister had heard from their dying father.

Just that morning fifteen-year-old Frank had been invited, for the first time, to bring out a gun and fire the fatal shot into a steer's brain. A rite of passage for the boy who'd been largely unhappy at the mission. Frank went back to class while the men finished up, wiping blood from their hands and knives.

And that's when the Cayuse attacked.

Frank leaped to the window, and so did Eliza, at the sound

of the gunshot and Mary Ann Bridger's screams. He saw men in the yard bleeding on the ground; he saw Saunders' body draped over the fence. The boy told Eliza and Matilda to push desks together and stack them with books so the children could climb into the eaves. The girls used the book stairs they'd constructed to scramble into the loft ahead of the others. Eliza, with Matilda next to her, lay down on her belly and hung her arms over the edge. Frank helped the younger children, one at a time, balance on the makeshift platform so the girls could pull them up. Frank hefted himself into the loft last, kicking with his feet to knock the books to the floor. He got the panicked children into the far recesses of the dusty storage space, warning them to be silent, as silent as they could manage, meaning not a sound.

Only a few minutes passed before Joe Lewis booted open the schoolroom door and came inside with three Cayuse men. "I know you kids are up there," Lewis called out in English, "come on down now."

Lewis promised the children they'd be safe, soon reunited with their mothers if only they'd emerge. At the mention of mothers, a few of the smallest children began to sob while Eliza and Matilda clamped hands across their mouths to hush them up. But they had no choice, really. The children ventured out of dark corners, lining up to leap into Joe Lewis's arms. "I was afraid to try to jump to the floor," wrote Matilda Sager many years later, "but Lewis said, 'Put your feet over the edge and let go and I will catch you.' He failed to do this and I struck the floor hard, hurting my head. When he helped me up I was dazed when he asked me, 'Where is Frank?' I replied, 'I don't know.'"

Frank had stayed hidden in the shadows of the loft. "I know you're there, Frank. Don't make me get you," Lewis shouted at the boy. More promises of safety. The killing was done, Lewis said. Apparently that was reassurance enough, because Frank, too, ventured into the light.

Eliza and the still dizzy Matilda followed the others to the house, through the kitchen door. At the back of the room, they found John. Frank pulled the cloth from his brother's neck, and the children stood by as John bled out and died. "I'll soon join him," Frank told his sisters. Not ten minutes later Joe Lewis shot Frank in the head.

"You who can see your friends die peacefully," Catharine Sager wrote in her later-years account, "after doing all for them that love can suggest, can form but a faint idea of the feelings of those who see them ruthlessly murdered and thrown out on the ground, mutilated and covered with blood, exposed all night to anything that may disturb them. And you denied even the relief of tears."

# 10

When she was twenty-four my great-grandmother, Hazel Maude Long, jumped on a train with a gangly man she'd met at a dance near Holbrook, Nebraska. It was 1912, quite a stretch after the finish of the Oregon Trail migration, and yet still a time when the West was considered largely unclaimed, open for the taking. Leslie Nugent Gwartney, who was called Mick, was her man, and he'd had a foul upbringing. His mother died in 1890, when he was barely two. His one memory of Fanny was her giving him a smack across the face one day out in the yard of their house because he'd fed the cow a cob of corn she'd intended to boil with other cobs in water for soup stock—a thin meal, but something at least. After she died, Mick's father couldn't care for his four children and farmed them out to relatives. Just like Marcus after his own father's death, just like the Sager girls after the Whitmans' deaths, young Mick was shuffled from one house to another, tolerated as long as he could be put to use doing farm or ranch chores, sometimes housework.

Over on the plains of Nebraska, Hazel had mostly a stable, happy family life—similar to Narcissa's. During Hazel's childhood, the family was poor. She was born in a sod house, as were her four siblings. But Mike Long's fortunes expanded as his children grew to be adults, and he was able to build a nice home with clapboard siding and an expansive front porch where he could sit in his rocker and survey his land. Hazel received an education; like her next older sister, she was hired as a teacher at the Scott School House in Kimball County. She had several offers of marriage, some from young men who practiced her Baptist religion. And yet it was wily young Mick she fell for, a man with a hot desire to travel west to the frontier where he would conjure from the rocky canyons and brush hills any damn life he wanted for himself—reminiscent of the Sager father, that gung-ho nimrod for the West.

Hazel, for reasons I can only guess at, traveled to Colorado to meet up with her fellow and marry him with no family to witness the ceremony. She wed a cowboy who'd not stepped in a church. A man with few prospects and meager savings. A man who must have admitted to her at some point (though it could be he never did; none of us knows what was said and what wasn't) that he'd been married before—to a woman named Alice who gave birth to stillborn twins, after which the pair parted ways (whether he and Alice were formally divorced remains a mystery).

What did Hazel mean to pry from this new place for herself?

Two years after reaching Salmon, and with her first baby (my grandfather) on her hip, Hazel rode a train back home to Holbrook. Her husband, Mick, who typically took his first daily drink in the Lantern Club around 11:00 a.m. and his last after his wife was asleep for the night, had cheated on her. This is what I heard from others who told tales after my great-grandparents were dead, though maybe Hazel took off because she'd discovered the truth about the first wife. It could be that Hazel had found a card written to Mick from Alice, such as the one Aunt Janice showed me a few years ago, a picture of a dark-haired woman astride a horse with a soft pencil inscription on the back: "Dear Old Pal, Please remember me kindly, and if you ever feel that you can forgive me for the sorrow I have caused you, I wish you would tell me so. It would help to ease my heart some, I think." The card is signed, "your wife."

I have a few scratchy photos of lovely young Hazel standing next to her parents' white clapboard home in 1918, the one she had not lived in but was only visiting because of troubles in her marriage. She is strikingly beautiful, thin and self-contained, a swirl of hair on top of her head. Her face is contorted. She soon chugged back to Salmon and to Mick—what choice did she have there in the early years of the century?—but going back wasn't an easy decision; I can tell by the shadows around her eyes and the forced smile in this series of photos in front of the Long home. And yet after a week or so with her mother, her father, her sisters, she did return to Idaho, marriage illusions shattered, and she remained there in Salmon, raising two other children and working nearly every day at the implements store, married to her husband for over fifty years. I can find no evidence that she returned to Nebraska again, not even for her parents' funerals, her father first and then her mother. She stuck it out in Salmon, and she died there. She's buried in the cemetery on the hill whose backdrop is the Beaverhead Mountains. From her grave on a sunny day, you can see the Continental Divide.

When I was around ten years old, spending summer weeks at my father's folks' house, Grandma Lois woke me up late one night. She told me to put a sweater on over my nightgown and come along with her. Once we were outside on the gravel driveway, my grandmother opened the back door of her boat of a Chevy and told me to slide in. It was July, but cool—a mountain town's typical shivery night, and I did that: I shivered on the chilly vinyl seat while I wondered what in the world we were up to. My grandmother's agitated mood—she was the one, after all, for riled tempers—was a signal for me to keep my mouth shut. I'd find out soon enough what our middle-of-the-dark-night venture entailed.

In minutes we were parked in front of the Owl Club downtown, about halfway between Gwartney Equipment and my other grandparents' newspaper offices. Grandma Lois stormed into the bar, hitching up one of her legendary muumuus that covered her wide hips and thunderous thighs. I stayed in the car and waited. And waited. Finally, here she came again, pulling my great-grandfather by the arm. Her father-in-law. I swung open the back door to a rush of wind that swept in with a mix of cigar smoke, cheap whiskey, the sound of my great-grandfather bellowing about how he wasn't ready to go home, his demand that she goddamn leave him *be*. Grandma Lois ignored his noise, piling the man in the back seat with me, shoving on his flat butt to make sure he was in, slamming the door shut. I was, she instructed me once she was back in the driver's seat, to hold on to my old great-granddad—he must have been in his late 70s—so he didn't try to escape the car and shuffle back to the tavern. His head drooped so that it rested against the passenger seat in front of him, and he did not recognize, or so it seemed to me, that I was sitting a few feet away. I put one hand on the seat between us, flat, my fingers pressed together, the closest I was willing to get to this father of my father's father, who I figured would do exactly whatever he pleased, as he always had—what could I do to stop him?

The smell of my great-granddad wasn't unfamiliar, just more ripe than usual, wafting off his clothes, his breath. This man who challenged me to a game of cribbage about every time I went to the old Gwartney house. This man who loved to regale me with stories of his younger years, most of which I couldn't sort out, all those names of people and valleys and gullies and make-it-rich plans of his, grand success that might have been but never was. He told us jokes, my sisters and me. We laughed to please him though we didn't get some of the punch lines—like the one about how he decided to be mayor of Salmon because City Hall was a former whorehouse and there were still "plenty of screws in the walls." He called my father "Miguel," and he was the man, I was certain, that this grandson admired second best of anyone (Grandpa Bob was first on the list) and in fact fashioned his life around. He was the great-grandfather who read us poems he'd written about the solitude of the woods, the tendril of smoke from a campfire and paddling in a canoe with a beautiful "squaw." Poems recited outside the earshot and purview of our great-grandmother Hazel, whose own hours were spent in the kitchen, mixing dough for the most airily perfect biscuits you could put in your mouth, or for her famous cinnamon rolls soaked in caramel, or tending to the pot of beef stew she kept hot on the stove. She swept every corner of their old house and scrubbed the counters until their place was spotless.

It took only a few minutes to get from the Owl Club to their house. Grandma Lois pulled up in front of the old Gwartney home, on Gwartney Street, and there was my great-grandmother on the porch, illuminated by the lamp, which struck me as terrifying (the harsh light deepening the lines on Hazel's face, the resigned slant of her shoulders). Her hair was untwined from its bun—only the second time I'd seen it down. It fell to her waist, all that gray hair, the ends lifted by the soft night breeze as if making a feeble attempt to drift away from a troubling state of affairs. Hazel stood under a midnight cloud. My great-grandmother had forever struck me as unbendable, tough, reliable as any rain. But on this night she was whittled, her hands clasped in front of her sagging breasts as if she could hardly keep herself together.

Grandma Lois got me to help her extract the old man from the back seat, to totter him up the steps of the porch and hand him over to his wife. No words were exchanged, but the message was clear: the women will stick with their marriages, and they will endure the men's behavior, and they will also, when they can, fix what's wrong, or learn to ignore it staunchly. To this day I don't know what had gone down at the Owl Club. No idea what elicited a call to the house, or why Hazel was instructed by the owners or the bartender to get him out of there as quick as she could, which prompted a call to my grandmother, a daughter-in-law not well-liked by either Hazel or Mick. Grandma Lois would barrel in and get things done. You could count on her for that.

And why was I brought along? I have the feeling that my grandmother thought it was time I understood what women did late at night while the children slept and the men caroused. Another lesson learned from a woman of the West who might have been trying to shape me into a proper woman of the West.

I prefer the memory of another late evening, when I was eight or maybe nine years old, some time before the Owl Club rescue: I was spending the night in the old Gwartney house by myself—rare enough that I doubt it happened again (usually I was accompanied by at least one other kid, sibling or cousin). My mostly silent great-grandmother asked me if I wanted to take a bath in the clawfoot tub, and yes, I did. I sat naked inside the cold porcelain as water trickled in through ancient pipes while she grunted her way up the stairs with a pot of water to pour over my legs, so hot I nearly cried out, though I managed to not wriggle away from the stream. She suffered no nonsense, no fussing, no complaining. This is the same great-grandmother who, one day when I was barely six, told me to get my stringy hair out of my face by putting it in a braid. When I admitted I hadn't yet learned, she slammed down the spoon she'd been using to mix some dish on her stove, turned off the heat, and went off to find an old pillow-case. She cut the cloth into three strands and sat with me at her small kitchen table until I got it, the outer piece becoming the middle, over and over until a braid came together in my hands. "There," she said, and went back to her cooking.

Sometime after the clawfoot-tub bath and bedtime, I woke up frightened, aware in that prickled-skin, wide-eyed child-hood way of a locked door across the hall from where I slept. Behind the door, I'd heard from my Salmon cousins who drifted in and out of this house as if it were their own, was great uncle Larry's room, left exactly as it was when he died at age twenty-six. His clothes were in the closet, his war medals on his bureau. He worked for Idaho Power after the war ended and was out near New Meadows with his crew, changing the fuses on a bank of transformers on a July day in the late 1940s. "They tested the line and it was dead," my great-grandfather wrote years later, describing "the saddest day of our lives."

"While Larry was on the ladder someone somewhere along the line throwed a switch and energised the line. Larry lived until they took him out of the ambulance. He died on the hospital lawn."

Larry was gone ten years by the time I was born. I grew up with the rumors of his unsettled ghost, and on this dark night a jangle or creak from across the hall got me out of bed in a rush and onto the curved staircase—black treads, white risers—in search of a great-grandparent pat on my head (Hazel was not a hugger) or maybe a cup of milk. About halfway down, I stopped. I hunkered on a step and pulled my flannel nightgown tight across my knees. Between the slats of the railing I spied on my great-grandparents, who were settled on fluffy pillows on the floor in front of their huge brick fireplace, the crackling and popping of logs having muffled, I'm guessing, the sounds of my approach. He was brushing her hair. Lifting a long strand of her gray locks with his left hand and drawing a boar-bristle brush from crown to the end, her hair pulsing with electricity in the light of the flames. Hazel sat cross-legged on a pillow while he was up on his knees. He now and again stopped to rest a hand on her shoulder, a show of an alliance they did not display around others. Here it was, confined to their private world, to be witnessed by no one.

Like Narcissa and Marcus Whitman long before them, my frontier-seeking great-grandparents had, at least in their later years and probably long before that, made some kind of peace with each other. Like the Whitmans, they'd lost a child. Like Narcissa, Hazel had to figure out how to go on. And like the long-dead missionary woman that Hazel may have heard about once she settled herself in the West, my great-grandmother was intensely loyal to the choices she'd made and the man with whom she'd made those choices, right up to the end.

And now I'm remembering another afternoon in Grandma Lois's car—this memory rising from the pool of the hundreds of times I drove around with her. I was in high school then, in Boise, and she was dropping me off at my job. I worked in the lingerie section of a department store on what was then the out-skirts of the city, a small store that elderly Basque women often frequented to buy stout stockings for their "very close veins."

I don't know why this day, but I started to ask my grand-mother questions while we sat there together in her wide sedan. I prodded her into reentering the past in ways she usu-ally avoided. She'd made cryptic remarks over the years about her husband's parents, who'd been against her from the start, she said, and she'd once told me about how Hazel and Mick had sent their stubborn daughter Janice to the East Coast to get her away from a boy named Jack, though Janice would marry the Carmen Creek rancher anyway and would stay married to our kind and sweet great-uncle for sixty years until his death. Grandma Lois told of Great-Uncle Larry's redheaded girlfriend, who showed up at the funeral, but Lois said little to me about her own dead daughter, born during the war with the umbilical cord around her neck with no doctor left in town to revive a strangled newborn. She did not speak about her grief, or Hazel's silent rumination over her lost son, which filled every corner. Lois didn't complain about my grandfather's lover, the woman he'd been seeing on the sly for twenty years or more. She did not remind me of her disappointment when my father came home one afternoon to tell his parents that his new girlfriend was pregnant, the day her grand schemes and plans for her brilliant oldest boy fell to pieces, his future slithering away because of the child who was me. Let the past stay in the past seemed to be Grandma Lois's attitude. The past left her churlish; it stunk like a dead thing decomposing in the basement. She wouldn't address it.

I sat in the car with her, minutes ticking toward the start of my shift, the engine humming under the hood so heat would blow on us from the vents, my grandmother huffing and puffing as she did for the last quarter of her life, as if no amount of effort could get a full breath of air in her emphysematous lungs.

*What can you tell me, Grandma?*

*If you knew the half of it,* was all she said, staring straight out the windshield. *You'd have a different opinion of these people if you knew.* But knew what? She wouldn't go on.

They're all gone now, these women of my past, and what I'm

left with is the memory of Mamie's sadness, of Lois's temper, and a knowledge that Hazel's plans to go west and find her fortune with her new husband ended with a simple life in Salmon, the first years spent on this and that ranch in the county until they finally landed in a house on the corner of Gwartney Ave. and Post St. not far from the implements shop she worked in every day until her death. I am sure she and her husband had good times in that home, because I had good times with them.

And on one firelit night, he brushed her hair.

When I went back to the Gwartney house a few years ago, sold now to strangers who entertained the prospect of remodeling for a few months and then walked away from a half-assed unfinished disaster, I found the back door unlocked. Two of my daughters were along that day and followed me inside. We snuck through the empty house, the falling-apart home of my great-grandparents, no scent of biscuits in the oven or snap of cribbage pieces on the board, no roaring fire or bucket of freshly pumped water on the counter. I showed my kids a tiny closet and told them about the day Great-Grandad rocked himself out of his chair to retrieve a coffee can hidden in the back of that storage space. He snapped open the lid to show me what was inside: wads of Confederate dollars. *Worthless*, he said, laughing at his own folly at saving something that had no value. I don't remember if he said where he got the currency or why he'd hung on to it—except my great-grandfather was not one to let a possible windfall pass by.

When my daughters and I got as far as the dining room, we saw that the living-room floors had been ripped up, every strip of stippled oak gone, the planks my great-grandmother once kept polished to a golden hue. We stood on splintered and washed-out subflooring, broken apart enough that we could peer down a cold dirt hole into what was the crawl space of the house.

Here was the perfect metaphor for being in Mick and Hazel's home once again, my feelings about being in Salmon— returned this time with my children and reminded constantly of my separation from the town. No matter how long I stood in my family's empty living rooms that had been left in disarray, I couldn't bring back the past that had once taken care of me, that made me who I am. These places once so familiar, emptied of us. Of me.

When she was near eighty (and I was a sixth grader), Hazel, ever the tidier, was sweeping one day in the back of the implements store. She gathered metal filings and dirt on the concrete floor in the room where Grandpa Bob did his welding, planning to return with her dustbin to scoop up the waste. He'd been working on a horse trailer that morning—more specifically on its spring-loaded gate. When she jammed her broom under the trailer to get at dust in the shadow, the gate sprung open and hit Hazel smack in the knee. She lay on the concrete for a half hour or more, her kneecap shattered in a hundred slivers, before the men, gone out to the City News Stand for lunch, found her there and called an ambulance.

Again, my great-grandfather: "While not being in too much pain, she was uncomfortable. The doctors said she would have to be in traction for thirty days. On November 2, 1968, I had to go to Leadore to make an inspection, so I stopped at the hospital and told her I would come by again as soon as I returned. She answered, 'Well, I suppose I will still be here.' But she wasn't. When I got back, she was dead."

At her funeral my great-grandfather stumbled to the nave of the church where she lay in her coffin. He reached inside to take one of her arms, pulling on her, pulling hard enough to raise her head from the pillow. "Mrs. Gwartney," he said, "it's time to get up. The children are here." My grandfather and father on either side had to coax him back to his seat.

These great-grandparents weren't the first of my forebears to reach what was to become Idaho—the first were Grandma Lois's relatives, who beat the Gwartneys by about seventy years. But there's something in Hazel and Mick about best-laid plans. Something about the impulse to go, to discover the untamed corner of the country no matter the cost. The ache to be someone different in a brand-new place. A new you reinvented by the old you. It's no wonder this gambit struck Mick Gwartney as just the route to take, and somehow the journey West appealed to Hazel as well. My stoic great-grandmother was like hundreds of thousands of other women who moved to our part of the country to make something of themselves. And in her own way, I suppose, that's what she did.

# 11

Catharine Sager wrote in her journal that her brothers planned, in fact, to leave the mission not long after they arrived, in keeping with Morrow's tale. The true-life boys told the Whitmans they intended to locate a parcel of land that had been promised to their father, get settled, and return for their sisters. But Marcus Whitman insisted the girls could stay at Waiilatpu only if the boys did too, and only if they pledged to work around the place. The boys reluctantly agreed. They'd remain with the Whitmans for the benefit of the sisters. But all seven would leave as soon as John reached adulthood. Everyone shook on it.

Except by the spring of '45, Frank, nearly fourteen years old, was fed up with the "strict discipline" at the mission, as his sister described it. Catharine wrote that the second Sager son couldn't bear the severe beatings by the teacher Hinman, nor the Whitmans' rigid rules, day after day. One afternoon, after threatening to do so for months, the boy got on a horse and rode off. He had a scheme all worked out: he'd meet up with emigrants who'd settled near Fort Walla Walla and find a way, eventually, to travel the last few hundred miles to the promised land to claim his father's reward. He'd had it with Waiilatpu; no going back. That is, until letters started reaching him and chipping away his resolve. A few from his sisters and many from Narcissa, missives sent with settlers passing through that somehow got into his hands. Each note urged Frank to return.

"It took some time to convince [Frank] that Mrs. Whitman laid up nothing against him, and to win his confidence," Catharine says. But one day the boy slunk back, half willingly (if that), to Waiilatpu.

John also balked at the overwrought discipline, but instead of running away, the oldest boy slipped off to his tiny cubby-hole of a room in the evenings, where he wrote page after page in a hefty journal he let no one else read. Finally, though, the teenager reached a point when he too needed a change of scenery. In early fall of 1847 he announced that he, having recently turned eighteen, would overwinter with Henry and Eliza Spalding at Lapwai among the Nez Perce. Maybe once John heard that young Eliza was moving to Waiilatpu to attend school he figured he could exchange places with her for a season and perhaps more easily move on from there to find his father's property and establish a homestead. But, no, Narcissa said. She was wounded, indignant about the boy's plans, and then she was outraged. He couldn't go, especially if he might let the Spaldings in on even a hint of his discontent with the Whitmans—she couldn't bear to give Henry Spalding one more reason to defame her. She argued so vehemently against the move that John gave in and stayed at the Whitman mission, soon too sick with measles to travel anyway. A month after he'd broached the idea of leaving, his throat was cut and he was dead on the floor of the kitchen.

Fifty years after watching their brothers die, a sister succumb to measles, their adopted parents killed, many friends and loved ones stabbed, hacked, shot, the three Sager women went back to Waiilatpu for the half-century commemoration. After they were rescued in 1847, the Sager girls were shuffled off to families that couldn't afford, or were unwilling, to take on the burden of an additional child. Catharine, Elizabeth, and

Matilda were split up, offered lodging and food if they agreed to work as unpaid housekeepers in mostly dismal situations until they married—each escaping into marriage as soon as she was able, hitched to men (significantly older) at young ages, and all bearing many, many children. The final wish of their mother, Naomi, which was for her own children to stay together, turned to dust in the wake of the deaths at Waiilatpu. The girls saw each other only rarely after the dawn of 1848, and though Henrietta, the youngest, moved in with Catharine and her new husband for a time, she didn't stay long. As soon as she was old enough, the youngest of the Sagers went to California and got into the "acting trade." Her sisters were beside themselves with shame and disappointment over the decision. The sisters wrote her, begging her to return and find a suitable husband. But one evening, when she was twenty-six, and married by now to a man of questionable behavior, Henrietta was shot dead in a bar.

For nearly fifty years the bones of those who'd been killed had stayed buried under a heap of soil, beneath the wagon that Joe Stanfield had jammed on top of the communal grave back in early December of 1847. In 1897 civic leaders in Walla Walla and those who'd built Whitman College in honor of Marcus and Narcissa announced that they planned to disinter the remains and move them to a more pleasant and appropriate location at the mission. A lovely corner, where a soft breeze blew through Marcus's apple orchard and a patch of tansy grew at the base of the trees. The Sager women, in letters to the college president, to the mayor of the city, to newspaper editors, begged for that to not happen. They wanted the remains to be left where they were, in peace. The answer back to the Sagers was *Stay out of it.* In the summer of '97 the bodies were exhumed despite the survivors' adamant reservations. No one consulted with the women about when or where or how this would happen. The last survivors of the attack, the women who'd lost so much, were given no voice in the matter.

In the fall of 1897 Catharine wrote an angry letter to the *Spokesman Review* in Spokane, recalling the original burial and disclosing a fear that had haunted her for half a century: she dreaded finding out that most of her loved ones' remains had been hauled off and eaten by animals. "The [original] grave was only about three feet deep, so it was soon dug into by wolves, and Mrs. Whitman's leg was dragged out and the flesh eaten off to the knee. We reburied it. Before we left the remains were again dug up, and morning after morning we would see the wolves at their ghoulish work and hear their snarling. . . . Where the bones are now, God only knows. I am sorry the grave was disturbed, for doubt has now become a certainty."

Matilda wrote to the *Walla Walla Journal*, expressing her own dismay at the "disturbance of our sacred dead." This time the editors responded in print: "If you desire the bones of your brothers to remain where they are, you can come and pick them out and do with them as seemeth best to you."

Matilda did walk around the table where the unearthed bones were displayed in the days before the fiftieth anniversary celebration. She rolled around the femurs, poked at the ulnas and scapulas, doing her best to identify John and Frank from an old scrap of cloth or square of decomposing boot leather. Then she and her sisters stood by as the comingled remains (any effort to organize parts of the dead was quickly abandoned—Catharine was correct, there weren't enough bones left to reassemble whole bodies) were reburied at Waiilatpu, the last scraps of Marcus and Narcissa and the twelve others covered with a marble slab that lists the names of the victims. The three sisters searched the grounds for Louisa's grave on the afternoon of the celebration, but they could locate no sign of their little sister's resting place—nor the grave of the girl they'd never met but were well acquainted with, Alice.

Catharine lived for another thirteen years beyond the ceremony, and her sisters even longer—growing into old age with the memories of the attack and their loved ones' deaths (but never meeting Morrow, despite what the author claimed). The women were the final witnesses of a collision between whites and Native people that altered the course of the West.

The Sager women's accounts, along with several others written by survivors, are still available to anyone interested, stored in the rare-book rooms of local libraries. But the hundreds of pages written by John, a heap penned so furiously that his sisters deemed him the family's "most avid journal keeper," disappeared in the fires set by the Cayuse after every white person was gone. John's was, no doubt, a remarkable true story. But no one will ever know what he set down, what he worked out on paper, night after dark night in his hidey-hole at Waiilatpu.

# 4 Memento Mori

# 1

A few years back, a woman wrote me to ask if I knew about a strand of Narcissa's hair stored in the archives at a university in Oregon. The school she mentioned, Pacific University, near Portland, happens to be where I teach summer writing workshops. In fact, I'd sat many times on stiff pews in the chapel of Old College Hall to listen to student presentations without an inkling that above my head in a storage room, contained in what I figured had to be a plain wood box or a raggedy old cloth bag, was hair off Narcissa Whitman's own head.

That is, if the stranger who'd written me had her facts right and a piece of hair had been wrapped up and preserved for posterity. And if it was up there in the musty museum, it had to smell like old feet by now; a spider-infested wad well on its way to decomposing into dust.

I had to see it, though I wondered why. I don't like to think of myself as a looky-loo, a gawker, standing out here a century and a half past Narcissa's death and reveling in the gruesome remnants of her end. Even though I'd already seen one piece of her hair that didn't do much for me, I wanted to believe that another, this swatch of hair at Pacific University, might make her more human than anything I'd yet come across, including her scrawled handwriting and including the two (only two, strikingly different from each other) likenesses painted of her while she was still alive. She had grown that hair. She'd combed it, braided it, touched it. And now maybe I'd get to touch it too.

The archivist at Pacific University was young and kind and, it turned out, somewhat tantalized by the story of Narcissa's hair. My version of the story. I told her how the thirty-nine-year-old woman, after eleven years of proselytizing that went nowhere at the mission, died with her husband and more than a dozen others during an attack. How Narcissa, shot in the shoulder and later the chest, was rolled into an irrigation ditch. How, once she was dead, a Cayuse man took a shovel and split open her skull. I told the archivist that Narcissa's hair—it had to have gone down this way—was released into the cold wind, strewn out across the compound. Left there for lucky men to find and fold into their shirts.

I'd seen the first single curl of Narcissa's hair, which was picked off a field at Waiilatpu, in Walla Walla. The blonde strand is looped into a dainty circle, tied with a ribbon, and glued to cardstock. It sits in a gold frame inside an antique cabinet in the Whitman College archives—beyond reach. "A lock of Mrs. Whitman's hair found at Whitman Mission March 1848 by James Ballieu, presented to Whitman College in 1888 by Mrs. America Grant."

Mountain men had tromped through Waiilatpu the year after the attack (around the time, apparently, that our unknown person plucked the tansy). James Ballieu must have been one of the curious stragglers; maybe he found the strand of hair, yellow as fresh butter, on the ground and carried it in a pocket until he could give it away to Mrs. America Grant, whoever the heck she was. She tied the hair with the red adornment and sent it to Whitman College, and now it rests behind glass and, frankly, fails to disclose a single thing about Narcissa. At least it didn't when I stared at it, waiting for the wisp to cough up some idea of the woman.

One thing did strike me as odd, and that's the color: a

whimsical, sun-kissed blonde. Narcissa, in my mind, was anything but whimsical.

So what did I think yet another unloosed hank of hair stored in the Pacific archives would tell me about Narcissa Whitman that I didn't already know? Hard to say. I was sure Pacific University's hair was found by someone who'd ventured onto the mission grounds post-attack. A nineteenth-century mountain man who wanted his own souvenir, like lucky Ballieu. But, still, it was worth having a look at whatever hair was stored away in the archives, and I'd driven to the campus, about four hours from my house, to locate it.

Once the archivist had unlocked the closet door in the far corner of the second floor of Old College Hall and we'd both squeezed into the narrow space of the storage area, she began pulling down boxes. She apologized for the mishmash of stuff upon stuff, for the lack of strict organization, though it seemed quite organized to me. The university was the first one west of the Continental Divide and is thus packed to the gills with history of the frontier, including all kinds of artifacts from the Eells and the Walkers and even the Spaldings.

The young woman set a container the size of a shoebox and promising gems of history on the center table and opened the lid. Inside was a hill of cracked and yellow human teeth piled against one side. I ignored the creepy coat hanging behind me made entirely of horsehide and horsehair (except for lining and buttons—I don't want to know what those were made out of) and concentrated on another box that held an early optometrist's case of glass eyeballs in many shades of blue. There were boxes of papers, of ratty clothes and shoes and crocheted linens. At one point the archivist pulled out a thick, long hank of jet-black hair, bound with a strap, and I clapped my hand over my mouth. Not Narcissa's, but *goodness*. After that came a whole lot of stuff, though no strawberry-blonde mane. No tangles scooped up from the gravel or picked out of a clump of sagebrush near Narcissa's death place. I slipped past the archivist, sneezing from things grown dank, and pointed to a high shelf. I stepped on a stool to reach for a box myself, wanting to see it all, the whole of what was here, sure that somewhere on a back edge we'd find Narcissa's hair. But the woman held up her hand. Stop. That's enough. She needed time to sort out what was squirreled away in this closet. She promised she'd investigate, she'd search, and, she told me as she ushered my pushy self out, she'd get back to me.

I drove home disappointed. I hadn't seen the hair. But I did have hours between the campus and my house to work on the mystery of what had happened in relation to it.

Let's say that someone had picked up a handful of hair off the bloody compound (about three hundred miles from Pacific University) not months but days, maybe only hours, after Narcissa's death. My guess was one of the Sager girls, though none of the three survivors mentions hair in their separate accounts of the attack and its aftermath. Maybe she—whichever Sager picked it up—didn't think it worth noting. But, never mind, that wouldn't have happened. If hair was gathered, it would have been written about. Nevertheless, I stuck with my idea that either Catharine, Elizabeth, or Matilda had retrieved the strand of hair. Henrietta was too little. I narrowed it further to Catharine, because she was thirteen at the time, or possibly Elizabeth, because she was eleven, and because these two, along with Eliza Spalding, were the ones sent out to the field to gather torn-apart pieces of Narcissa's body, those dug up and scattered remnants, giving the girls plenty of access to hair stuck in the reeds and rushes or banked up against a frosty tumble of boulders.

The day Peter Odgen hurried the girls toward a boat to get them clean away from the mission, Catharine or Elizabeth, either one, could have stuck the hair into a satchel. Catharine did pack Mother Whitman's coffee box, which is to this day stored at Whitman College. Attached to its handle is a handwritten letter from Catharine Sager Pringle: "This was the coffee box in it was left the green coffee after the masacre of Nov 1847 an indian name of Tim-Tim mesa came to the door of the mansion house where we were held as prisoners called for me and gave me the Box and Dr. Whitman's compass. The compass I afterwards gave to Cushing Eells and I now present the Box to Whitman Colledge."

That left a riddle for me to solve: How did the hair get out of a girl's keeping and onto the shelves of this small museum storage closet at Pacific?

The university, at its advent, was named the Orphan Asylum. It was started in the late 1840s by a woman named Tabitha Brown, a widow in her late sixties, who was determined to care for children who found themselves in the middle of a vast nowhere without family or a place to settle because their parents had died on the trail. It turns out that the two Sager boys and five girls were not the only ones to suffer this fate. In September of 1849 the school, recently renamed the Tualatin Academy and supported by the Home Missionary Society of the Congregational Church (one of its first hired teachers, none other than Eliza Spalding), had grown large enough to get the nod from a nascent Oregon Territory government. The school was officially certified as the territory's first educational institution and needed trustees. One of those trustees, a man most eager to take on the role, was Marcus's old pal, Alanson Hinman.

It took me some time to figure it out, but here was my lynchpin: Hinman.

Alanson Hinman showed up in Oregon Territory at the height of the mad rush of migration. He was a single man in one of the early wagon trains to roll through Waiilatpu in the fall of 1844. Like the others in the train, he was hungry when he reached the Whitman station. Exhausted. Sick. Doubting his decision to upend his entire life to move west for—for what? All he saw was a desolate landscape and extraordinarily few human amenities. That is, until he stepped into Waiilatpu. Narcissa's tidy home and fairly decent cooking, if you ignored the preponderance of horsemeat. Hoards of children and other families were pitching in, making a compound that was, basically, well functioning. He decided he wanted to stay right there, safe and sound with the missionaries in their enclave.

Marcus hired him on the spot as the compound's schoolteacher for the boys and girls under the Whitmans' care, Helen Mar, Mary Ann, a few others, plus the Sagers. Also the children of the families who'd opted to overwinter at the compound, the Osborns and the Kimballs among them.

What Hinman knew about religious pedagogy was little. He promised the Whitmans he'd do fine with teaching, despite only minor experience. He was just the man to shape up unruly children. Perhaps most thrillingly to Marcus and Narcissa, he said he was ready that very day to convert to their faith. Hinman was the first in line when Marcus offered a day of river baptisms in the fall of 1844. No Cayuse takers again (eight years running), but there was Alonson, eager for the dunk. Save his soul, dry the man off, give him a teaching job.

In the schoolroom Hinman made up for any lack of skill or demeanor by becoming a bully. He shouted, he yelled, he cursed, he ridiculed, and he hit. Hinman often dragged a boy to the front of the room to receive a beating in front of the others. Frank Sager, again, got it the worst. Hinman was, wrote Catharine Sager in one unusually stark passage, "one of those small-souled tyrants that could take delight in torturing helpless children and who, under a cloak of religion, hid a black licentious heart."

But when the children complained to Narcissa and Marcus, they were told that "whatever the teacher did was right."

Hinman moved on from Waiilatpu after less than a year—to the relief of every child at the mission. He left because he was ready to seek a different sort of fortune and not because the adults had finally decided to protect their children from daily corporal punishment. In fact, the Whitmans were fond of their newly converted friend and were sorry to see him go.

Hinman carried his teaching credentials to a different frontier school. Two years later Marcus convinced the Boston mission board to let Hinman take over a failed Methodist mission near the Dalles called Waskopum (where Narcissa once recovered from her hardship). Neither the Eells nor the Walkers wanted the post, so Hinman was shuffled in. Marcus sent his nephew Perrin, who'd traveled west from New York State, to help restart the mission. How teenaged Perrin fared at the hands of this quick-to-violence man, who knows, but at least the boy was away from Waiilatpu and certain death when the Cayuse killed every male over age twelve. Reports tell of a small band of Cayuse headed to the Dalles mission for the express purpose of killing Perrin, an effort that sputtered out—though Perrin was told by a trusted Nez Perce man to run and run fast, as "the Cayuse have offered one hundred horses for your scalp."

(My sister sent me a link to an Idaho history website that said Perrin ended up moving to Lewiston to work as an interpreter. His daughter, Elizabeth Auzella Whitman, known for her raucous and entertaining music—a regular Annie Oakley, "a one-woman orchestra on the new frontier"—married Harry K. Barnett and gave birth to a son, Marcus, who became father to Virginia, who became mother to a girl named Grace. Grace Slick, that is, lead singer of Jefferson Airplane. Narcissa spins in her grave.)

When Hinman heard about the attack on Waiilatpu, he rushed away from his new post along the Columbia River, which was obviously a good idea. He hurried as far from any hint of violence as possible, avoiding Waiilatpu and eventually heading to the recently established town of Forest Grove. One thing led to another, and he was soon trustee for the college. The location of one strand of Narcissa's hair.

Here's where my story suffers another gap. Narcissa dies, head is crushed, hair is broadcast about, then someone picks up a piece (I've still assigned this role to a Sager daughter) and . . . passes it on to Hinman? Probably not. The Sagers had no affection for the man. Once he'd left they didn't want to see him again. Hinman, like Spalding, left it to others to rescue the fifty-some women and children held hostage by the Cayuse. There's no indication that Hinman contacted the four surviving Sagers after they were free, nor did he arrange to have the twice-orphaned girls—who simply had nowhere to go after their second set of parents, as well as two brothers and a sister, died in front of them at Waiilatpu—brought to the school created expressly for Oregon Trail orphans.

A line often muttered by Grandpa Bob seems apropos in regard to Hinman: *If the man isn't a son of a bitch, he'll do until one comes along.*

But how did Hinman come by Narcissa's hair?

I asked if I could return to the Pacific Archives for a search.

210

This time the answer was no, I wouldn't be granted access to the storage room. The archivist—a new hire, another young woman and not the one from my first search—would do her best to locate the hair, and she'd let me know when she had.

I waited. I wrote her again. I waited some more. I thought about driving to Pacific—if I was standing in front of her, she'd have to let me look though the boxes, right? She wrote and asked me to hold off, as she had not yet had a chance to locate the hair.

Then, a week or two later, I received an e mail from her with a scan attached. Narcissa's hair. I printed out the photo and sat in the soft chair in my room, staring. There it was, the bit of Narcissa I'd been after. To what end, I'm still not sure. Especially because the black-and-white image in my hands brought up more questions, and about zero answers, concerning Narcissa Prentiss Whitman.

Pacific's relic was not a loose lock of hair. Not in the least like the America Grant curl I'd seen at Whitman College, tied with a ribbon. This was not a strand picked up off the ruined grounds of Waiilatpu. The picture in front of me was of a wreath, maybe two inches in diameter. A complex, skillfully constructed work of art made entirely from human hair.

"Narcissa Whitman's hair, braided by her and sent to Alanson Hinman, who spent the winter of 1844 at the Whitman Station and was in charge of the Dalles Station in 1847 at the time of the massacre." So states an anonymously penned note, in shaky handwriting—an aged person, maybe Hinman himself—that accompanies the washed-out blonde wreath of human hair.

So. The hair was shipped by post by Narcissa when she was alive to her friend Hinman as a gift. The man I had vilified, excoriated, was one held dear by her.

The discovery of the wreath of hair got me to contact yet

another newly hired archivist, this one at Whitman College. *Might you have any other pieces, besides Ballieu's, of Narcissa Whitman's hair?* She responded that in fact, yes, the archives at Whitman College (despite my visit to that room years earlier when I was told that the curl in the frame was the one and only) had acquired five over the years.

As soon as I could manage it, I got to Walla Walla and back into the basement of the Whitman Library to sit at a large table in the archives where a kind and well-informed assistant archivist named Bill had already piled five envelopes, each of which held, ostensibly, Narcissa's hair.

Out of the first envelope came a loose piece of brown hair looped onto a piece of paper. "This is supposed to be a lock of Mrs. Dr. Whitman's hair. It was in a book in 1867 when Reverend Cushing Eells gave the book to Mrs. Martha Jane Bessy. Signed, Marion B. Bessy." The note was dated May 22, 1929.

From the second envelope, an ever-so-slight strand of yellow hair, loose, without adornment of ribbon or twine, along with two handwritten letters.

Escondido, California, 9/29/1899
President SBL Penrose, Walla Walla, Washington
Dear Sir:
I have in my possession what is said to be,—a lock of Mrs. Mark Whitman's hair.

As a Mr. Rector and another soldier who had known Mr. and Mrs. Whitman were assisting near the spot where the unfortunate victims fell, at the time of that fearful Massacre of the Missionaries in 1845, a lock of golden hair lying on the ground before them caught their attention. On closer examination, the soldier whose name she had forgotten said, "There lies a lock of Mrs. Whitman's hair." Then gave it to

Mr. Rector, who gave it to his wife, who recently gave me a small part of it when I told her I thought I could find some surviving friend who would cherish so sacred a relic. Can you ascertain through some of her friends whether her hair was golden or if this probably belonged to some other victim of the massacre? If this can be identified, I shall be happy to send it to her nearest relative or convey it to the college at Walla Walla as a relic.

Hoping to hear from you soon, I will close this note of peculiar import.

Sincerely,
(Mrs.) Sarah M. Wyckoff.

Escondido, California 10/12
Pres. SBL Penrose
Dear Sir,
I am happy to return this lock of hair to the place that holds so dear the mission and devotion of Mr. and Mrs. Marcus Whitman. No doubt the cruel ax that "cut their quivering flesh" as they lay dying severed this lock from her head and it laid concealed for nearly two years—as I think it was in 1849 that it was found by the two soldiers of the war with the Indians of that time.

I have retained but a small part of the lock I send you. When we think of your college we can but pray that its future usefulness may be commensurate with the sacrifice it cost this sainted couple who gave their lives for it.

Sincerely yours,
Sarah M. Wyckoff

In the third envelope was a folded black square of card stock and a letter:

Narcissa Whitman's Hair

Hopefully this will remain with a sentimentalist for I am one when it comes to things like this. Inside is part of a single hair from a curl of Narcissa's, which she gave to a girlfriend prior to her departure in 1836 for Old Oregon. The curl is normally at this time on display at the Rushville, N.Y., Central School with Marcus Whitman's 1826 license to practice medicine. One short hair, which had become loose, was saved and divided into three pieces, of which this is one. *Be Careful Please.*

Signed, Ross Woodbridge, Pittsford, NY, December 12, 1970

I opened the black card stock and, right away, called Bill over from his desk. "I think you've been robbed." I handed him the card. He studied the surface in his quiet way and then pointed out the faintest—and I mean faint—inch or two of human hair. I peered in closer and there, on the black card, I saw it, stapled and then scotch taped. One third of one single hair.

From the fourth envelope came two letters and what seemed to me an old loop of gray. Maybe it was dusty, maybe its color had aged away in harsh light, but it was too far off from the others to add up. The gray hair is glued to a thin piece of paper, on which is written, "Mrs. Whitman's hair."

San Luis Obispo, Ca. July 2000

Dear Mr. Dodd,

When my parents, Roy and Kathryn Eells had to dismantle their home, I inherited the writing desk of my grandmother and the lock of hair I've sent you was in the small drawer. At Sarah's death, the desk was acquired by my parents and subsequently came to me.

According to the book "Father Eells," by Myron Eells, Cushing Eells arrived at Waiilatpu a day after the massacre and therefore he probably would have acquired the lock of hair at that time. This information is partly from "Father Eells" and partly from my parents.

Sincerely,
Florence Eells McLennan

The first four envelopes were laid open in front of me, their letters unfolded on the desk, each strand of hair sitting atop the note that described its origins. Bill left me alone unless I called him over in a mistaken panic about missing hair. The young archivist stayed in her office. They let me handle the letters, even the ones over a hundred years old. They let me touch the hair. *They let me touch the hair!*

And look at this array before me. Isn't it something that we all had our own Narcissa Whitman hair stories, these people who'd donated their strands of hair, and me? Such desperate measures to get close to a woman who each of us felt we had a connection to. I mean, we'd studied her at practically the microscopic level. My body buzzed as I sat there with her hair, even as I was questioning what in the world I wanted out of it.

Cells from Narcissa's body. Blonde hair and brown hair and one strand with a reddish tone, and that one twist of crinkled gray. I sobered up and started to actually look over the material in front of me on the table. The letter writers, not to mention America Grant, each wanted to believe the hair in his or her possession came off Narcissa's head. But how could that be? The blonde so light, the brown the shade of dark chocolate. No way were these cut (from "quivering flesh"—Mrs. Wycoff's theatrics) off the same person's head.

I read the letters over again, this time starting to notice

mistakes of sequencing and dates, picking up now on how these people (and I'm one of the people, I admit) got their facts wrong. We bend stories to reflect our notions of who we want her to be, and the seven of us (Mrs. Grant included), I suppose, felt we got to *own* Narcissa somehow because we'd held a smidge—one third of one single hair!—of what was once (probably/maybe/doubtfully) attached to her.

The Eells great-granddaughter, who'd found the ring of gray hair in her grandmother's desk—let's start there. No, Mrs. McLennan, the missionary Cushing Eells, living at his mission near Spokane, did not go to Waiilatpu on November 30, 1847. If he had, he would have been killed, and I'm sure he was keenly aware of the risk. He was right to save his own skin and the skins of his family by avoiding the Whitman mission altogether. I have no beef with his rush to get out. The Eells, like Hinman, hurried away to a nearby fort, and then to Oregon City, and then to Forest Grove (and after some years, back to Walla Walla, where Cushing Eells started Whitman College), veering from the disaster at Waiilatpu and their dead companions.

Still, I can't help but envision the relief it would have been for the survivors at Waiilatpu if Eells had shown up. The children, especially those left without any adult to tend to them, knew this man; his family had traveled to Waiilatpu many times for mission meetings, and they had, in turn, traveled to the Eells and Walker homes. The Reverend Eells, if he'd managed to survive, might have wrapped up the extremely ill Louisa Sager and the extremely ill Helen Mar Meek and driven them to safety, rather than leaving the children upstairs, soaked in blood and dying of dehydration. He might have rescued Lorinda Bewley from being raped in public and dragged away for weeks. He might have prevented her brother from being

216

beaten to death in the center of the compound, witnessed by the other terrified survivors.

At the very least, he could have buried the dead in the way they would have desired to have been buried.

Mother Whitman had taught her foster children that Catholics, the Black Robes, were the very definition of evil. Catholics, the kids heard again and again, were the devil's representatives on earth. They drank the savior's blood! Ate his flesh! Henry Spalding regularly called Jesuits "The Cannibals."

The children were told that it would be better to die than to even greet a Catholic with a friendly hello.

And yet it was a Catholic Jesuit Priest who rode into Waiilatpu three days after the killings—not Cushing Eells. ("I was more afraid of him than I was of the Indians," Catharine wrote years later of the priest.) This was Father Jean-Baptiste Abraham Brouillet, a Canadian who prayed over the dead at Waiilatpu, who blessed them with the sacraments as they were placed in the ground once again, covered with Stanfield's wagon. It was the Jesuit who ate dinner with the Cayuse without saying a word to the survivors—not a single word—before disappearing back into the forest.

Henry Spalding, who spent the rest of his life blaming the Catholics for the attack at Waiilatpu—the priests had incited the tribe, was his accusation—condemned Brouillet for his callous behavior toward the women and children suffering at Waiilatpu in the aftermath of the attack (my response to that: Where the hell were you then, Henry?), to which Brouillet responded that any show of emotion during his hours at Waiilatpu, "would only have endangered their lives and mine."

The great irony here is twofold: Brouillet had arrived as a Jesuit missionary at the newly constructed Catholic diocese on November 27, only two days before the attack. Despite the fact that other Jesuits had been communicating with the Cayuse, he could not possibly have wielded the influence Spalding accused him of. Second, and here's the real head-scratcher, Brouillet risked his own hide by sneaking to Five Crows' camp once he'd heard about the Whitmans' deaths, expressly to warn Rev. Spalding about the outbreak of violence at the mission and to tell him word had spread far and wide that a band of Cayuse men was on the hunt for the Lapwai minister. They meant to kill him as mercilessly as they had the others.

Spalding snuck away in the dead of night. For six days and nights he creeped and crawled through thick forest, away from any trodden path, to make his way to Lapwai, where he'd been given up for dead. He arrived bruised, scratched, and hungry—with no news to give his wife Eliza about their daughter Eliza—but alive. And it was a *Catholic* who saved him. And yet Spalding seemed to forget about that kindness almost immediately and went about a defamation so severe that Brouillet finally published a book in an effort to clear his name: *The Authentic Account of the Murder of Dr. Whitman and Other Missionaries, by the Cayuse Indians of Oregon, in 1847, and the Causes Which Led to That Horrible Catastrophe.*

Horrible, yes. The children watched in horror as the priest arrived and quickly left again. Several of the Sagers later said the Jesuit man's presence, his secret conference with the Cayuse, convinced them more than ever that they, too, would be shot or beaten to death. What the girls could have used at that moment was a friend, a true friend, someone like Cushing Eells. But Eells did not show up, even if his son's book later claimed he did.

On to the Wyckoff woman, the spinner of the Western Tale, who knew nothing of the Whitmans until she saw the hair and heard the story of the missionary couple (Mark!) from her neighbor. What gets to me most is that she strong-armed the Rector woman to hand over part of the hair, and then she decided to *keep some.*

Who did she think she was, creating her own version of how things went down?

But of course I'd done the same. I'd been sure—and in fact told about anyone who wanted to listen to my hair story—that the Pacific hair had come from Waiilatpu, post-attack. I recited this version often, describing how the strand had been retrieved by someone who'd watched Narcissa die. I was certain one of the Sager girls, conflicted as they were about Narcissa at times, had saved the hair. A remnant from the woman who they sometimes, on the days she allowed them to use such a term of endearment, called "mother."

Instead, that tidy wreath for Hinman.

I shouldn't have been surprised, then, by packet number five. When I opened it at the archival table in the basement of Whitman College, what emerged was a second wreath of hair. Not unlike the wreath stored at Pacific. Except. Except the hair is dark brown. Except the weave is neither skilled nor intricate as is the Pacific wreath. Nowhere near as elegant. This one, the accompanying note explains, was made by Narcissa and sent to Perrin Whitman. Delivered by post to the Dalles Mission.

By the early 1840s Narcissa's eyes were ruined. She needed eyeglasses, badly, and eyeglasses—unless a certain someone had brought a pair or two from Boston when he made a year-long trip (harrumph)—were not to be had. Also, Narcissa was busy. A houseful of children, many of them sick (someone always, forever, sick). She was surrounded by families too pummeled from months on the road to continue on to the Willamette Valley, and who were thus dependent on Narcissa and Marcus for mechanical help, spiritual guidance, food. Every meal was a chore. She began each morning with a 4:30 a.m. recitation of scripture by the children of the household, and then moved on to laundry, and then baths—especially for the most ill among them—and then breakfast, and then . . . always more, and more, and more to do.

When did Narcissa find time to squint over a board, moving her overworked fingers through taut strands of hair, wrapping and weaving them around the pegs, shaping a wreath?

Two wreaths, though I refuse to believe she made them both. Either she wove her shining blonde hair into a tight and perfect wreath for Hinman, or she wove her dowdy brown hair into a rather poor emulation of the same for Perrin. Which was it?

When I held that second wreath, loose as it is, oblong rather than round, with wisps of hair escaping at the edges, I had a glimpse of Narcissa Whitman at her work, and I was taken aback again over this breath of affection in me toward the woman. I pictured her in her small sitting room, side-by-side with a Sager girl. Elizabeth, probably, for Narcissa was very fond of Elizabeth. Night has fallen. A lantern burns on a hook above them so the two can better see their work. The girl works at her wreath, the woman at her own. They talk softly, laughing, their heads close together. The next day, Marcus will wrap the gifts in paper and deliver them to Fort Walla Walla, along with his own letter to Hinman and another to Perrin. The package will be delivered to two lonely men hundreds of miles away on the Columbia River.

But whatever happened, in the end the Sager girls almost definitely walked away from the mission without Narcissa Whitman's hair. Still, I'd argue the three knew her best. Catharine and Elizabeth had a relationship with the matriarch more intimate than even Marcus, who was so often away, often distracted by his own concerns. The final years of Narcissa's life she was not once apart from Catharine, Elizabeth, Matilda, Louisa, or baby Henrietta. I suppose that's why I'd figured one of the girls, on her way to collect scattered bones and torn strips of sheets, found a single strand of hair half ground into the soil that would remind her and her sisters of their time at Waiilatpu, and of the woman who at least tried to love them. But no. The Sager girls departed Waiilatpu with only Marcus's compass, the battered coffee pot, and their skinny little lives.

A few years after their rescue, flung apart from each other now, and their adopted parents just another sad memory like their biological parents, the Sagers heard from their own father's brother, a man named Frederick Sager. He sent Catharine a letter after he read about the attack in a local newspaper. Henry Sager's brother wanted her to know he existed and that his father, too, was still alive. Catharine managed to get the letter to Elizabeth, who'd spent desperate years wondering if anyone out there ever thought of Henry and Naomi's kids.

In her response, a long letter to a relative she didn't remember and would not meet again, the second of the Sager daughters pours out her soul.

Five weeks after the attack that killed the Whitmans and their brothers, plus Louisa, the Sager girls were abandoned. They heard nothing from their adopted parents' relatives, no offers of help or safekeeping. They were not taken in by other ABC missionaries, not the Eells, not the Walkers, certainly not Hinman.

Unbelievably, the Spaldings did little to help resettle the Sager children and made no effort to keep the girls together, in a safe place where they could begin to deal with the many troubles of their past.

Curses on the Spaldings. Especially Henry, who spent the next years writing letters to every newspaper that would give him space, long missives about his "dear departed sister" Narcissa, who he now praised to the heavens.

The Sager girls were stuck in heinous conditions. When she read her uncle's letter, Elizabeth was separated from the last members of her family, her sisters, as alone as she'd been in her life.

There could be no more plaintive letter than the one she wrote.

In it, Elizabeth begs him to continue the exchange, to be her friend (there's no indication that she heard from him again). She shares gory details of the attack, as if she suspected his true intent was to get the insider's take on the mayhem that was the great gossip of the East.

"We went down[stairs] and raising the cover from Father's face beheld a sight we will never forget," went one passage. "His head was cut literally to pieces."

Elizabeth does not, in her letter, refer to Narcissa's hair. However, she asks if she might share a piece of herself with those she'd love, who she'd fiercely love, devotedly love, if only she could meet them. What did she have to send her relatives in the East except gruesome tales of death and survival, and a strand of her own auburn hair?

I have a great many questions to ask and I expect you will think them silly, but I have such a curiosity to know everything. When you write to me I want you to answer them if you can. I want to know if you are a married man and who you married and if you have any children and what their names are. How many brothers father had and their wives names if they are married and I want to know what my father's mother's name was before she was married. And what grandfather's other two wives names were. I want to know what my father's age would be if had lived and my mother's. What state he was born in and what month and what day of the month. If you have a lock of his hair please send me a piece, and a piece of Mother's if you have any. Send me a lock of yours and dear Grandfather's, too. Sister Catharine wrote you a letter the 24th of December. She wrote you more particulars than I can. She is older and remembers more than I do. She sent you a lock of all of our hair. And if you could send us Grandfather's Daguerreotype we would prize it as highly as if it was Grandpa's own self. I don't know what I would give to see him. I always said if I had a Grandpa I would be so happy. I always thought he was dead. I was a little surprised when you wrote us that he was still alive. I will send you three pieces of my hair. Please give one to Grandpa and give one lock to your oldest daughter, if you have one, if you have none keep it to yourself. Give the other one to my other Cousins if I have any. Write to me as soon as you get this letter if you please and give me all the particulars. Your affectionate niece. Elizabeth M Sager.

2

Grandma Lois was dead, and Mamie was in a memory care unit of a nursing home: not many reasons to go back to Salmon. But I made the long drive from Oregon one Thanksgiving weekend partly because I wanted to be in on a get-together with our grandfather, and partly because I had a piece of unfinished family business weighing on me. And on Thanksgiving morning itself, the sky as pale as a pink dahlia, I bundled up and took my two youngest daughters to the Salmon cemetery so they could look at the graves of those who'd gone on. Behind us was the Lemhi Range and beyond that, shimmering white, were the Beaverheads, a ring of mountains that cradled the valley where I once lived.

My father was there, too, along with his third wife, four years younger than me. We were the graveyard's only visitors, surrounded by scrawny pine trees, tossed-about plastic flowers, and thigh-high granite headstones poking out of the crusty snow. Up on the hill the wind squirmed under our jackets and past the cuffs of our mittens and, because he'd worn his old cowboy hat rather than a knit cap like the rest of us, around the edges of my father's bright-pink ears.

My daughter Mary kicked the ice off my great-grandparents' headstones with her fat snow boots. A few steps downhill, Mollie scraped the frozen snow off my great-uncle Larry's grave. Past that headstone was the smallest marker, this one for my father's sister, the baby who'd been pronounced dead and whisked from the room before Grandma Lois could float above the dose of ether that had knocked her out for the birth. All that remained of the child sixty years later was this, a white rectangle. Flat on the ground. No year or epithet carved in the stone; no etchings of lambs or angels. It simply said, "Baby Girl."

I stood up from pushing snow off the infant's grave, about ten minutes into our time there, and could tell my fidgeting daughters were ready to get back to the house and to the turkey roasting in the oven, to the wood stove my grandpa was tending during football game commercials. Later that afternoon I'd put together a pecan pie because it was my father's favorite, and my sister Rebecca from Seattle would rice, not mash, the potatoes because she said they were tastier that way. My thoughts had already moved toward the meal and the overheated house and away from the people interred in this ground when my father said, out of nowhere, "Where's my mother's grave?"

His wife laughed. "Oh, Mike," she said.

I leaned against a frozen headstone that seared a line through my jeans and reminded my father that Grandma Lois had no grave. Years past her funeral, past my last trip here, her ashes were still around the house somewhere—in Grandpa Bob's bedroom, probably.

My father stared at nothing for a few silent beats then turned and crunched back through the snow to his diesel truck, which he'd left idling. He climbed inside and turned up the music that'd been a low drone during our visit to the graves. His wife watched him go and kept watching as he slammed the door, tossed his hat in the passenger seat, and crossed his arms across his chest. "He doesn't like this sort of thing," she said to no one in particular.

When my grandmother died at the age of eighty, she left a thick pile of yellow lined paper covered with her handwritten instructions. She'd signed and dated each page at the bottom, and so had her witness—a woman named Frenchie who came in every few days to keep house but who did more eating and gossiping than keeping. In this pseudo will my grandmother attended to every detail: who got which dish, which piece of furniture, which piece of art that had come down from her family. The family that had started out with almost nothing, gained wealth, slipped into poverty again. Grandma Lois decided who should have her books and clothes and the few dollars in her savings account. She wrote out instructions for her funeral in the Episcopal Church down the street—"Moon River" sung, blooming peonies in vases, Tennyson recited, a PEO reception with white cake and Folgers coffee. She also described what should become of her body. She'd return as a corpse to Boise to be buried next to her mother and grandmother, some miles from another graveyard where her great-grandparents were buried. Decades earlier, she'd purchased a plot at the Rose Hill Cemetery for this purpose.

When Grandpa Bob had her cremated the day she died, I figured we'd bury the box of ashes in her Boise plot at some point. But no such plan was mentioned at the funeral or after the potluck dinner at the house. Not brought up again. My sisters sometimes reported to me by telephone about furniture gone missing, china disappeared from the cupboards, books packed in boxes and hauled off to who knows where— taken by cousins, or friends of the family, or anyone who dropped by with room on their truck bed. We got plenty worked up about the disregarded will, but most of our worry was focused on our grandmother's remains. And yet we did nothing about them.

Now here I was in Salmon again. This was my chance to set things right.

My father was bumping back down the frozen gravel of the cemetery road toward his childhood home when I leaned forward from the back seat, where I was wedged between my daughters, and asked him about my grandmother's ashes. He's the one who brought her up, after all, and I figured that gave me an opening. But without turning his head from the road, he waved a leather-gloved hand in front of my face. "Keep me out of it," he said. "Ask your grandpa what he wants to do, don't ask me."

I sat back, considering this directive to go straight to Grandpa Bob. Besides chitchat about my kids and job and such, I hadn't had a serious conversation with him. Wait: had I ever had a serious conversation with him? I couldn't remember one. Not in my whole life. Mostly I avoided direct contact with my grandfather, largely due, I think now, to a deep-down suspicion that I was in his way, that I'd been in his way since the day of my birth. Anything I had to convey to him in the past, if there'd even been news or information, had gone through Grandma Lois or my brother. I wasn't even sure talking to me was something he would put up with after my long time away from Salmon.

As far as the grandchildren go, I'd known Grandpa Bob the longest. But it was the men in my family who *knew* him—my father, my uncle, my brother. Ron moved back to Salmon when he finished college and learned how to weld from our grandfather, as he had earlier learned to hunt, to raft, to fish, to repair a tractor, to mix a drink from our grandfather.

Whatever I took in about Grandpa Bob was through distant observation, and through stories. His mostly, but also my grandmother's. She told me plenty of tales, though only once in a rare moment of vulnerability near the time of her death did she talk about Baby Girl, how Grandpa Bob was the one who'd taken the dead child from the delivery room while she, Grandma Lois, was still unconscious from a dose of ether; how he later informed his wife that they would not speak of it again. They didn't, and, because she'd not seen her stillborn infant, Lois believed the baby had been offered up to another family, a different woman—for what reason she couldn't say. Sometimes she'd spot a girl on the street and convince herself that this was her daughter because of the red highlights of her hair or the shape of her nose. It wasn't until Hazel died and Lois went up to the family section of the cemetery that she knew, for the first time, that there was a grave for her child who would have been in her mid-twenties then. Her daughter who was dead.

I went along with the other grandchildren when Grandpa Bob drove out into the sagebrush hills to feed his horses, though I wasn't fond of horses. I didn't like riding them, I didn't much like their smell or the way they swished their tails to keep the flies away, I didn't like setting one of his apples in my palm for a horse to lip off my hand, mostly because I preferred keeping my fingers. I wanted to like every bit of what he offered, but I couldn't seem to snap into the regular things of my family no matter how I tried. What I did like was watching my grandpa lean against a barbed-wire fence, a bucket of oats at his feet and a cowboy hat low across his eyes, his buckskin-gloved fingers gripping a post. He'd make a sound, a low-throated whistle, that I could barely hear even when standing a few feet away over by his Scout. Within a couple minutes there'd come the rustle of brush and the sound of April or Amber's snorts and whinnies—their antiphonal call. *We're coming.* Crow ambled in after the two females. These horses had the entire hillside to roam, but they somehow understood to get back to this one straggly portion of fence line when Grandpa showed up and made his sound. He lifted the bucket to give each a mouthful and ran his hand down their long, smooth necks.

What was it about my grandfather that he elicited such awe? What was it about him that he could do no wrong?

Grandma Lois didn't care all that much for horses either. She tolerated hunting camp, and even pushed her way in a few times. She appreciated the stores of meat brought to her every autumn. She put up with basketball, probably because she loved the noisy gathering of young people out on the concrete slab next to her house. She saved a few dollars from each Salmon High School teacher paycheck so she could get to London once a decade or so to see a genuine Shakespeare play. When money was tight she drove over to Oregon for that year's *Richard IV* or *As You Like It*; too few dollars for even that trip, she'd lecture us with *Hamlet* or *Macbeth* soliloquies or tell one of us to run and find a volume of verse so she could read a poem aloud, her many chins and the flabby skin on her upper arms trembling through the recitation. She introduced me to the Beatles, a band my young parents had no use for, and to Herman Hermit's "Mother-in-Law," which she played on her hi-fi at top volume while my sisters and I hopped from one end of the living room to the other in our bare feet, avoiding cats that slithered through the house. How she'd hooked up with my grandfather, whose fingers were a stubborn black from years at the hot welding torch, and who spent his evenings reading Zane Grey and Louis L'Amour in his reclining chair in the den, I couldn't imagine.

Yet I do imagine. Here was Lois in the early 1930s, with her brown waved hair and browner eyes, setting up her spanking-new appliances at Gwartney Equipment, in the back of which

Bob ran his welding business. For the week she was in town, this darkly handsome young man—smoldering, I'd say—sat in on each of her morning sessions about the ease of doing laundry (while his mother scowled from the far end of the shop, unhappy about newfangled washing equipment and unhappier still about the flirtation), and Lois pretended not to notice.

Lois's grandfather was John Case, he who'd bought tracts of land in what became Boise City. He started a mercantile there and soon a hotel. Later on he built a mansion and filled it with furniture from Asia and Europe. By the time Lois was born, John Case was dead and a new husband (the doctor who'd attended Case's death and who'd married up the widow lickety-split) had gambled away the family's fortune. Even when the coffers were nearly empty, shop and hotel long ago sold, the women kept up the big hats and fine dresses, whatever travel they could manage. Until the crash. Lois lost her teaching job when the high school shut down, and she left her mother and grandmother in a home that covered a square block, now a crowded boardinghouse. She went on the road in a pickup truck with the washing machine strapped in the back, trying to keep at least a few dollars coming in.

When Grandma Lois returned to Boise, after her sales trip to Salmon, to Idaho Falls, to Mountain Home, she found a letter from Bob proposing marriage, and a few days later she accepted. Who can guess why? Why he asked, why she said yes. Except that the mismatch may have struck them both as exotic, a romantic preoccupation when everything else in those days fell under the heading of hard times and endurance. On their honeymoon night in the hotel in downtown Salmon, Bob admitted that though he'd claimed to be her age, twenty-five, he was actually not yet twenty. Lois had married a boy, and as far as family lore went—as far as my own personal lore went—she spent the rest of her life regretting it.

By the time I came along, my grandparents' lives were as separate as their living room: One half was decorated with the last of the Rawls family pieces, carved trunks and golden statues, the French purple velvet fainting couch we weren't to touch with sticky fingers and dirty feet (though she let me stretch out there once to read *Lord of the Flies* in a single afternoon). The other half of the room was filled with Charles Russell prints my grandfather had framed with barn wood, and on the wall was a set of six point buck antlers draped with beaded necklaces from the Shoshone.

Now, on a Thanksgiving Day after her death, the living room had become Grandpa's own—the velvet couch gone, the trunks and statues and the wind-up bird in its cage disappeared. Most of the books sold. He'd moved his recliner in from the den and bought a larger-screen television, arranged under the dusty antlers and the final strings of the dustier beads. This room is where I found him when we came in from our trip to the cemetery. I sat on the footstool next to the rocking chair he'd settled in, near the crackling wood stove, knitted blanket over his lap, football game roaring in the background. I told him we'd made it to the top of the slick road and had a look at the family graves. He leaned in so he could hear me, nodding to urge me on. Once he was close, I decided to blurt out my questions: about the ashes, about his intention for them.

"By golly, I haven't thought too much about it," he said, sitting up straight, his furry eyebrows popping halfway up his forehead. "Did she tell anybody what she wanted?"

My grandfather was eighty-four years old on this day and possibly forgetful, but I also detected a coyness that made no sense to me. Except, maybe he was telling the truth. Could it have been that while we were whispering our disappointment, no one had told him that Grandma wanted to be buried in Boise?

I looked around, suddenly afraid that my father was close, ready to pounce on me for upsetting my grandfather. I'd been sure for all these years that Grandpa Bob was keeping his wife's ashes in his room out of spite, or stubbornness, or as a sign of power over her. I'd rolled into town partly to be her defender, her protector, but now I wondered: Protector against what? Maybe he'd simply neglected to read her yellow legal-pad papers and no one had suggested he should.

"We could sprinkle them at hunting camp," Grandpa said. "No," I said quietly, and then I explained the details of her burial plot in Boise, how she'd written out that this was where she wanted to be. He sat back in his rocking chair, and after several seconds I suspected our conversation was over, that I'd crossed a line with him. I'd started to get up, to skitter away, when he said, "I'll go ask her." He pulled himself to his feet to hobble to his bedroom at the back of the house.

Maybe five minutes later he returned to the living room with a plain black box in the splay of his bent fingers. "She's ready to go," he said, and he handed me the container, which was lighter and smaller than I'd expected. And the moment the wood surface of the box was set in my hand something burst in me like a boil—I rocked back on my heels. Suddenly I wanted to leave things be, to be the defender of no one. Not the trouble-maker others talked about, complained about. I wanted to shove the box back to him and say, *Forget it.* I should have kept my mouth shut.

The last conversation I had with Grandma Lois before her death was a brief one by telephone. By then I'd heard about my grandfather's other woman, who lived on the other side of the valley. They'd chosen not to divorce their spouses, he and she, but they did not keep secret their desire to be together. I was surprised my grandmother had put up with this other wife—somewhere in those three decades, she had to have found out that her husband had wound his life with another's. Grandma had her own money, her own profession—she could have moved back to Boise and started over. I couldn't understand why she hadn't.

When she called that last time, my grandmother had my marriage on her mind, not hers. She reached me in Tucson, where I was going to graduate school, to talk about my recent separation from my husband—a fact I'd tried to keep from her until I'd sorted out an explanation of why we were splitting up, as if the complexity of that decision (let's start with four children under the age of ten) could be boiled down to a few simple words. Apparently a relative had blabbed, a sister, a cousin, and now on the phone Grandma Lois flat-out told me to pack up my kids, turn the keys to the apartment I'd rented in to the landlord, and go back home.

"Things aren't so good there, Grandma," I said.

"Who said they were going to be good?" she said. "Nobody promised good. But you promised to stick it out, and that's what you'll do."

I hung up and went back to my sole occupation: getting out of the marriage and moving several states away with my children. To hell with my grandmother if she couldn't get behind me. What did an old woman know about the troubles of modern marriage?

After the call I was furious, shaking with anger, and then I was sad. Grandma Lois was often difficult, consistently loud, a tempest at times, critical to the max, and yet she was also high,

high up on my list of those I adored. She had given me books and music; she encouraged ideas. My ideas. She threw back her head and laughed with utter joy when she was joyful. She'd introduced me to books, so many books, and she showed me *The Reluctant Dragon*, a brief animated film that helped me shape my sense of the world, truly. Yet, the phone call was as harsh as any conversation I'd had with her, as if the institution of marriage was all that mattered, the people in it just its pawns. She refused to hear my side of things.

Sitting in Salmon with the ashes in my hands, her name typed on a label on top, my bones ached from squabbles with the husband from whom I was now separated, from the damage being done to my children, from the knot hardened in me since I'd decided to end a no-good marriage. Maybe there was something to be said about hanging in if you can. I couldn't. I wouldn't. My grandparents were the inverse of that conviction. They'd cooked at least some small strain of peace between them for fifty-plus years and did not let it go. What was it I thought I knew better than them? Than her?

Before he put the ashes in my hands, my grandfather said a few words about *The Price is Right* on television. Lois was a fan, he told me, so he turned the show on every morning and set the box in front of the screen so she could watch Bob Barker. It hadn't occurred to me until his story that maybe he liked having her ashes in his room. It hadn't occurred to me that he might miss her, even if he did have a true love on the far side of the valley. What weighed on me now was stepping into a situation that was flat-out beyond my ability to manage. I'd taken time off work, spent a good portion of savings to get to Salmon that Thanksgiving to insist things be made right. But what was right?

Saturday morning, as we got ready to head back to my father's house in Boise, I was weary from worry, which increased by some measure when I noticed my father was stiffer than usual, snapping at this person and that. I made sure the girls stayed at a steady clip while putting their things in the bed of the truck, and I looked around to make sure we cleaned up our messes in the house. But it wasn't clutter or timing that bothered him. I found out what was frying a blister in my father when I began to climb back to the pinched jump seat with the box of ashes tucked in one arm. "Those aren't going in my truck," he said.

"What do you mean?" I asked him.

"I mean what I said."

I didn't argue with my father or remind him of his statement the day before about keeping him out of things; I just stood on the sleety sidewalk with my jacket zipped up to my neck and the box in my hands, not knowing what to do. There was no other option for getting to Boise, and I wasn't about to head into the house at this point and return the ashes to my grandfather—that seemed worse than pushing on. In some flimsy way, I still felt I must act on behalf of my grandmother.

"Here, give them to me." It was my father's wife's voice; she was speaking from the truck bed where she'd been arranging luggage. Since Grandma Lois had pretty much despised the woman, I didn't think I should hand the container over, so I climbed into the bed as she opened the truck's built-in toolbox. She moved aside a few wrenches and a tire iron, and I put the ashes in the cleared space. The two of us packed tools around to prevent slippage, our white breath mingling in the air, and my father—who might have been watching and who was most certainly taking account of what we were doing—didn't object. So I assumed, with some measure of exhaustion and resignation, that he could live with it.

That evening, Ron and Cindy brought their families over to

our father's house a short distance outside Boise so we could see each other before my two daughters and I left for Oregon the next morning. We'd had a couple of cocktails, and my father was settled in his leather recliner, half watching a football game. He hadn't spoken to me the entire six-hour drive back from Salmon. Not a word. Now he hardly rustled in his chair when Ron brought up the idea of a raft trip—wasn't it time, my brother said, that we did it again? I recoiled at his suggestion, though a small voice in me wondered what it might mean: a trip down the Salmon that I would help put together, that I'd figure out how to make my own. Possibility turned and looked straight at me, bumped against my shoulder. *How about it?*

The booze and the family hum had loosened me up. Made me braver than usual. First, I half agreed to a river trip in the future and then mentioned, under my breath, that I'd brought Grandma Lois's ashes back from Salmon. That one sentence out of my mouth, mild though it was, propelled my father to his feet. He stood in front of me and suddenly he was shouting; his hands were fists. I slipped halfway behind my equally stunned sister as our father gave me what he thought I deserved, what in retrospect I might have deserved. It's not like I hadn't shouted the same words at myself all day: Who did I think I was, he said, to talk my grandfather out of that box? If Grandpa Bob had wanted to bury the ashes in Boise, he would have done it. I had no right to horn in on something that had nothing to do with me.

My father finished with his yelling as fast as he'd begun. He returned to his game and his drink, and I slipped out the back door into the chilled, still night. Horses whinnied over from the far pasture, including Grandpa's old Crow, and the faint sounds of laughter and clinking dishes sifted through a square of bright window. I counted up the hours—eleven—until Mary and Mollie and I would be in an airplane on the way to my own house, my own bed, my own way of being in the world, where I didn't have to explain myself to anybody, even myself.

I'd tried to be my grandmother's self-appointed defender. Now I think I did so because I had so little idea how to defend who I'd become to my family. I couldn't explain my choices to my father, my grandfather, to any of them. And anyway, if Grandma Lois could have chosen among family for her champion, would she have landed on wobbly me? Probably not. No more than Narcissa Whitman would have tagged me to tell her story—in fact, it would have struck our missionary friend as a ridiculous notion for me to be her spokesperson. An outrageous proposal. What could I know about what she did and why she did it? But back to my grandmother: It dawns on me now that she actually had made herself right with her Salmon life, her marriage, her home and profession. It's a balance she sought constantly, some days more successful than others. Who was I to say she should have wanted more than what she was given?

Any writhing in that regard belonged to me.

I stepped back into my father's Boise house and asked Ron to meet me in the garage. In the over-bright light, I asked my brother if he'd take the ashes. When he shrugged and said he guessed he would, I moved our grandmother's box from the toolbox in my dad's truck to the front seat of my brother's truck, and I went inside to pack.

After that night—decades have passed—I've done nothing about burying my grandma. None of us have discussed the ashes. Except once. I brought them up with my brother one time, and he laughed, crossed his arms as he does, and said his wife had recently named him the ultimate redneck because he had "an elk rack in my living room, a shotgun in my truck, and my grandmother's ashes in my closet."

I laughed along with him, but the joke was a drop of acid on my tongue. I remember how determined I'd been that year driving to Salmon, ready to do what I had to do to give my grandmother the honor, the respect, she was due. Somehow I'd managed only to make it worse.

# 3

I suppose that by the last time I went to Waiilatpu—which happened to be on a hot summer day—I was touting myself as an authority in the field of Narcissa Whitman. I'd been to the site of her death many times. I'd watched the film, wandered through the exhibit hall in the visitors' center. I'd read dozens of books and articles about this First Woman of the West and had published my own essays about her. I'd touched her hair.

I figured that, at this point, I probably knew her better than just about anyone else alive.

Not long before this visit I'd received another letter in the mail, this one from a stranger who told me that her mother, and her mother's sisters, had once played with what she swore was "Narcissa's very trunk." *That* trunk. The one tossed off a cliff by an impatient husband and later rescued by a gallant witness. A simple wooden container that the letter writer's family was sure once held the missionary woman's most cherished possessions from her home in upstate New York, including her "please the savages" dresses.

The letter writer said the trunk had belonged to her mother's grandmother, whose parents had supposedly procured it from one of the surviving Sager sisters, and she also added that at one point the family had a letter proving this was all true. A letter that had been, for at least a generation, missing.

I read the note she'd sent to me, aching for the trunk

business to be real. But how could it be? It was impossible to believe that either Catharine or Elizabeth had hauled the long-ago gift from sister Harriet away from the mission on their final night, during the clandestine under-the-cover-of-darkness escape, especially since Catharine carried the coffee pot and Elizabeth, I'm guessing, carried the toddler. Highly doubtful that the trunk made it out, but the letter writer insisted it had, and she wrote that she'd recently done the right thing by history: she'd crated it up and shipped it to the mission. The end of the letter expressed dismay about having heard nothing from the archivists. She'd expected an acknowledgement, a call thanking her profusely, a squeal of delight over such a rare artifact related to the Whitmans. Now she urged me to go to the mission and see it for myself—Narcissa's precious trunk.

The visitor's center, sparsely visited, is one of those rich-with-antiquity spots located in an out-of-the-way field, this one appointed with a brown, carved sign: WAII-LAT-POO. It's easy to picture people centuries ago living a good life on such wide-open land. A visitor can also wander around the interior display room and peer through smudged glass to study items excavated from the site, some of which belonged to Narcissa and/or to Marcus—a pair of broken eyeglasses that might have been his (not hers—I have to rub it in one last time). A few chipped plates and cups. This and that tool. A torn Bible. In the middle of the room a set of mannequins enacts the first encounter between Cayuse and missionaries. On one side a tall man and woman—her knees bent as if in prayer, her long arms stretched out, palms raised in supplication—who look down on small, brown Native women on the other side. Most of the Native women are kneeling in the dirt, planting seeds (I suppose this is the idea) with woven reed hats atop their heads.

Every time I take in this scene, I find myself wishing that both sides had remained exactly this far apart for the decade they were around each other. Curious about each other, but protected from whatever harm they could inflict.

Back to the display room; it holds many Whitman items, but nothing, to my mind, with the weighty importance of the trunk. At least I've spotted nothing there as revealing of the couple's overland journey and their time at Waiilatpu as this, Narcissa's box hauled all the way from home. I couldn't wait to set my hands on it and, if I could legitimately do so, announce it to the world as hers.

The young ranger who met me at the mission, whose name was Ben, led me through a skinny hallway at the back of the visitor's center building, past office-like cubicles that felt curiously out of place—Ikea modern rather than nineteenth-century traditional—and into a small room crowded with metal shelves. On a table in the middle of this stuffy room, a table that left Ben and me practically no room to maneuver or even comfortably stand, was the trunk in question, and right away he began to tell me why it could not possibly have belonged to Narcissa. His affect was pancake flat, as if he were reading a press release to a room of bored reporters. Ben pointed out faded nursery-rhyme-themed decals that had been pasted to the interior of the lid, overly modern for Narcissa's times. *Couldn't they have been added later?* He showed me the hinges, early twentieth-century style and definitely not from the early 1800s. *What if the first ones wore out?* The wood, the shape of the trunk, the screws and nails holding it together, none of those pointed to the year 1834, when Harriet Prentiss either purchased the trunk for her sister or had it made by a craftsman in Prattsburg. "But what if . . ." I said, reminding him that, after all, the trunk had taken a Marcus-propelled dive off a cliff at some point and likely needed repair, but the stern look on this young ranger's face shut me down: experts had checked it out. This was not Narcissa's trunk. There was nothing I could say that would make it otherwise.

I'd speculated about Ben's age. Around nineteen, based on his doughy skin and mop of hair but mostly on his pants sagging to the bottom of his hips, held in place (sort of) by a belt so that his boxer shorts bloomed from under a regulation button-down shirt in a muddy shade of brown. I amended the nineteen guess to early twenties after he shyly mentioned, on our way back down the hallway and out to the main room of the visitor's center (my trunk hopes dashed, and me crushed—I'd set my sights on being *the one* to unearth a newly discovered Narcissa relic), that he'd recently returned from the Congo, where he'd served in the Peace Corps. He described a grant he'd been awarded, funds to transform a program he'd developed in Africa into one suitable for Waiilatpu, and, by the by, he said, at 1:00 p.m. on the nose he'd be leading a tour, the premier of his presentation, that would encourage visitors here at Waiilatpu to "walk a mile in the other's shoes." Would I like to go along?

I glanced at my phone. It was 12:40. My only plan for the afternoon was to watch for a second time the revised film—it showed several times a day and at last included a Cayuse perspective, interviews with tribal elders and a context that made the tribe finally matter—and then I wanted to walk through an art exhibit at the hotel whose subjects were Narcissa and Marcus. I'd looked over the paintings a year earlier and found them garish and ghoulish—as if Cayuse and Whitman faces were carved out of soap, fake pink and faker orange, and clumsily pasted to thick paper—but I felt I had to go back to study this so-called art again. (When my husband and I were checking in at the Marcus Whitman Hotel a day earlier I'd asked the young clerk about the name: *Who was that man?*, pointing to the inn's title. She didn't even look up. "I'm not sure," she muttered, "some kind of minister?")

I'd arranged to meet back up with my husband at the end of his own workday, so Ben's program might be a squeeze— but I decided to go for it. I was the first to sign up. I had far more knowledge of Narcissa than this young man in front of me, or so I applauded myself, but why not find out what his thing was about? His Congo-Waiilatpu connection, whatever he'd hatched it to be.

Ben led me to the starting point, and we waited in tree-dappled sun for other tourists, stepping under an awning in an attempt to stay cool, though I itched and sweated under the thick overhang of oak and maple trees surrounding the building. I looked out on fields of tall grasses, reeds, and bulrushes— an effort, Ben explained, to restore at least some parts of the mission site to its original ecosystem. I nodded at him, my own thoughts brimming. *I could tell him a thing or two about the grasses.* But I stayed quiet. I watched the wind rustle the tips of the purple-green foliage and wondered about Waiilatpu as it once was. Pre-plow. Pre-wheat crops. Pre-Marcus.

At 1:00 p.m. on the nose Ben suggested we give it another ten minutes, in case people were still making their way over, and I managed a wan smile and then sweated some more, taking swigs from my water bottle. I figured it was best not to mention that so far that day I'd been the sole visitor to the mission.

"Hey," I said instead of griping about the heat like I wanted to, "could I ask you something?" When he flinched as if to agree, I went on: "How do you pronounce the name? You know, the word that means 'place of the ryegrass people.'"

Ben said it, *Waiilatpu*, that long word with its tidy collection of vowels and bilabial consonant, a word I had seen in books and journals and typed out dozens if not hundreds of times. He said it again, a retry, this time without a zing of authority, more like a droopy stab at a mangled foreign term, and I was sorry I'd asked. My regret had to do with, well—why would this kid pronounce the word better than anyone else? And also, I didn't want to give him any reason to believe that I didn't know *everything*, that I wasn't steeped in Whitman history to my eyeballs, meaning that he should pick up on the fact that I was actually more suited to decipher what had happened in this place a long time ago. He should have asked me how to sound out the name of the mission.

A less-than-charitable treatment of this young guy just starting out in his historical-site career. I might as well have been sneering at him: *I know more than you do.* And I remember that's what I'd decided—that I knew more than he did—when young Ben jerked his chin at me, resigned to his single customer, and the two of us set off alone.

The idea of his project, I soon learned, was to provide the person visiting Waiilatpu, the location of past discord, a sense of both sides of the roiling dispute. Whitmans versus Cayuse.

*Imagine you are the mother of a family traveling on the Oregon Trail, pulling into the mission after months of an exhausting trip through hostile territory; your food is gone and your children are sick.* Ben gave me a moment to become this unfortunate soul as we walked on in silence. *Now imagine now that you are the mother of a Cayuse family whose children have died, watching as more settlers arrive at the Whitman Station, demanding food and care and eager to take land that has historically belonged to your people.*

Okay, I got it. Five minutes was more than I needed of the relating-to-each-side he was after, Ben's effort to transform an extraordinarily complex story into history-lite, suitable for a tourist from Kansas or Illinois who'd stride back to his car at the end like he'd actually learned something.

I walked alongside my guide as we shuffled through hot, dry grass, breaking in with questions that had nothing to do with Ben's presentation. I did it to rattle him. I had most of the answers, but I asked anyway. *Where was the Cayuse camp exactly? Has anyone ever found Alice's grave?* (I knew no one had.) *How about Louisa's or Helen Mar's?* (Ditto.) We walked past the location of the second Whitman home, the house set away from the river with an attached schoolroom. The only sign of the house these days are white lines painted in perfectly groomed grass, irrigated to a sheen, that remind me of those around the dead bodies on *Law and Order*. We stopped in front of the house site, where Ben began asking me to imagine myself as one of the Sager children standing at the window as the men in the center of the courtyard—butchering that steer—were killed one after the other. I interrupted again. *Where was the side door of the house? I mean the one that Andrew Rodgers came out of, carrying Narcissa on the settee, you know, just before she was shot?* I lathered on the details so Ben was reminded again of my full command of all things Whitman.

This time he stopped and turned toward me. He stared hard. I noticed annoyance on his face, and also some measure of woundedness. "I've allotted time at the end for questions," he said. "If you could let me get through the program. It has a particular order."

I shut my mouth.

I was more than twice his age. Old enough to be his mother. But for some reason I needed to compete with him, as if I were outdoing the boy on a TV history quiz. I ground my teeth together and did my best to listen to a young man who had his own story to tell about Narcissa. Different than mine, different than any of the others. Ben's version of the tale of Waiilatpu, which he had no interest in amending.

Any more than I was interested in amending mine.

I slunk back to my car at the end, pushing away thoughts of Ben and the trunk that wasn't to be, forgoing the viewing of the film, forgetting already this bust of a visit to Waiilatpu.

I also decided to skip the ridiculous art. So what if there was a display of Whitman hagiography up in the old hotel, the Cayuse painted as bloodthirsty demons and buffoons? What would be satisfied in me to stand in judgment, again, of an artist who'd been paid handsomely by the city fathers to chronicle exactly this take on the Whitmans' story? A modern-day reassurance to visitors that white people were *in the right*.

Better to pause in the center of Walla Walla, about eight miles from the Whitman mission, and read again a plaque in the community square that recognizes a treaty formed in 1855. "The sovereign nations of Walla Walla, Umatilla, and Cayuse secured a reservation of 510,000 acres in northwestern Oregon," it states. Though from the beginning, the Confederated Warm Springs Reservation encompassed only 245,000 acres, a miscalculation chocked up in the 1800s to a "surveyor's error."

At least two Cayuse chiefs were among the tribal leaders who'd appeared on this very Walla Walla corner to negotiate the treaty in 1855. One of those was Stickus, the last Cayuse man to engage in friendly discourse with Marcus Whitman before the latter's death. Stickus was also the Cayuse man who accompanied the Sager girls and other hostages down to the boats once Peter Ogden appeared and offered a means of escape. Stickus, a peacemaker to the end, and Five Crows, too, both chiefs forced eight years after the attack—no way around it—to sign a treaty giving up millions of acres of their ancestral land to white settlement. Under the 1855 treaty the chiefs sacrificed the dwindling tribe's access to traditional hunting and fishing grounds in order to walk away with something, anything. But Stickus didn't go along happily. He's the one who spoke loudest to the new Territorial Governor, Isaac Stevens, in opposition: "If your mothers were here in this country who gave you birth, suckled you and while you were sucking some person came and took your mother and left you alone and sold your mother, how would you feel then?"

I arrived at the hotel after my visit to Waiilatpu, the mission where I'd behaved like an ass, and walked through the lobby of a hotel whose fancy appointments would have infuriated Marcus and Narcissa both. No glory to God in the thick drapes or the sparkling chandeliers, not to mention the scrumptious duck breast with morels served in the restaurant (I ordered it twice). I made my way to our room and stepped into the shower to wash off the heat of the day, the confusion of the day, the jumble inside of me now about my objective with Narcissa's story. It would still take me a while to admit how I'd made her a character of my own creation. Entirely. I'd put thoughts in her head. I'd ascribed motivation, intention. I'd even concocted her voice, the hardness in her when she spoke to the children in her care, the even harder hardness when she communicated with the Cayuse. I'd rarely allowed her to be real, a woman who'd suffered a crippling loneliness and who'd died alone. I'd endlessly criticized those who rewrote history to serve themselves, only to discover my own capacity for doing the same.

Days after this trip, when I was home at my desk again, I reread a letter that Rev. Henry Perkins wrote to Jane Prentiss after her sister's death. This is the man Narcissa stayed with, along with his wife, when Marcus was away defending the mission to the board, that time when Narcissa pulled herself from her darkest terror.

Perkins, who describes a real woman and not a myth, tells Jane that Narcissa was simply "out of her sphere" in the West, a person who could not adapt to her work with Native people and never would be able to. "The truth is," he wrote, "your lamented sister was far from happy in the situation she had chosen to occupy." She wanted "something exalted. . . . She longed for society, *refined* society." He went on: "She loved company, society, excitement & ought always to have enjoyed it. The self-denial that took her away from it was suicidal."

In one of her own letters home, Narcissa comes close to copping to the same: "I am entirely unfitted for the work, and have many gloomy, desponding hours." She ended that letter with this: "I find one of my most difficult studies is to know my own heart."

Yes, Narcissa. Me too.

Out of the shower in our room at the Marcus Whitman, I pooled lotion in my palm to rub on my legs. That's when I noticed, on one inner thigh, a black dot. I looked closer to see tiny legs wiggling from my skin. A tick. My husband had returned during my shower, and I called to him now. I moved over to the desk, bending my leg at an unlikely angle until it was directly under the lamplight. With a pair of tweezers, he plucked the tick out of me and held it close to the bulb so I could study it. Before I squished it dead, I turned it around, peering at all sides. A tick from Waiilatpu, sucking my blood. Set there by Narcissa, maybe—ha, wouldn't that be something. I could almost see her scowling in my direction: *There, woman. Exactly what you deserve.*

# 4

In the middle of one night, my sister Cindy called me at my home in Arizona to tell me that our father had been crushed by a horse. She meant what she said: most of his vertebral column had turned to rubble. A lung punctured, his spleen burst. Cindy told me our father probably wouldn't survive the surgery he'd been rushed into, that he was in the middle of as we spoke.

I pressed the phone to my ear.

Once I'd hung up I stood on the cool tile floor of our living room. I didn't switch on a lamp, as light might have made the news more fact than rumor. I leaned against an armchair and let myself feel forgotten by my father, already thinking more about myself than about him. It doesn't surprise me now that this was my response to news of his possible death nearly thirty years ago. After all, it was a familiar state for me. I'd often felt left alone in the dark, afraid to consider what it would mean to lose a father with whom I engage in maybe three or four conversations a year, a man I'd seemed to let down at most turns, and who I'd often suspected would have done better with his own prospects had I not been born.

After I hung up with Cindy, I stayed up the rest of the night, packing quietly so I didn't wake my daughters. In the morning I'd have to call the still-husband, the almost-ex, to come get the girls and care for them while I was away. I would seek no comfort from this man I'd been married to for twelve years. We were ground to nubs by then. We barely endured each other's presence for the sake of our kids. Maybe we were also lulled into an apathy that comes from waiting for the other one to actually say the words: it's over, done, finished. I stuffed a bag with clothes and books; I paced the kitchen and pinged the caps off bottles of beer, drinking in long swigs. I sent mind messages to my father, as if he could pick up my thoughts from hundreds of miles away. I asked him to stay alive until I got there and could sort things out with him. What there was to sort out, I wasn't quite sure, but it seemed like certain words should be said between us.

At least he could give me that.

At dawn I started phoning airlines (no internet then to help me make arrangements) to get my ticket to Boise, although when I spoke to my father's wife later in the morning, she encouraged me not to come. He'd survived the surgery, but he was unconscious and in rotten shape. What good could I do in Idaho? There was nothing now but the waiting. I told her that I certainly did not plan to sit by in Tucson, where we had moved so I could go to graduate school, and where my husband could live closer to his family. If I had to bide time for my father to resurface, if he *was* to resurface, I'd be in the ICU ward along with my two sisters and two brothers. Hovering.

My father, by the year of this accident when he was forty-eight, was doing fine. He'd climbed the corporate ladder and made the right investments. After divorcing my mother he'd married again right away. He divorced that second wife and married his third. Over those years, while he was between and with his wives, he'd invite me now and then to go along with him to an event, a bank board or a political meeting.

I'm tall and thin at one of those, dressed in my best skirt and top, my long, blonde hair pinned on my head. I lean against a wall with a glass of expensive red wine in my hand, not one to warm easily to a crowd of strangers, wishing I could be anywhere else besides here, with my father's people who I don't know and won't meet again. My father stands next to me, swirling his drink, when another man dressed in a strikingly similar suit saunters over and slaps my father on the back. They both laugh. *How the hell are you?* The other man notices me, raises an eyebrow. "Oh," my father says, as if he's just noticed me too. He explains that his wife couldn't come along and that he'd spotted me on the street outside the hotel. He nods in my direction, a jerk of an elbow. "I talked her into being my date." My face burns, my arms grow limp in that way when you feel undone, but I say nothing. This isn't a new trick he's pulling—it's one of my father's favorites. Meant, I guess, to throw off his business pals who've been let in on little of his personal life. My part is to appear irritated and to fidget and, after a pause—just long enough—to set forth the correction. "I'm his daughter," I say this time, laughing along with the men, though I find none of it funny. And yet I remember how I excoriated myself on the way home: *I'm thin-skinned, too thin-skinned to take a joke, to laugh it off, to remember this is simply my dad having a good time.*

I wonder how many times I've repeated the same line: *He doesn't mean anything by it.*

With midlife money, a new marriage, and plenty of friendships around the business of horses, my father decided to go back to territory that still had heft for him: on the weekends he'd be a rodeo cowboy. This sounded right to me. My father is a wonder on a horse. He and Grandpa Bob often ventured on weeks-long pack trips, deep enough in the Idaho wilderness that they saw not one other human being—days of riding in silence except for the squeak of saddles and the rustle of brush. That's my idea of their time out there, anyway. Horse hooves sparking off scrabbly rock as one man follows the other into a distant ravine. My father has a way of merely standing next to a horse that makes it behave, ears pricked for the rider's commands. I've seen him slide up on the saddle, one liquid movement, tick the reins in his hand, and ride away.

In the spring of the year of his accident, my father bought a large tract of land along the Boise River. He and a partner called the place Lonesome Dove because they were fans of the book, and they had a replica of the little town built, the Dry Bean Saloon, the Livery Emporium. In the center was a rodeo arena surrounded by shiny bleachers. Local rodeo groups, including one from the university, started holding competitions there at the spiffy new grounds. During the second rodeo—fortuitous, as the recently churned-up ground was not yet pounded hard as steel—my father volunteered to act as flagger for a cutting competition. It was never explained to me why he rode a strange horse that day rather than one of his own. I don't know what happened after he got on that horse, because my father hasn't recited an account of the day within my hearing. I doubt he's spoken about it to anyone. What I heard is that for whatever reason their heads collided, man and animal, and my father was knocked out, seeing stars, falling backward with the reins still tight around his arm, pulling the nine-hundred-pound horse on top of him.

It happened that a paramedic driving home had, an hour or so earlier, noticed the rodeo and turned in to watch the action out on the sawdust. A nice way to end his day, he figured. From the bleachers he watched my father's fall; he was the one up from his seat and hopping the fence by the time others had rolled the horse off its rider. The paramedic used CPR to get his heart restarted and later said that when my father opened his eyes he was muttering through sand and dust coating his forehead and cheeks, his lips and teeth. The paramedic leaned in close. "The truck keys are in my pocket," my father said, as if he were going to drive himself to the hospital, and then he went back under.

When I entered the room up in the ICU—way up, the top floor of the hospital, with windows that overlooked the parched valley—I found my father looking like a turkey stuffed for the oven. His body was a pale hue of raw meat; he was swollen into a mound. Tubes of various colors sprang from his skin and dripped into containers hanging from the rungs of the bed.

I stood over him that first afternoon, not all that certain he still had an eye under the glob of grape pudding between his nose and left ear. I thought about poking at his puffed flesh, oddly soft, nothing like the sinewy man I might recognize. But I didn't touch him. I wandered back into the dim hallway and met up with the doctor, who was scribbling notes on a chart. He seemed more delighted than concerned about my father's condition. It was as if the doc was complimenting us, actually, as in, *Hey, look here, your family's own remarkably true story of the West.* A story of blood-curdling excitement, of horses, of survival. A tale of the unsettled frontier at the tail end of the twentieth century. The doctor told me that he planned to cart X-rays around to medical conventions so others could get a load of this case. "You know, when he came in," the doctor told me, whispering as if this were gossip just between us, "he was folded in half the wrong way."

The difficulty for this surgeon, and for any medical facility in Idaho, was in deciding what to do next. When they'd opened my father up stem to stern—and he has the riverine scar down his back to prove it—the team of surgeons found only fragments, each vertebrae of his thoracic curve and several of the lumbar vertebrae turned to dust. The surgeons mopped up the mess around the exposed spinal cord, repaired the damaged organs as best they could, and sewed him together. This meant that our main job—my sisters, brothers, and me—was to make sure he didn't move, this man who rarely stopped moving. Cindy and I stayed over most nights, watching him sleep—if sleep is the right term for being that unplugged. Other than regularly punching the morphine button, though we'd been strictly warned to keep our hands off of it, we sat in chairs, watched bad TV, caught each other up, and we waited.

A week was what I felt I could spare: I had four children, classes, work. A marriage that, splintered as it was, had to break for good. A week should be enough to be certain my father was going to live. That was my plan, anyway. He might revive a bit; maybe he'd say a few words about being glad I was there. Even a couple of squeezes of the hand to let me know he was pleased by my presence. I'd take it. I settled in my chair, right next to his bed, reluctant to leave for even a little while in case any of those things happened.

In the hospital my siblings and I—who didn't see each other all that often anymore—started telling stories about our childhood because, I think, the memories allowed us to believe that we'd been a family once upon a time. Ron talked about the night he drove our dad's new Audi into a ditch, Cindy about sneaking out of our bedroom window to meet up with her high school boyfriend, who was now her husband, and I told about a few Saturday nights driving our old Volkswagen van down windy roads, heading home from a kegger in the hills, too drunk to be at the wheels of the bobbing, weaving billboard of a vehicle, which just might have flipped right into the river. I sucked on Lemonheads, as did the friends with me. We passed Lemonheads out by the handfuls. We'd heard somewhere that enough of the candy would let you pass a breathalyzer test.

This chatting about the old days: it was like running into someone on the street who you once knew, studying his face, the slope of the mouth, for some hint of recognition. *Didn't we live together in a big brown ranch house a long time ago? Weren't we the ones who ate Sunday-night tacos and jumped the fence to swim in the neighbor's pool? Didn't we play One-on-One in the driveway, hide boda bags of Annie Green Springs in the garage, ride bikes down the canal road with our hair streaming?*

Whether our father heard these versions of the past, I don't know. He wouldn't have said one way or another. He's too tough for sentiment. I get it. He doesn't talk things over or out or around or through. Years after we were all rescued from the Salmon River, our father's second wife—who'd been in the yellow raft that day—told me that as soon as our belongings came bobbing along in the current, our flip-flops and hats and the floating cooler, our father insisted that Grandpa Bob let him off on a nearby bank. He spent hours, or so I've heard, bushwhacking the edges of the river and its tributaries, backtracking in our direction, pushing in toward the water wherever he could while calling our names, looking for evidence of any of us, dead or alive. I have no idea how many miles he covered, no idea how he eventually got back to Salmon. No idea if he was hurt, afraid, exhausted, spent. He's not once spoken of it. And until he stood in the doorway of the kitchen to say, *Get the hell out of here,* I hadn't thought to ask where he was that day.

Now he'd had an accident. He was the one who was disassembled. Broken bones and torn flesh, parts gone for good.

Which parts? Was it only bone and blood and tissue gone missing, or was the essence of him changed too? I was determined to wait, as long as I could, to find out.

The third day of our hospital vigil he began a kind of muttering none of us could make out. I got up to bend close enough that his drug-laden breath was sticky on my face. I noticed gray grit in his hair from the fall, a bruised earlobe. I'd not seen my father in a vulnerable state like this, not ever, and I pulled the sheet up around his neck so the lacerations around his stubbly chin were hidden. Then I leaned closer to hear what he was saying. He asked me why we'd tied him to a tree, why we'd left him there to die. He flinched, as if a rope had tightened across his arms and chest. *Get it over with*, he said. *Hurry up about it.* I stood and punched the button twice to flush him with what he'd later call his feel-good juice. I punched it two more times to make sure the machine got the message. I didn't call out soothing words or rub my father's shoulder in comfort. I just wanted to stop this kind of talk. I hadn't been lingering near his bedside to hear him give up.

The third afternoon is also when my grandfather arrived. I don't remember that Grandpa Bob said anything to the rest of us in the room, although he must have. What our grandfather did was pull a chair up to his son's bed. He didn't read or watch sports; he simply sipped coffee from a Styrofoam cup and sat there, a man who objected mightily to the sitters of the world. He wore a buckskin vest made by Camille George. Hand-beaded red vines decorated the front panels, and she'd used cross-sections of antler for the buttons. The next time I saw that vest was twenty-two years later—my father wore it on the day we spread Grandpa's ashes at hunting camp. On this day in the hospital, Grandpa Bob crossed his legs, wagged his boot, drank more of that weak coffee, and now and again reached over to pull a wire away from my father's face. He didn't appear particularly worried or sad, nor did he beg my father for a reaction to his presence or seem to expect much of anything. He was there, that was all, and I envied his calm, his acceptance of whatever, which I could not manage to find in myself.

On the sixth day our grandfather, having been assured that his son would make it just fine, packed up and returned to Salmon. I felt released too, as if whatever bubble we'd been surviving in had finally burst. I needed a hot shower, a few glasses of wine, and a walk, so I left the hospital and went to my sister's house. Cindy and I sat in her backyard, two mothers with small children who probably weren't as well acquainted as we should have been—our respective friends knew us better than we knew each other. We started out a little stiff, chatting about our kids. I didn't mention the end of my marriage to this sister whose own marriage was considered ideal by the family, as stable as any—a certainty among us that she and her husband would stay together until they were done on the earth. I wasn't about to admit to her that I'd do just about anything to get out of mine while I was still young enough to start again.

We sipped at gin and tonics, tart with lime, while chicken marinated in the kitchen. I was more exhausted than I could remember being, my skin creeping with guilt about being away from my daughters. I needed to go home, soon. I was saying something about that when Cindy jumped up to answer the phone. She came back to say it had been our youngest sister. "What happened?" I said, and Cindy told me that our father had, in our absence, perked up. He'd opened his good eye, looked over the room, asked for water. In past days he'd been having trouble figuring out who was around him, but now he recognized Rebecca, calling her by name. "I guess he started talking about all kinds of things," Cindy said, rubbing her face before she took another sip. "And, you're not going to believe this, but he said that he loved her."

Love? No. That wasn't a word our father used. He hadn't said it to me, anyway. Not on the day of my wedding. Not when my first child was born or any of the subsequent daughters. Not after I'd been pulled out of a river that seemed determined to swallow me whole. I do recall a letter he wrote us while he was away studying at Harvard—he went there when I was thirteen and he was twenty-nine—that was signed, "Love, Dad." We'd passed around the page of writing back then, examining that word that was not his way. But this? *Love* said out loud to our sister? I was stunned, and not in the way I could have predicted. It wasn't gratitude that filled me, not a relief that our remade father was one who loved us and could say so. Instead I had a sudden impulse to borrow Cindy's car and race back to the rodeo grounds, to scrounge in the sawdust until I found the missing pieces of my father's vertebrae like teeth lost in the dirt, to hand them off to the surgeon so he could rebuild exactly the man he'd been to me since I was born, the sixteen-year-old who snapped the bottoms of my feet to keep me awake long enough to eat, who told me from my first day to, in essence, buck up, to breathe, to look around, to *live*.

Cindy and I were quiet for a few seconds. "Are you sure?" I said. "Maybe she didn't hear him right?"

My sister shrugged and got up to check the chicken in her oven. She stopped in the doorway and turned toward me. "You think this is going to change him," she said, "but it's not."

I couldn't have explained my muddled mind to her or, actually, to myself. For reasons I'd be sorting out for years, I suddenly couldn't bear the thought that our father would be anyone but who he'd always been.

I ended up being the only one in my father's room on my last night in Boise. I don't think I twisted arms to get the time with him, though I probably hinted that I ought to have a shot at his sudden rush of affection, too, wary as I was of that very thing. I was topsy-turvy about it after a night of thinking the matter over. Maybe it would be a good thing, after all, to hear my dad express affection. *Love.* Cindy lived in town, she'd have other chances to hear it, and Rebecca had gotten what she came for. Well, she'd gotten what I'd come for. Or what I thought I'd come for. That Friday evening before my Saturday morning flight, I had no idea what would satisfy or settle me.

I coaxed my father to eat a few bites of Jell-O and scooted the sheepskin under his back. He asked about my children and what was happening with the marriage, and I mumbled a few words about our current state of erosion. He sipped water from a straw, and I wiped up the dribbles on his chin, and then he opened his mouth as if he were going to offer advice. I pushed back in my chair, already resisting whatever plan he was about to propose. He'd given me that rescue check for attorney's fees some months earlier, and now I was afraid he was going to tell me to go home and get the lawyer to finalize the damn deal. I didn't know how to say that on this one, I needed to take my own time.

Before he could say anything about my disaster of a life, I picked up the remote and rushed to find him a movie on TV, and miraculously I came upon an old John Wayne film that he could slide in and out of without losing track of any plot.

"You know what I'd like?" my father said then, distracted enough from topics related to me that I could breathe again. "A cup of hot chocolate. That sounds like about the best thing right now."

"I'll find you one," I said, thrilled by the request. So direct, so unfraught. I grabbed my purse and hurried down the hall. The nurse at the station thought there might be a machine a few floors down. I found it and dumped in my quarters, and a thin stream of cloying brown liquid, piping hot, dribbled into a cup. I slipped on a lid and headed back to my father's room, the drink hot in my hand. I was determined to spill not a drop. A western movie with themes of conquest and bravery and all bad guys dead by the end, the hero on a horse atop a sherbet-sunset hill, and now a treat he'd been yearning for: I beamed with pleasure at making him happy, hurrying to his bedside to reap my reward. But when I reached his door, I stopped again, hesitant to go in. Yes, I wanted him to say he loved me, or at least liked me, at least could stand the idea of me, and yet I also could not manage the thought of those words coming from his mouth.

And the reason I didn't want him to say such things? Probably so I could keep wishing he would.

I walked in to the room after a few seconds to find my father asleep, the low drone of John Wayne's voice buzzing about the room. I put the chocolate on the table and settled into the chair that my grandfather had occupied earlier, pulling a blanket around my shoulders in a mix of relief and disappointment that's been with me ever since.

The unraveling of my marriage took more months, the same time period in which my father was flown to a hospital in Baltimore where a surgeon opened him up to implant a twenty-inch rod that encases his spinal cord. For months he wore a cast that started at his chest and went to his knees—he often rested against a pole seat my grandfather had welded in his shop, the perfect (of course) relief for my exhausted father. Once he'd mended, my father cut the cast off with a hack saw and threw it in the back pasture to disintegrate in the rain. He refused to see another doctor. And one day he got on a horse and rode along his river during a dewy pink sunset fit for the same John Wayne movie we'd seen in the hospital.

That night in the hospital room—and let's say that ten hours passed between the time the others left and when Cindy arrived to take me to the airport—remains the longest stretch I have spent alone with my father. During those hours I probably thought about nudging him awake again. Off his pins as he was, I might have shaken his blankets until he came around, and then I could have badgered him into a few reassuring platitudes, hinting that since my youngest sister got the word I should get it too. Yet it seemed for the first time since the accident that he had given in to rest. My father had sunk into a place of healing, of—I like to think—assurance that no one here would hurt him or frighten him or turn their backs on a pain he could not admit to. Or is that me I'm talking about? I stayed wrapped in my blanket, dozing but mostly watching his face grow slack, the bruise around his eye receding, rimmed with greens and browns. His reflated lung accepting air. I watched and waited for morning, and though I didn't think so at the time, I suppose the hours passed as they should, with a familiar silence between us. We stayed true to what we have been to each other from the beginning.

After that I didn't know how to think about my fantasy father anymore, the one I'd carted around since I was a kid. The man who would take me out to lunch just because or proudly introduce me to others as his daughter. I'd still like to meet that guy, but I doubt he would have had the ferocity to fight his way out from under a horse, nor could he have taken on a child at age sixteen and raised her up along with four others. Sometimes I even glimpse how my actual father provided in spades what I've most needed from the time I was a little kid until now: the gumption to get back up off the ground every single time I fall. And here's another thing: it's taken me many years to realize that he's never called me out on my own lack during that week in the hospital. I sat there for seven days with beeping machines and flickering lights, all the time the fully conscious one in the room. But never did I utter the word I profess to have wanted from him. Not once did I say it out loud. *I love you, Dad. Please survive this.*

# 5

I pulled into Whitman Cellars parking lot downtown on our last day in Walla Walla. I was hot and I was thirsty and I was after some Narcissa Red.

Whitman Cellars—which closed its doors for good not long after (hard to figure out what happened, since the Columbia Basin is renowned these days for fabulous wines and other wineries seem to be thriving)—was housed in a warehouse-type building, walls lined with barrels, and when I walked in the place was hopping with bluegrass music. I paid a $5 fee that allowed me a few tastes of wine, and I strolled past the tables of viogniers and pinot noirs, searching out the blend that was the only one I wanted to get in my mouth and swirl across my tongue: Narcissa Red.

"Ask about the story of Narcissa Whitman, the namesake of Whitman Cellars' red blend, and you know you're in for a serious wine." Or so stated the description on the website.

The 'W' on the bottle stands for Whitman, the brave and idealistic young couple Marcus and Narcissa, who traveled west to set up a Christian mission amongst the Cayuse people only to be killed before their time. Narcissa was one of the first women to cross the Rocky Mountains and make it to Walla Walla. Along with their religious ideas, the Whitman's [sic] unfortunately brought disease with them and their pathology wiped out the children of the Cayuse. So it was a matter of survival for the locals that the Whitman's [sic] be killed and the buildings of the mission destroyed. This is just the kind of story that inspires strength and perseverance, and the story has resonated in the area ever since.

I looked around the winery, hoping the person who wrote that description was here, though how would I be able to tell? If I met him (I'd fixed him as a man) I'd question him about this peculiar slant on Narcissa's story. This one different than Ben's, different than Mrs. Morrow's, different than the fable told by the woman who was convinced her grandmother had stored dolls and toys in Narcissa's trunk. Different than mine, which had grown on me like a carbuncle for years.

Anyway, I was curious. Which part of the Whitman tale "inspires strength and perseverance," and which part still resonates? I wanted to ask the writer, too, about why there was no mention of Narcissa's hard line regarding alcohol, and why only the lightest touch about the Whitmans' religion, the very reason the couple had traveled all that way, their laser-beam focus on saving souls? Plus, the Whitmans hadn't brought illness to the valley. That came from measles- and typhoid-ridden wagon trains moving down the Oregon Trail—four thousand wagons in 1847 alone, a good number of those stopping at Waiilatpu for rest, food, relief. The Whitmans cared for sick people traveling through their compound but did nothing—no historian has ever suggested, anyway—to intentionally spread disease to the tribe.

Once I had a taste of Narcissa Red in my cup—and I was sure glad for it (every swallow as satisfying as the website promised, rich on the tongue, lingering in the throat)—I wandered about the building, snacking on sample cheese and chocolate, kicking up sawdust under my feet, quickly losing interest in talking to the website writer even if he was here.

After all, that person was no historian (nor am I). I didn't have to ask him why he'd posted paragraphs loosely based on the truth for visitors to the site to read as actual history. I already knew the answer. Obviously the writer had a single task, and that was to whip up enough interest in a historical figure, Narcissa Whitman, that he could sell a wine named after her. A marvelous wine. I'm guessing he felt that if he had to hedge on the facts a bit, so what?

If I was going to interrogate anyone, I might have started with myself. Since when was I a member of the Narcissa defense team? I still believed it was largely her deeds and actions that led to the November 29 attack. I still blamed her, in good part, for the decimation of the Cayuse tribe, for those killed in retribution and the five chiefs publicly hung in Oregon City. I could not consider her a stellar mother to the children she'd taken in, not just the Sagers but the ones who'd been dropped off like so many sacks of sand by their parents. But I also had to admit that Narcissa had lived through a whole lot of difficulty. Her loneliness and endless hard work and constant loss were probably more than most of us could have shouldered. More than I could have shouldered.

Back at Waiilatpu, next to the communal grave for the fourteen killed, is a tall headstone for William Gray, showy enough that I'm surprised Whitman fans let Gray's family put it there in the late 1850s. Gray's tomb casts a long shadow, detracting from the simple and flat-to-the-ground slab that lists the November 1847 dead at Waiilatpu, weather-beaten enough now that it's almost impossible to make out the names. I'd taken a few minutes to stand at Narcissa's grave before I met up with Ben the day before, and I'd turned my back, as I had in the past, on Gray's fancy list of accomplishments on his fancy pillar. The Gray projectile reminds me every time why the man is high on my list of Narcissa's Bad Guys: Spalding, Hinman, Joe Lewis, Stanfield, Gray. Each one more deserving of opprobrium than the last.

William Gray, hired by the board to travel with the Whitmans and Spaldings as a mechanic, trudged along for five months, insolent and grumbling about being tied to the ineffective doctor and his stuck-up wife (as if Narcissa needed another detractor). Once at the mission compound it was Gray who took an instant dislike—distaste—to the Cayuse. Not only did he poison the melons, he's also the one who urged Marcus to drag any "misbehaving" Native man into the center of the compound for a public whipping. Gray, to me, was a small and pinched human.

After the attack on Waiilatpu Gray unleashed an excoriation of the Native people he'd lived among for years. The dead Whitmans provided him a reason to bellow. In one letter published in newspapers he describes his take on the tragedy:

The tribes below the Cascade Mountains were the first that had any intercourse with the whites. Diseases never feared or shunned by the profligate youth and sailor were introduced to them. So prevalent was vice and immorality among the natives that not one escaped. Their blood became tainted, their bodies loathsome and foul, the communication corrupt continually. The flattened head of the royal families, the round head of the slave, were no protection from vice and immoral intercourse among the sexes; hence, when disease of a different nature, and such as among the more civilized white race are easily treated and cured, came among them, they fell like rotten sheep.

And then Gray dishes out a last condemnation of the

266

deceased Whitmans, just because he could: "The little moral influence brought by the first missionaries was like pouring water upon glass; it only washed the sediment from the surface while the heart remained untouched."

Whatever the winery copywriter's take on Narcissa's tale, it was nothing as damning or damaging as Gray's, or Spalding's with his years of attack on the Jesuits and the many (many) articles he wrote defending himself and his faith in the wake of the attack at Waiilatpu. The winery's prose was simply a string of misstatements. Suggesting refinements to the writer would be a silly exercise—at least my self-congratulatory self had been humbled that much by the afternoon with Ben.

I was thinking about getting out of there, heading back to the hotel, when the man pouring my second sip of Narcissa Red pointed out the winemaker—the very person who'd developed the blend I was about to sip. I watched out the window as the vintner slipped out the front door and headed to his car, finished with crowds (and questions, I suppose) and done with work for the day. I hurried out the same door, wine in hand, to catch him. His foot was already inside his Subaru when I said, "Could I talk to you for a minute?" He wanted to refuse, that was obvious, his required hours entertaining wine lovers on a Saturday afternoon had been met and then some, but good winery man that he was, he nodded.

Why a wine named after Narcissa? That was my first question. He startled a bit; I got the idea others had dragged him down the same road and he was a little sick of it. His answers to that question and the others were, in fact, rote. Yes, he was aware of how she'd died. Yes, and her distaste for booze of all sorts. He tightened his grip on the door handle as I grilled away—Did he realize that she abhorred the Catholic use of red wine for communion? Did he know that several of her adopted children were soaked in her blood when they died of the measles? Did he at least think about a white wine instead of a red? He sent out a vibe that was not exactly unfriendly but impatient. What was my point? *Make it*, he seemed to be saying, *and then leave me alone.*

I don't recall, exactly, his final words to me, but I turned the gist of his statements over in my mind all that night. I turn it over still. Basically his opinion was that the Whitmans had their time in this region, they'd had their chance, and they'd spent it. It didn't work out the way they'd wanted, true, but the couple set in motion a series of events and episodes that eventually led to the way things are now—a lively city, a nice community to plant a family, a means to make a living and buy a house. The Whitmans' time here led to young clerks at a fine hotel who didn't care a whit about its namesake, to a college whose students had recently demanded a change of mascot, from the doddering *Whitman College Missionaries*, which probably put most in mind of a bland sex position, to the *Whitman College Blues*.

And so what about erasing the past? Now was about continuing a legacy of wheat growing, of sweet onions, and the discovery of fertile terroir where wine grapes ripen perfectly in the sun. The vintner said it wasn't up to him to preserve Narcissa's history or her legacy. His job was to make nice wine, and he'd made one in honor of her. He owed her nothing.

His explanation wasn't that crass or callous. I'm remembering it with a blunt edge. Because though he was talking about his region's history, I'd later realize that he was also saying, without any inkling that he was doing so, plenty about me. The reading of more books and articles, the research, the one more visit to Waiilatpu—I let myself believe that if I kept at it some increment of knowledge about Narcissa would finally, somehow, illuminate my own plight. I knew a whole lot more about the history of the West than I had when I started this project, and I had file cabinets of Narcissa information, but that wasn't going to synthesize into self-understanding after all. That part, it finally dawned on me, I was going to have to figure out on my own.

I watched him drive away, this man who'd dreamed up Narcissa Red, while I stood on the sidewalk with my now empty plastic glass of wine, his words ringing. We are destined to repeat the mistakes of the past, and we will indeed repeat them. Not because we choose to ignore what history can teach us, but because there's so little clarity about what actually happened or why it happened the way it did. That's the slippery fish we can't seem to keep hold of and probably never will.

I went back into the winery and, pushing away any qualms about doing so, bought a case of Narcissa Red. Now every time I pop a cork in my own house, I think of her way back there at the start of the frontier, a legacy that wends its way to me, to me and to other women whose lives are entwined in the mythology of the West, including those related to the survivors of the attack at Waiilatpu. It was Nathan Kimball's daughter who described the scene of pulling into Oregon City, the lot of them squeezed into Peter Odgen's boat. Men had lined up on the shore, hats in hands, offering themselves up to the weary, hungry widows released from their month of captivity. And what could the women do but accept?

Narcissa wouldn't want me to raise a glass of wine in their honor, or in her honor—she wouldn't want that moment of recognition even in her secret heart. So I don't do it. Instead I toast to this: I'm still here. I'm still figuring it out. Somehow or another, I'm trying to make my way through a miasma of doubt to give permission to call myself a woman of the West, even on the days I can't quite grasp what that means.

# 6

The lore of my family's hunting camp was tight around my neck as a single line of us—my father, uncle, aunt, and several of their children and grandchildren—climbed a winding trail into the Lemhi Mountains. The weight of this mantle, this history, this place that I was going to step into for the first time in my life. I'd told myself when I'd pulled out of Salmon, three days after our grandfather's death, that I most likely wouldn't be back. And yet here I was, boomeranged again, whipping about and sailing into the center of my past.

I'd had to return. For one thing, I couldn't resist seeing hunting camp, a place that had lived strictly in my imagination—the setting of men-family stories: the cold mornings of the hunt, the early start with bacon and coffee in the belly, the animals shot, gutted, dressed and hung high, away from coyotes and bears. All that whiskey consumed, the guitars played and songs sung around the evening fire.

And now I was there. Or almost—the group of us, including my youngest daughter, Mollie, in front of me, had driven for nearly an hour, and now we hiked a couple of miles toward the creek-side swale, the location where the men in my family had set up wall tents and cookstove and latrine and gun rack for two or three weeks every November for nearly a century.

We'd come to spread Grandpa Bob's ashes.

I marched along behind my daughter, her strong legs and back, her easy way in the world. She laughed with Amy, the cousin next to her, both girls in their twenties, their young ringing voices caught in the trees. When it got warm enough Mollie slid the hat off her head and stuck it into her back pocket, unleashing a cascade of hair that fell nearly to her waist. It took my breath away—so much like Hazel's hair, just as thick, as alive, and as sparkling under the light.

I also watched my brother ahead of the girls, roving over this path that he'd walked since he was old enough to think. What would that be like to fully inhabit this land as he had?

Ron, at the age of six, was given a chocolate bar and a whistle to put around his neck as dawn gleamed over camp. With a rifle slung across his shoulder, my brother was sent out alone, for at least part of the morning, to toughen him up, to keen his senses. *Whistle if you're lost or if you've brought down a kill.* Ron knew to keep to himself otherwise. He learned to shoot, to hit his target square on. He could bleed out and gut a buck, a bull elk, by the time he was ten. He taught himself guitar so he could join in on the songs around the campfire at night. When we got to be adults, Ron told me stories, at least a few. He tended to stop when he saw envy in me, bubbling to the surface. I remember a story about how one night they'd chained Grandpa Bob's truck to a tree so the drunk old man (though he wasn't so old in his drinking years) couldn't act on his threat to drive to Salmon to load up on more whiskey.

It wasn't long after that chained-up night that our grandfather gave it up. He took his last drink and smoked his last cigarette, both habits quit the same day. One time when I asked Grandpa Bob if he'd ever been tempted to partake again, he answered by raising those eyebrows and staring at me like I was out of my skull. Okay. That was a good thing. But still, I wouldn't have minded being in on a single night of our wild grandfather in camp. A chance to see that version of the man too.

Once we'd reached the swale, ringed with massive trees, where camp had been set up over the years, the lot of us arranged ourselves on a long meadow next to the creek—as familiar to the men in my family as their bedrooms. I had a yearning to stay for a string of days, a desire that grew thick in my throat. I'd walk around the grasslands and between the looming pine and spruce, and I'd study the things my grandfather had left behind: a stack of poles he'd carved and painted red and blue and numbered in his slanted writing, piled just so under tarps, so that every year he could set up the kitchen tent in a matter of minutes. Also the cup hooks and compact metal shelves he'd screwed into trees, a small square of mirror for shaving. I found one of Grandpa Bob's ingenious swinging grills at the cooking pit, the pieces he'd welded himself to make living easier in a location that swelled with the fruit of him. So much of my grandfather in this place, and of course this is where his dust should mingle with other dust, including the last remains of animals he'd killed and roped up, a cairn away from bears, the meat he'd packed out and grilled and consumed through Salmon's long winters. Even while Grandma Lois's ashes sat in the back of some closet, a fact that spun a weeping sore spot in my stomach and will keep spinning while my obligation to her remains unfulfilled, Grandpa Bob would soon blend in where he belonged.

The twenty or so of us, mingling together under a surprisingly hot sun, sweating in our flannel shirts and long johns, our hefty boots, circled up in the meadow. It was too warm for October, but that's the weather we'd been given. Better than rain. Better than snow. My uncle held the cardboard box of ashes. He'd announced that the idea here was to take a handful, tell a story about Grandpa Bob, and toss the ashes you had fisted in your hand up into the air. Our uncle went first, reciting a story that made us roar. I don't remember how it went, overly concentrated as I was on my lack of grandpa anecdotes, steeling against any awkward pauses when my turn came around. Our uncle took a giant step into the middle of the circle of us and threw his fistful in the air. The gray smoke of our grandfather was caught by a breeze so that it splatted into the faces of those on the south side of our throng. They started to cough and spit. I wasn't in the direct path, but I got some in my eyelashes and on my lips. I wondered how to sweep it off with any modicum of respect.

*Okay,* my uncle said, *change of plans.* Tell your story, test the wind, and walk a few good strides before you fling Grandpa into a breeze blowing away—not toward—the rest of us.

That's what we did, discovering that there were a lot of ashes. A human body, apparently, produces a heap, enough to pass the box around the circle three times, four, story after story, *remember that time, remember how he always . . .*

But what did I have to give to this group? The only story on my mind was one I'd heard the last time I saw my grandfather. He had a bandage on his finger, and I'd asked him what happened. He said he'd been up at Panther Creek at the cabin where he stayed most of the time with the woman I think of as his true companion. When he sat on the porch in the bare mornings, light just cracking the sky, a bear cub rolled up to him. An orphaned cub. Grandpa had taken to feeding it scraps, the only way it was staying alive. "Well, the little son of a bitch finally bit me," Grandpa said, holding up his hurt finger. Only a day or two after the nip of sharp teeth, Grandpa Bob's companion died of a breast cancer that she'd refused to have treated. A day after that, her children asked our grandfather to move out for good. "What about the cub?" I asked him.

"I don't know," my grandfather shrugged. "Dead, I guess."

I didn't tell that story up at hunting camp. It felt like something I shouldn't know, too private for me to be in on. Instead, I recited a few thin memories of him, while Ron and our uncle and aunt had us laughing from the start, big, full laughter that filled the sky over us. Grandpa tales that were so exactly the man that he was nearly made manifest. I liked the notion of it: that Grandpa Bob had hiked in, too, and was just over there, sitting on a boulder with his legs crossed, his hat pushed back on his head, hearing himself talked about. He would have relished such a gathering.

Our father could have told the best and worst of his father, endless tales through the dark of night and into the next day, but he said nothing. He took only one handful of ash and only on the first round of the box-passing. He walked off a few paces and opened his hand to let loose the remains of the one person he loved best. Then he moved over to sit on a stump in the copse to wait us out.

I spent the day watching my father, my uncle, my aunt, my brother, those with an insider's knowledge of the man who'd glued us together, the man who was simple and direct in his needs and complex in his character. And maybe it started to sink in that I would not know Grandpa Bob in such a way. It simply couldn't happen, no matter how I wished for it. This bright-blue day offered me an opportunity to let it go, to end this particular hankering. I'd link arms with my daughter, who wandered over the grounds as I did in that dizzying fall air, examining everything. Mollie, with such brightness and curiosity. Unburdened. She's the one who'd give me courage to throw a handful of ash in the air and tell my grandfather good-bye.

That evening, well after the box was emptied, after a hike out of hunting camp that seemed longer, more somber, than going in, after the windy drive to town dodging excited deer on the road, we met at the Shady Nook for dinner. Mollie had never been there, and I hadn't since my grandparents' fiftieth anniversary, a party that took place in this locale a few years before Grandma Lois passed. She'd insisted on a big family to-do at the Shady Nook instead of her house, and she'd given the cook a menu, with clam fettuccine as the main dish. The Shady Nook recipe: boiled spaghetti noodles tossed in the slimy contents of a can of bivalves, sprinkled with bagged Parmesan. My grandmother was delighted with her deluxe meal and its execution. The rest of us pretended to eat the goo while she huffed and puffed at the end of the table, the emphysema that would eventually kill her already clogging her lungs and sending inky streaks of black up her shins.

That anniversary night Grandpa Bob was in rarer form than usual, regaling us with story after story, including one about the night he and our other grandfather, our mother's father, had drunkenly chased down a bear they'd spotted in the wee hours out in the woods. The bear had climbed a tree to rummage through a food cache, making noise enough to wake the men. The bear, a small one, ran off, but within the hour it was hunted down, shot, dragged back to the campsite, and laid out next to the fire that had been reignited, burning bright enough to glow the edges of its dead body. Grandpa's story of that night ended with Ron, no more than about four years old, storming out of his tent in his pajamas with his pocketknife drawn, telling the men to get out of the way because "I'm going to get that bear."

After the laughter died down I said to my grandfather, "I was there too." He looked over at me as if such a thing wasn't possible, as if the words I'd spoken were gibberish. "You were?" he said, though I was fairly sure what he meant was,

"No, you weren't." But I had been there, and so had Cindy. It was summertime, and the men wanted to get into the cool of the forest, and the women had probably insisted the two oldest girls be taken along with our brother. I remember being in a sleeping bag in the tent and waking to a scuffle, the shouting, the ruckus, the doors of Grandpa's Scout slamming shut, the engine roaring off into the night. Then silence. Cindy and I sitting up now, staring at each other in the dark, acute to sound and smell because the air around us was impenetrable. I scooted closer to her, and we huddled in the tent until the men roared in again, and then we ventured out to see the dead bear. That bear. Over and over again during my childhood, I made my way to its tanned hide to stretch myself out on it, to read whatever book my grandmother had passed on to me. The bristle of its hair itching through my shirt and shorts. The teeth gone orange, sharp no matter how many times I rubbed my fingers over the points. I was with it when it died, a memory I knew to be true, and one I have claimed often, silently, fiercely.

Now I was back at the Shady Nook for, I figured, the last time. The final Shady Nook Jim Beam on the rocks and order of medium-rare steak and potatoes. Mollie sat with her cousins at one end of the table while I was at the other next to my father, who, though he is not much of a drinker, ordered another round while our glasses were still half full. He took a sip and started to rib me as he tends to. When was I going to get it? Stop the liberal bullshit. Vote for the right men, defend the right causes. And wasn't it about time for me to get a real job instead of this business of writing and teaching?

I waved him away, turned to talk to my brother. But then my father pointed to Mollie and knocked against my shoulder. "Hey," he said, "it's not too late. My wife can still teach those girls how to be real women."

I should have laughed. I should have slapped a palm on the table to jostle the cherries in our cocktails. *Good one, Dad.* I should have insisted that he had it backward, that my daughters had plenty to teach him about real women. But I said nothing.

Mollie moved up behind my chair and laid a hand on my shoulder. She pressed hard enough that I understood that she'd heard him too. Let's go, she said, and I agreed it was time.

My daughter and I walked to the door of the café. She said she'd wait outside while I told my aunt we were leaving. I found my father's sister standing at the hostess desk, but before I could say much of anything, Mollie leapt back in, a gust of cold air pushing her toward us. "A buck!" she said, and she gestured out the window at a deer trapped in a patio that was closed for the season. The three of us squeezed together at the entrance, watching out of a small frame of glass. It was too dark to see anything but shadows, but I heard the clatter of tables and chairs, the panicked bellowing of the animal. Mollie opened the door and slid onto the sidewalk. I tried to yank her back inside, but she was strong, stronger than me, and she pulled at my arm until I was in the night air too. I stood against the wall next to her, my filmy breath and hers puffing into the darkness. We listened to the sound of a buck out of its mind, and we willed it to be free.

I remember that night: how Mollie and I stood under a crystal sky, a clear and star-studded sky, the sidewalk glittering under the café's porch lights. My main thought was keeping her safe; my main thought was holding her tight while she held me, keeping me safe. Only later did I let myself wonder about which part of me was trapped on the patio with the deer, banging around in all that folded-up vinyl and rusted metal. My grandmother's ashes still waiting to be put to rest; my inability to act on her behalf. Or it could be that the buck's dilemma was some kind of first bumbling step toward acceptance and resolve. This time when I left my best place, I'd better do so with the determination that Salmon, Idaho, was mine. No one could say it wasn't, no matter how far I drifted and even if I never again returned.

I squeezed my daughter's hand, both of us wide awake to the noise and the trouble. I could do nothing for the animal but stay out of its way, a good distance from sharp hooves and its mad, heated body that screamed from one end of the enclosure to the other.

And then, like that, it was finished. Mollie and I watched as the buck made its escape, as if the way out had been crystal clear and right there all along. It was over the wrought-iron fence of the patio in one long, graceful thrust of release, landing with a messy grunt of exhalation on the edge of the parking lot, hoofs clattering against the asphalt.

In a split second the buck was away, its tawny coat rippling under the pulsing beam of consecutive highway lamps, antlers slicing the air. In the last light I watched as it veered off the road, bounding on the scrub hills that led to town. From there it would go on to the mountains that surrounded us, that had always surrounded us, into the trees and across streams and up rocky cliffs and far from human confusion. Away from questions and histories and sorrow.

The buck ran hard and fast into the heart of Salmon, Idaho, freedom in every expelled breath. And not once did it look back.

# Acknowledgments

I was some years into the research, writing, and revising of this book when I received the thrilling news that Gretel Ehrlich had selected it for the 2018 River Teeth Literary Nonfiction Prize. I am humbled by her faith in this project. I'm honored to join the other books in the series and delighted to be associated with this top-notch journal. A huge thank you to Joe Mackall, to Dan Lehman, to Cassandra Brown, and everyone else at *River Teeth*.

I'm grateful, too, to the talented and committed staff at the University of New Mexico Press—James Ayers, Elise McHugh, Felicia Cedillos, Katherine White, Stephen P. Hull, and others— for their patience with me and for their diligent care in creating and marketing this book.

Thank you to Gail Hochman. I thank my lucky stars that I am in your camp.

I worked on this book at UCross, Playa, and Hedgebook, and I am appreciative of the time and peace (not to mention delicious food) each offered so generously. I also found invaluable help with research at the American Antiquarian Society in Worchester, Massachusetts. Thanks, especially, to Jim Moran for making my days there so richly productive. And thanks to Dr. Susan Armitage, who gave me perspective on western history, as well as Lawrence Dodd from Whitman College and the many others who aided in me in searching through libraries and archives.

A long-haul project requires long-haul support, and I've received that from many colleagues and friends, particularly Cai Emmons and Miriam Gershow, who've read more versions of this book than any human should be subjected to. Thanks, too, to Cheryl Crumbley, Kathleen Kochan, Valerie Laken, Kellie Wells, Laura Hendrie, Rick Bass, Laurie Parker, Ellen Bass, Alice Tallmadge, Dondeana Brinkman, and Carolyn Coman. So many others, too—I hope you know who you are and how grateful I am to you.

Two women who meant the world to me, and who offered sage advice and loving care through the writing of this book, left too soon: Katherine Dunn and Sandi Morgen. I'd give about anything to bring a copy over to your respective houses. I think you'd be glad to see it finished at last.

I am blessed by my four children, Amanda Mae, Stephanie, Mary, and Mollie, and their husbands. I am held aloft daily by my daughters' belief in me and tenderness toward me. Love to Owen, Ezzy, and Harry. Thanks also to the rest of my family, my parents and siblings. Ron Gwartney has been wonderfully supportive and helpful through this process.

My deepest heartfelt thanks are reserved for my husband, Barry Lopez, who is my shelter in every storm. I'd be lost without you.

# Selected Bibliography

Allen, Opal Sweazea. *Narcissa Whitman: An Historical Biography*. Portland, OR: Binfords & Mort Press, 1959.

Belknap, George N. "Authentic Account of the Murder of Dr. Whitman: The History of a Pamphlet." *The Papers of the Bibliographical Society of America* 55 (1961): 319–46.

Bonde, Deborah Dawson. "Missionary Ways in the Wilderness: Eliza Hart Spalding, Maternal Associations, and the Nez Perce Indians." *American Presbyterians* 69 (1991): 271–82.

Boorstin, Daniel J. *The Americans: The National Experience*. New York: Vintage, 1967.

Carrey, Johnny, and Cort Conley. *River of No Return*. Cambridge, ID: Backeddy Books, 1967.

Dodd, Lawrence. *Narcissa Whitman on the Oregon Trail*. Fairfield: Ye Galleon Press, 1985.

Drury, Clifford. *Marcus and Narcissa Whitman and the Opening of Old Oregon*. Vols. I and II. Seattle: Northwest Interpretive Association, 1986.

———. *More About the Whitmans: Four hitherto unpublished letters of Marcus and Narcissa Whitman*. Tacoma: Washington State Historical Society, 1979.

———. *Where Wagons Could Go: Narcissa Whitman and Eliza Spalding*. Lincoln: University of Nebraska Press, 1963.

Edwards, G. Thomas. "Narcissa Whitman." *The Oregon Encyclopedia*. Updated May 21, 2018. https://oregonencyclopedia.org/articles/whitman_narcissa_1808_1847_/#.W6VePPlRepo.

Farnham, Thomas J. *An 1839 Wagon Train Journal: Travels in the Great*

*Western Prairies, the Anahuac and Rocky Mountains, And in The Oregon Territory.* New York: Greeley & McElrath, 1977.

Gwartney, L. N. *My First Eighty Years.* Boise: private printing, 1976.

Jeffrey, Julie Roy. *Converting the West: A Biography of Narcissa Whitman.* Norman: University of Oklahoma Press, 1991.

Johnson, C. T. "The Evolution of a Lament." *The Washington Historical Quarterly* 2 (1908): 195–208.

Jones, Nard. *The Great Command.* Boston: Little, Brown and Company, 1959.

Lansing, Ronald B. *Juggernaut: The Whitman Massacre Trial.* Ninth Judicial Circuit Historical Society, 1993.

Limerick, Patricia Nelson. *The Legacy of Conquest: The Unbroken Past of the American West.* New York: W. W. Norton & Company, 1987.

Morrow, Honore. *On To Oregon!* New York: William Morrow and Company, Inc., 1926.

O'Donnell, Terence. *An Arrow in the Earth: General Joel Palmer and the Indians of Oregon.* Portland: Oregon Historical Society Press, 1991.

Ross, Nancy Wilson. *Westward the Women.* New York: Alfred A. Knopf, 1944.

Sager, Catherine, Elizabeth Sager, and Matilda Sager. *The Whitman Massacre of 1847.* Fairfield: Ye Galleon Press, 1981.

Saunders, Mary. *The Whitman Massacre.* Fairfield: Ye Galleon Press, 1977.

Stewart, George R. *Earth Abides.* New York: Random House, 1949.

———. *Names on the Land.* New York: NYRB Classics, 2008.

Thompson, Erwin N. *Shallow Grave at Waiilatpu: The Sagers' West.* Portland: Oregon Historical Society, 1969.

———. *Whitman Mission: National Historic Site.* Washington, DC: National Park Service Historical Press, 1964.

Unruh, John D. *The Plains Across: The Overland Emigrants and Trans-Mississippi West, 1840–60.* Urbana: University of Illinois Press, 1979.

Warren, Eliza Spalding. "Letter to Clarence Leroy Andrews containing a brief history of the 1847 Whitman Massacre." Pacific Northwest Historical Documents, University of Washington Libraries Special Collections, 1894.

White, Richard. *It's Your Misfortune and None of My Own: A New History of the American West.* Norman: University of Oklahoma Press, 1991.

Whitman, Narcissa. *My Journal.* Fairfield: Ye Galleon Press, 1994.